Books about regulatio[illegible] this one. Written in a cl[illegible] and informed fashion, the authors of *Smart Regulation* lay out a sensible path for reforming one of the most important tools of public policy. It is a path that has room for elected officials and voters in both parties, a rare thing these days. For that reason alone, read this book!

—ROBERT LITAN, non-resident Senior Fellow,
the Brookings Institution,
member of CED's advisory board, and
co-author (with William Nordhaus) of
Reforming Federal Regulation
(Yale Press, 1983).

With the increasing speed of technological advancement and the explosion of real-time data, the CED authors' call for data-driven, principle-based regulation is both timely and urgently needed. As they thoughtfully argue in *Smart Regulation*, there is a ditch on either side of the regulation road and smart regulations with clearly defined benefit-cost analysis are needed as guardrails. Whether you are most concerned with the environment or competitive markets, Smart Regulation is an excellent blueprint for a non-partisan dialogue on designing and maintaining regulations that create positive social and economic outcomes.

—MIKE MONAHAN,
Retired COO - Pitney Bowes Inc.,
Trustee, CED

Smart Regulation

Changing Speed Bumps into Guardrails

To Bob Gay,
My "go-to" economist
when the world makes
no sense . . .
-Hollis
1/20

Michael G. Archbold
Hollis W. Hart
Joseph J. Minarik

The Conference Board, Inc.
845 Third Avenue, New York, NY 10022

This book is printed on acid-free paper.
Manufactured in the United States of America

ISBN 978-0-8237-1384-4 (Softcover)
ISBN 978-0-8237-1386-8 (Ebook)

CONTENTS

ABOUT CED

THE COMMITTEE FOR ECONOMIC DEVELOPMENT of The Conference Board (CED) is a nonprofit, nonpartisan, business-led public policy organization that delivers well-researched analysis and reasoned solutions to our nation's most critical issues.

Since its inception in 1942, CED has addressed national priorities to promote sustained economic growth and development to benefit all Americans. CED's work in those first few years led to great policy accomplishments, including the Marshall Plan, the economic development program that helped rebuild Europe and maintain the peace; and the Bretton Woods Agreement that established the new global financial system, and both the World Bank and International Monetary Fund.

Today, CED continues to play an important role through its trusted research and advocacy. Comprising leading business executives, CED lends its voice and expertise on pressing policy issues. In recent decades, CED has made significant contributions across a broad portfolio, including: pre-K education importance and funding, bipartisan campaign reform, corporate governance reform, U.S. fiscal health, academic standards in K-12 education, post-secondary education access and achievement, importance of STEM education, immigration, free trade, foreign assistance, women on corporate boards, Medicare and broader healthcare reform, crony capitalism, inequality, judicial selection reform, child care, the role of business in promoting educational attainment, digital learning, teacher compensation and quality, corporate short-termism, federal tax reform, social security, innovation and growth, reducing global poverty, welfare reform, and more.

CED's work is based on seven core principles: sustainable capitalism, long-term economic growth, efficient fiscal and regulatory policy, competitive and open markets, a globally competitive workforce, equal economic opportunity, and nonpartisanship in the nation's interest. CED's research findings are disseminated widely, achieving tangible impact at the local, state, and national levels.

ACKNOWLEDGMENTS

LIKE ITS PREDECESSOR, SUSTAINING CAPITALISM, THIS BOOK is in many ways a collaboration among the dedicated Trustees and staff of the Committee for Economic Development of The Conference Board (CED).

Since its founding in 1942, CED's assembled business leaders have sought to advance the nation's collective interest through nonpartisan public-policy research. From their earliest accomplishments in their vital contributions to the Marshall Plan and the Bretton Woods monetary agreement, CED's Trustees have continued forward to reach national-scale milestones in campaign finance reform, and to place numerous stepping stones across the states through expanded access to quality early-childhood education. In their support for the production of *Sustaining Capitalism*, they perspicaciously foresaw a sound future for our nation's economic system. Now, in their contributions to this book through numerous discussions and seminars, they have helped the authors to focus on the issues raised by one of the key chapters of CED's earlier book. We thank the Trustees for their dedication to developing reasoned solutions in the nation's interest, rooted in their business experience and expertise.

We thank especially a group of CED Trustees, led by Kathy Hopinkha Hannan and Patricia A. McKay, and including Howard Fluhr, Michael Monahan and Jacob J. Worenklein, who read drafts of the book chapters and provided valuable comments and insights. Neri Bukspan, Bridget M. Neill and their colleagues at EY shared important research and helpfully reviewed our drafts.

Diane Lim, formerly of the CED staff, wrote an earlier CED policy statement on this topic that provided many important insights and formed the basis of a chapter of this book. Caroline Ferguson, Alanna Fuschillo, and Alison Snyder performed important research assistance. Connor Clendenen generously provided enormous effort in a highly productive internship.

Marta Steele greatly improved the manuscript with her editing. Ray Vella designed the cover. Peter Drubin and Pam Seenaraine of The Conference Board expertly managed the production of the book.

The authors accept all responsibility for any errors of commission or omission.

— Michael G. Archbold,
Hollis W. Hart, and
Joseph J. Minarik

1

INTRODUCTION

To some Americans, regulation is a dead weight hanging on the economy. To others, regulation is the last bulwark against killing exploitation of the citizenry at large. Given that many Americans have limited direct contact with regulation, public opinion is remarkably strongly held. According to Gallup, for 12 years in a row, more Americans say there is too much regulation compared with those who say there is too little or the right amount. The percentage of Americans who are willing to state an opinion, as opposed to "don't know," is remarkably high—well into the 90 range.[1] See figure 1.1.

There is a notable disparity in responses between Democrats and Republicans. See figure 1.2.

Although many Americans have limited direct contact with regulation, the real but less-than-obvious impacts of regulation on the daily life of John Q. Citizen are extensive. Food, clothing, and shelter are covered through food safety inspections and nutrition labeling, permanent-care labeling, and environmental standards for dry cleaning, as well as mortgage disclosure regulations, and zoning and structural code restrictions, among many others. Health care is regulated through occupational licensing and state insurance regulation, plus standards set by the federal Affordable Care Act ("Obamacare"). Transportation is affected by fuel economy and highway safety standards. Workplace conditions are determined by wages and hours regulations and

1 Art Swift, "Americans' Views on Government Regulation Remain Steady," Gallup, October 11, 2017.

FIGURE 1.1 **Americans' views on amount of federal government regulation (%)**

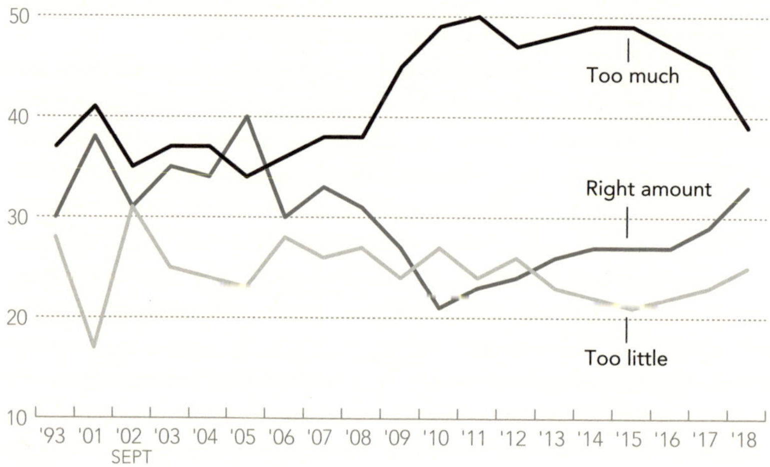

Source:
https://news.gallup.com/poll/220400/americans-views-government-regulation-remain-steady.aspx

FIGURE 1.2 **Americans' views on amount of federal government regulation (%) by party identification**

Source:
https://news.gallup.com/poll/220400/americans-views-government-regulation-remain-steady.aspx

occupational safety standards. Recreational and school facilities face safety codes. The bed to which Mr. Citizen returns at the end of the day must meet flammability standards. In short, the typical citizen does touch government regulation every hour of every day.

Probably more significantly, businesses, large and small, deal with regulation, and more directly, which affects the growth of wages and the number of jobs. Business collectively is often outspoken about regulation, usually in a negative way. Feeling the brunt of regulation makes businesses more cautious about investing or risk taking more generally.

Regulations come from different agencies, and even from different levels of government—federal, state, and local. The number of new regulations can be large in any given year, adding to the ongoing effort needed to comply. Businesspersons report that regulations are too often written for the community of regulators, not for the nonspecialists who must comply. The business resources that are devoted to compliance with regulations are diverted from other endeavors that could make the businesses more competitive and more successful. Smaller businesses, without the economies of scale to have specialists to deal with regulation, have their own unique problems.[2] For example, rigorous cost-benefit analysis is reserved for "economically significant" rules—those with large aggregate economic impacts. But regulations with smaller total impacts that focus on small businesses can affect them crucially.

There is another side to the regulatory coin, however. Regulation addresses problems about which our society cares. Episodes of food- and water-borne disease, and airway and highway accident, arouse public concern.[3] Worker safety regulations are controversial for business and labor alike, but workplace injury and illness have been financially costly

2 William Dunkelberg, "The Hidden Costs of Regulations," *Forbes*, July 12, 2016; Clyde Wayne Crews, "Ten Thousand Commandments 2018," Competitive Enterprise Institute, April 19, 2018.

3 Kristine Phillips, "Five Dead, Nearly 200 Sick in E.coli Outbreak from Lettuce and Investigators Are Stumped," *Washington Post*, June 2, 2018; Associated Press, "More than 200 Eggs Recalled Because of Salmonella Risk," *Wall Street Journal*, April 15, 2018; Associated Press, "Key Events in General Motors' Ignition Switch Recall," Fox News, September 17, 2015; Hiroko Tabuchi and Danielle Ivory, "Takata Airbag Flaw Linked to 10th Death; 5 Million More Vehicles Recalled," *New York Times*, January 22, 2016; Christopher Jensen, "Ford Explorers under Scrutiny for Exhaust Fumes inside Vehicles," *New York Times*, July 7, 2016; John Greenwald, "Inside the Ford/Firestone Fight," *Time*, May 9, 2001.

and have taken a serious human toll.[4] Citizen attitudes surely are shaped by pressures from this side of the regulatory coin as well.

And not surprisingly, different interests in society feel differently. A regulation may have a favorable ratio of societal benefits to costs; but that is of no comfort to the affected business, which cannot incorporate the benefits into its own balance sheet. Those who enjoy the benefits may not even recognize them (for example, the benefit of one regulation may be a problem that does not arise as a result) and certainly do not feel the costs; those who bear the costs may not directly enjoy the benefits. That leaves Americans at loggerheads over the value of regulation.

For these reasons, regulation involves inherent tradeoffs. The fundamental tool of regulatory evaluation, you will be reminded in these pages, is cost-benefit analysis. Regulation, like any intervention in a market economy, entails costs. Regulation is worthwhile for society as a whole if the benefits exceed the costs, but even such regulation that passes a cost-benefit test can leave businesses and individuals who are regulated worse off. And measuring benefits and costs is exceedingly complicated.

THE OPPORTUNITY

There is tremendous economic potential in the establishment of sound regulatory policy in the United States. One important reason is that the federal government has failed to review its existing regulations as time has passed. Our regulations are too often out of date, and the federal government lacks the data necessary to perform meaningful review. Although it will take time and money, an up-to-date regime of informed regulatory review could greatly enhance efficiency, yielding both greater benefits and lower costs. Among those lower costs will be reduced administrative burden for the regulators and the regulated alike. American business will be more competitive as a result.

A second opportunity will be political and civic, rather than economic. We will discuss the history of regulatory policy, a modern highlight of which was a period from the early 1970s through the early 1980s, when Democrats and Republicans in the executive and legislative branches collaborated on significant regulatory modernization—"deregulation."

---

4 The Occupational Safety and Health Administration (OSHA) reports some success, as reflected in falling instances of illness and injury over the last 15 years. Bureau of Labor Statistics, "Employer-Related Workplace Injuries and Illnesses—2016," November 9, 2017, accessed at https://www.bls.gov/iif/oshsum.htm.

Many regulations that had outlived their useful lives, notably in transportation and telecommunications, were swept aside. Businesses were free to offer new services to serve consumers better. The result was greatly enhanced technical innovation, and faster economic growth, in the affected industries—and indirectly, throughout the economy.

The deregulation of the 1970s and 1980s cannot just be repeated. Those opportunities were to a notable extent figurative low-hanging fruit, which was grown by technological innovations of earlier days. Today's situation is more complex, with no such obvious opportunities. However, the underlying principles remain the same. Both Republicans and Democrats can agree that the economic and social benefits of necessary regulation—such as fair competition and a healthier environment—should be achieved at the lowest possible cost. Both Republicans and Democrats can agree that businesses empowered to deliver the highest value—the greatest quality at the lowest cost—and in free competition with one another, will innovate, create that value, and along the way create good jobs at rising wages. And Democratic and Republican cooperation toward that end—achieving their own objectives, but at the same time recognizing the legitimacy of their opponent's—could change our current oppressive Washington environment. Every recent year has had its perceived political hostilities. But by today's standards, the decade from the early 1970s through the early 1980s was marked by notable harmony. The bipartisan cooperation on regulation was probably an important reason. Thoughtful regulatory cooperation could play that role again today.

TODAY'S REGULATORY SETTING

Regulation is a major focus of Washington policymaking today. The current Administration has made perhaps its largest strides in pursuit of removing regulations that it perceives as economically stifling. Following are the goals of some of its most prominent initiatives, many of which are still underway or under challenge:

- **Technology and Telecommunications**: Roll back "net neutrality," under which all users have equal internet access; repeal a requirement that users must agree to some commercial uses of their data; loosen rules restricting concentration of ownership of local media outlets.
- **Energy and Environment**: Withdraw the "Clean Power Plan," which would have reduced carbon emissions from coal-fired power

plants; withdraw a rule that required disclosure of chemicals used in hydraulic fracturing ("fracking") on federal lands; delay a rule to restrict emissions of methane gas from oil and gas wells; ease safety rules on off-shore oil drilling; restrict the coverage of the Clean Water Act to navigable waterways, not their tributaries; withdraw some protective designations of habitat for endangered species; narrow the protections against toxic chemicals and pesticides.

- **Labor**: Withdraw some gender- and ethnicity-reporting requirements for wages; reduce coverage of overtime pay rules; permit the distribution of employee tips to non-tipped employees; limit the ability of contractors or workers at franchises to unionize.
- **Finance**: Restrict the so-called "Volcker rule," which limited investment activities of banks; reduce consumers' ability to bring class-action lawsuits against banks that specify arbitration as a remedy in their contracts; limit conflict-of-interest rules against providers of financial services; loosen requirements of the Community Reinvestment Act.
- **Agriculture**: Loosen some restrictions on contents of federally provided school lunches; loosen requirements associated with "organic" designations of livestock and poultry; limit the ability of poultry and livestock farmers to sue food dealers.
- **Transportation**: Loosen proposed future "CAFE" fuel economy standards; withdraw requirements that airlines disclose baggage fees when specifying fares.
- **Health care**: Loosen standards for "short-term insurance" and "association health plans"; freeze a rule restricting workplace exposure to beryllium.

These steps individually are controversial, and collectively they could be described as moving in a single ideological direction—which is not surprising for any Administration; some describe the previous Administration similarly.[5] Experts in regulation might focus on each individual regulatory step and stress that every rule change should be considered on its own merits, and that in each case the cost involved must be weighed against the benefits. And that turns us more to the state of the regulatory process than to individual regulatory decisions. Here, too, the current Administration

5 Among the critical voices is Clyde Wayne Crews Jr., *Ten Thousand Commandments*. More favorable was Keith Zukowski, "Trump's Own Budget Office Admits Obama-era Regulations Brought Billions in Benefits," Environmental Defense Fund, March 6, 2018.

has been highly active. There have been two major executive orders that have given some direction to all future regulatory decisions.

On January 30, 2017, the President signed Executive Order (EO) 13771, "Reducing Regulation and Controlling Regulatory Costs."[6] This EO specified that whenever an executive department or agency proposes a new regulation, it must identify at least two existing regulations to be repealed. This EO also specifies that the incremental total cost of all new and repealed regulations (without considering any benefit resulting from the regulations) must be less than zero.[7] And in future years, each agency will have a budgeted amount (which may be positive or negative) for the net cost (again, without regard to any benefit) of new and repealed regulations.

A second EO, number 13777, dated February 24, 2017, builds on the first.[8] "Enforcing the Regulatory Reform Agenda" holds that each agency is to name a Regulatory Reform Officer and a Regulatory Reform Task Force. Each Task Force is to identify agency regulations that (a) eliminate jobs or inhibit job creation; (b) are outdated, unnecessary, or ineffective; (c) impose costs that exceed benefits; (d) create a serious inconsistency or otherwise interfere with the President's regulatory agenda; (e) rely on data that are not publicly available (or similar criteria);[9] (f) were called for by past EOs that have since been rescinded. Notably, having costs that exceed benefits is a sufficient condition for a regulation to be nullified, but it is not a necessary condition; the February 24, 2017 EO would potentially target for repeal other regulations whose benefits exceed their costs.

As was suggested earlier, we are encouraged that US regulatory policy should receive an energetic review. We believe that there is enormous potential to improve regulatory outcomes in terms of both improved achievement of the intended outcomes of existing regulations—more competition, greater safety, and so on—and at lower costs, with consequent lower prices and stronger economic growth. We will explain how we believe that the nation can achieve all of these objectives not merely

6 https://www.federalregister.gov/documents/2017/02/03/2017-02451/reducing-regulation-and-controlling-regulatory-costs.

7 Notably, the EO does not include the word "benefit," except once in legal boilerplate language that specifies that the EO does not create an entitlement to any "benefit" to any party.

8 https://www.federalregister.gov/documents/2017/03/01/2017-04107/enforcing-the-regulatory-reform-agenda.

9 This requirement is controversial, in that some argue that non-public data can be an important basis for sound regulatory decisions.

through rescinding regulations (though in some instances that would be constructive) or merely through adding more regulations (though in some instances those are needed), but rather through smarter regulation.

The nation needs to design regulations with more input from all of the various stakeholders, and with more thorough evaluation of all costs and benefits. And at least as important, we need to track regulations through time, to ensure that they were well designed from the outset, and that they remain effective as the world changes around them. This will require the collection of better data (in some instances, the first collection of ***any*** data) on the performance of regulations, rather than a perfunctory "set-it-and-forget-it" mentality. This will take time, and it will take money. It will not be simple deregulation, or more regulation. It will be regulatory reform, or smart regulation. It will follow cost-benefit comparisons as its primary measure of success.

And we believe the smart regulation, while a value in itself, will be a broader step forward for the body politic. Both Democrats and Republicans can—*should*—agree to a process that achieves the original objectives of the regulations better, while being less of a drag on employment and the economy. And Republican and Democratic cooperation to achieve something—*anything*—for the good of the country will be a veritable revolution in the way our federal government works today.[10]

It is our self-assigned task to try to explain how government could better perform one of its most important tasks.[11] We are optimistic, because we believe that it can be done—and it has been done before (as suggested above and explained in more detail below). This process can begin if Americans talk to one another, accept each others' good intentions, and find ways to achieve our shared objectives. Regulation is a good place to start.

---

10 The last Pew Research Center poll tracking "Public Trust in Government, 1958-2017" to do the right thing most of the time (or "just about always," the two groups combined) is near its all-time low (10 percent in 2011, shortly after the financial crisis) at 18 percent as of December 4, 2017.

11 Political science has identified "tools of governance," of which direct government action is only one (and perhaps of decreasing prevalence over recent years). Other tools, beyond regulation (perhaps in the ascendancy), include government-sponsored enterprises, insurance, public information, taxes, fees, permits, contracting out, grants, loans and loan guarantees, and tax expenditures and vouchers, among others. Lester M. Salmon, ed., *The Tools of Government: A Guide to the New Governance* (New York: Oxford University Press, 2002).

2

THE PURPOSE OF REGULATION

WHY IS THERE REGULATION?

To some, regulation clearly is a punishment for some past sin so terrible that we dare not speak of it. To others, regulation is the only force allowing our civilized society itself to hold on by a single thread.

In reality, the answer lies somewhere between these two extremes and is far more complicated than either.

Economists believe that competition in a free market is the life force of prosperity. As much as each individual would prefer to prosper in isolation, competition is what drives our society collectively to advance. Competition causes each worker to do his or her best, and each firm to seek ways to improve quality and reduce price. And the success of each worker and firm in one product or service market expands the potential of all those elsewhere in the economy, by improving their choices among business inputs for productivity growth, or consumption opportunities for every American's personal well-being.

So competition sounds great—and easy, too. Just let the invisible hand do its invisible work. If firms are competing with one another for business, competition should keep them honest. Give your customers a bum deal and, especially in these days of instant communication via social media, your competition will eat you for lunch. So why not just let the profit motive rip?

Well, it turns out that the vast majority of economists would agree: an unfettered competitive market does yield the best outcomes, and such markets should be left alone.

But problems arise when markets are not truly competitive. It is always a judgment call as to whether there is true competition. Actors in the markets can tussle over this with government regulators, both in and out of court, and legislators can debate the issue as well. Given the merit of market outcomes, there is reason for some diffidence about government interference. But on the other hand, the risk in the event of serious "market failures," as economists call them, can be very high.

So why is there regulation? In the textbook, at least, the reason would be that some of the fundamental elements of competition—economists talk about "perfect competition" as the quintessential, the ideal state—are absent. In those instances, economists describe such deficient markets as "imperfect competition," or sometimes worse.

So what is perfect competition? It is fair bargaining among a large number of fully informed buyers and a large number of fully informed sellers over a uniform (standardized) product. No one can take advantage of anyone else in the marketplace. Think of lots of farmers selling identical wheat to lots of bakers (but hold that thought for a few moments). No seller can step out of the behavioral line, because any buyer can simply move on to buy from someone else. No buyer can take advantage of the seller, because the seller can wait for one of the many other buyers to come along. The price that results is precisely what the market forces of supply and demand say it should be, and both buyers and sellers get exactly what they want, subject to the reality of those market forces. There is nothing for government to do but stand back and marvel at what the invisible hand hath wrought.

So what can go wrong? Why would government need to get involved? Well, basically, any one or more of the assumptions about this perfect market could be violated. And in fact, this probably happens more often than not; but whether government needs to get involved and regulate in any particular case is another question.

Let's think about how these assumptions of perfect competition might be violated such that some form of government regulation might improve economic outcomes. Economists can rattle off a long list of potential market failures that could interfere with the workings of the free market. Many combine attributes of several items on the list.

One classic market failure is the *spillover or externality*. Imagine a chemical plant located on a river. The plant generates foul wastes that might be just unpleasant, or outright dangerous. The cheapest way of disposing of the waste is just to dump it in the river. Then, it is the next town's, or even the next state's problem. If the firm wanted only to give its customers the highest-quality product at the lowest possible price, the firm would choose to pollute.[12]

Some might wonder how cynical an economist would need to be to imagine a business so unethical that it would dump its waste into a river. And that is a fair question. But imagine further that the business is on the cusp of survival, and that the added cost of safe disposal of the waste would render it non-viable. This raises a common element in numerous market failures—a potential "race to the bottom" under which the competitive pressures that we otherwise extol (some might add simple greed as an alternative driver) could lead to a breakdown of social-behavioral norms. In such instances, government regulation could remove that temptation.

A variation of the externalities theme is the so-called *tragedy of the commons*, so named because of the historical phenomenon of sheep herders allowing their flocks to eat their towns' common lands barren, to the ultimate disadvantage of all. A more common contemporary manifestation is the overfishing of particular species of fish or whales into extinction. Here, the "race to the bottom" problem appears with even greater intensity, because despite all good will on the part of an individual fisher or firm, there is a distinct anti-self-interest in holding back and watching others profit by exhausting the resource that the individual uses to make a living. Another potential example might be carbon emissions. Even business managers or householders who felt great concern about potential climate change might doubt whether they should incur costs to reduce their emissions of carbon while others did not. Therefore, there can be an urgent need for government regulation to protect a resource that might otherwise be lost to future generations.

12 "Externalities" can be positive as well as negative. For example, economists sometimes argue that a business would undertake more research if it were impossible for other businesses to observe its findings and use them for free. In such an instance, government could require that the research continue, but in lieu of that awkward approach, would more likely subsidize it (such as through our current research and experimentation tax credit) or would establish patent protection.

In some instances, there are benefits to *standardization* of products and services in the private sector, and there can be benefits to government making that happen. As one straightforward example, requiring all automobile bumpers to have a standard height reduces private-sector costs, because bumper-to-bumper contact causes less damage than does bumper-to-sheet-metal contact. Still, getting different manufacturers to act in coordination, when each would prefer that the others conform to its standard, could take some persuasive power. In this situation, creativity and openness could certainly help. Automakers should be involved in setting the standard, so that issues that matter receive the most attention and all ideas are considered. For example, the height of the center of the bumper from the ground matters, but so does the dimension from the top of the bumper to the bottom. Government acting in isolation might miss opportunities to make the standard both more effective and more economical to implement. But in addition to all such best efforts, the threat of governmental coercion might be necessary to get the deal done.

Public safety can be a moving force behind regulation. Beyond such issues as auto bumper height, government regulation requires insurance and licensing for taxicabs and drivers. When the taxicab industry was upended by new ride-hailing services such as Uber and Lyft, some suggested that those market disruptors were advantaged by lesser regulation, but these key safety provisions retained public support. In another example, highway safety regulators require that automakers preserve records of customer complaints and reports of incidents that relate to safety and reliability, and report when any similar or related complaints reach some minimum number. Official recalls might result. The reason for regulation is the concern that firms might conceal such information to avoid reputational damage despite a safety risk. And in fact, one manufacturer was recently cited for concealing relevant customer complaints.[13]

Also recently, along the lines of safety motives for regulation, a Member of Congress was annoyed at restaurant restroom signs enforcing regulations that food preparation workers wash their hands. He suggested that the market replace such regulation, and that restaurant patrons be allowed to choose between restaurants where workers are

---

13 Mark Magnier and John O'Dell, "Mitsubishi Admits Hiding Complaints," *Los Angeles Times*, August 23, 2000.

required to wash their hands and other restaurants where they are not.[14] It is not clear whether that suggestion was serious or in jest, but it does illustrate the sense of some that the market and open information can replace regulation, and the contrary views of others.

Some consider government safety regulation to be overdone. Take, for example, costly safety devices on lawnmowers. Manufacturers who comply with such regulatory requirements might receive a presumption against liability in the case of an accident. However, some might prefer that elaborate safety devices be made optional, giving consumers the choice of buying a cheaper lawnmower with the commensurate obligation to exercise more care.[15] Others might counter that this might constitute one step on a "race to the bottom," tempting the same kinds of consumers whose accidents during instants of distraction while using older pre-regulation lawnmowers motivated government regulation in the first place.

A similar complaint with respect to businesses might indict the Occupational Safety and Health Administration (OSHA). OSHA requires, for example, that ladders meet load-bearing, among other standards. A criticism is that workers should be allowed the choice of working with cheaper ladders in exchange, perhaps, for a higher wage. A counterargument might be that competitive cost pressures and deficient worker bargaining power might induce employers to force less-safe ladders and other equipment on workers whose only option would be to leave their jobs, setting the stage for avoidable workplace accidents.

All of these forces have occasioned regulatory interventions by governments—federal, state, and local. But two forces that can require regulation are monopoly power and asymmetrical information.

Monopoly refers to a market in which there is one seller of a particular good or service, confronting numerous buyers. Think of a grain market with only one farmer. The buyers have no choice. Simple economic models of such markets suggest that the seller will maximize his income (which of course is precisely what the quintessential "Economic Man"—the purely rational pursuer of self-interest—is expected to want to do) by

---

14 Veronica Stracqualursi, "Senator Suggests Restaurant Employees Shouldn't Have to Wash Hands," ABC News, February 3, 2015.

15 Greg Ip, *Foolproof: Why Safety Can Be Dangerous and How Danger Makes Us Safe* (New York: Little, Brown, 2015).

reducing output and raising the price. Society would be disadvantaged by both the lower production and the higher prices, compared with what would obtain under perfect competition.

One reflexive reaction to this scenario is that consumers always have some choice: they can simply refuse to buy the product. One response is that the economic model that we just discussed respects and includes that choice. Implicit in the notion that monopolists raise prices and reduce output is the tautology that therefore some consumers do not buy.

But more troubling is the reality that, in some instances, consumers might not have a viable option of refusing to buy. A recent round of enormous price increases for an unchanging life saving response to potential fatal allergic reactions raised this public-policy conundrum.[16]

Even though this concept is based on one seller, monopoly in practice is rarely an absolute. Often there are powerful sellers marketing similar, but not identical, products or services. In this context, economists speak of perfect and imperfect substitutes. So if there are a few, but not many producers of identical products, or of similar and partially substitutable products, economists use the term "oligopoly" rather than "monopoly." The policy problem is similar, however; sellers will still find it advantageous to reduce output and raise prices, thereby maximizing their profits but disadvantaging society.

The traditional regulatory discipline to remedy either monopoly or oligopoly is antitrust policy. Antitrust remedies, when invoked, typically prevent a merger or acquisition that is feared to create or aggravate such market power. Action is taken only rarely to address pre-existing market power. (So, for example, there was much sound and fury, but no action, over the price increases for the epi-pen device for allergic reactions.) However, there are remedies that address exploitation of existing market power, such as outright collusion among oligopolists to increase prices.

Monopoly often is in the eye of the beholder. One observer will see a firm that has acquired leverage over the consumer and is raising prices to exploit that power. But that firm could tell a story of innovation or disciplined competition to reduce costs and deliver quality, leading to market-judged success—precisely what we request from firms.

---

16 Charles Duhigg, "Outcry over EpiPen Prices Hasn't Made Them Lower," *New York Times*, June 4, 2017.

Furthermore, market power is defined in an ever-changing marketplace and technological environment. Some retail chain stores might be said to hold enormous competitive advantages over their peers with near-identical business models. But those same chains might be fighting for their lives against purely online sellers. Historically, firms like US Steel and Kodak were behemoths, dominating their markets. Now they are mere shadows of their former selves. For years, many considered that the restriction of taxicab operation to owners of medallions created an oligopoly. The rise of the ride-hailing industry has cut the value of medallions substantially and has challenged taxicab oligopolies nationwide.

So accusations of abuse of market power should be leveled with care. But sometimes they should be leveled nonetheless. As one example, market power can have a geographic dimension. Much of health care, for example, cannot be delivered via the Internet. One sector-specific problem today is local monopoly over hospital beds, which can exacerbate the problem of our notoriously uncompetitive health care sector and lead to higher prices in some parts of the country. There may be a new idea for a new model for the more-efficient delivery of quality health care, but if the proposed health care plan cannot obtain access to hospital beds, the pre-existing, more-costly health insurance plans can continue on their wasteful ways.

A final powerful motivation for regulation is *asymmetrical access to information* in the marketplace. Where competition is quintessentially perfect, both buyers and sellers know all about the product or service for sale. For example, in the quintessential perfectly competitive market for wheat, all wheat is identical across all sellers. If a buyer offers a price, he or she knows exactly what that money will buy. Deception is impossible, prices are held low by competition, and so there is no need for government to intervene.

That happy situation does not characterize a wide array of goods and services transactions today, even for wheat, in the real world. Think of just a few examples:

Many manufactured goods today are bundles of components and attributes so numerous that each product is nearly unique. Most customers have limited understanding of the complexities of those products. A small number of manufacturer-sellers, each with some degree of market power, build and sell those products. But those market positions could be exploited to the detriment of consumers.

One element of value in an automobile, for example, is fuel economy. It would be very difficult for consumers, acting on their own, to obtain accurate and comparable information about the fuel efficiency of different vehicles, so the market could not compare the relative merits and values of alternative makes and models to help consumers to make the best choices. For that matter, consumers could for whatever reason circulate misinformation about fuel economy to favor one manufacturer over another. Different manufacturers, acting on their own, could estimate fuel efficiency in different ways. So regulation to require standardized fuel economy estimates can serve the goal of fair competition.[17] Similar reasoning can apply to vehicle safety standards. In a very different product space, the same reasoning can apply to the nutritional and health attributes of foods.

And on the services front, complexity might again confound. Contracts in finance and insurance can be understandable only to specialist attorneys, leaving consumers at the mercy of these specialists and sellers when it comes to the rate of interest on a loan or the rate of return on an annuity. Honest differences among such sellers as to the "best" measures could lead to a proliferation of different estimates that could confuse and potentially mislead consumers. Differences in information disclosure by sellers of corporate bonds or equities could do the same.[18] Regulations to dictate standardized measures and disclosures can protect consumers, in part by heading off the temptations of a "race to the bottom" in standards of financial reporting.

Information asymmetry, as well as public safety, is sometimes cited as a reason for occupational licensing. Individual consumers might not be well situated to verify the qualifications of professionals, such as physicians or even auto mechanics, whom they hire. However, such licensing requirements can easily prove excessive. Professions not rising to the level of public safety, such as some branches of cosmetic services, can seek to impose and preserve occupational licensing requirements to limit competition and support member incomes.[19]

---

17 And the regulation must be effective; note the scandal over Volkswagen manipulation of emissions from its diesel passenger cars.

18 Financial Crisis Inquiry Commission, *Financial Crisis Inquiry Report*, January 2011, https://www.gpo.gov/fdsys/pkg/GPO-FCIC/pdf/GPO-FCIC.pdf.

19 US Council of Economic Advisers, *Occupational Licensing: A Framework for Policymakers*, July 2015.

CONCLUSION

There are valid reasons for regulation in our complex and fast-moving economic and commercial lives. There are also ways in which regulation can be overdone or can be excessively complex, stifling competition to the disadvantage of businesses and consumers alike.

On an economist's blackboard, competition can render the abuse of consumers impossible—or at least punish it when it occurs. However, even such perfect competition, with its razor-thin sellers' margins, can motivate sellers to try to achieve mere survival by finding minute advantages in a behavioral "race to the bottom." But far more common threats, such as consumers' knowing less about a product than sellers; monopoly or oligopoly market power; negative externalities like pollution; dangers to prosperity through the depletion of scarce resources like fisheries; threats to public safety through corner-cutting on standards; and the need for standardization or coordination among products and sellers, all can make regulation necessary or at least beneficial to a dynamic economy and consumer prosperity.

But at the same time, regulation can overflow its mandate—adding costs and stifling competition. Regulation can outlive its usefulness or overreach its mission. An accumulation of low-value regulations can overwhelm existing small businesses (or deter the formation of new ones) that are the economy's lifeblood. In short, either the benefits of good regulation or the burdens of bad regulation are certainly large enough to justify reading—or for that matter, writing—a book.

As in so many areas of public policy, there is need for sound judgment, weighing the foreseeable consequences and anticipating the unintended consequences of either action or forbearance of action. Hard-and-fast rules will not suffice.

And to hammer home that point, recall that most common example of the quintessential perfectly competitive, regulation-free market: the sale of uniform wheat by multiple farmers to multiple bakers. Move from the textbook to the real world, and you will find that one of the most government-intervention-laden of private markets is . . . Agriculture. Can government keep its hands off even such a textbook-free market? Regulation may in many instances be necessary; but must it be overdone? Can it be done better? That is the motivation of this book.

3

THE REGULATORY PROCESS

It all began with 10 simple words:

> *[H]e shall take Care that the Laws be faithfully executed. . . .*[20]

These words, which have come to be known as the "Take Care Clause" of the Constitution of the United States, were intended to instruct the President to implement the laws as passed by Congress. It sounds simple enough.

As the executive branch sought to accomplish this objective, it established government agencies. Together, the President and the executive agencies began to issue proposed rules, final regulations, public notices, requests for public comment, and similar information. Over more than a century, this panoply of paper grew cumbersome. So in 1935, Congress passed the Federal Register Act "to provide for the prompt and uniform printing and distribution thereof." This resulted in the first publication of the Federal Register at 2,620 pages which, given this demand, not surprisingly resulted in a dramatic increase in the quantity of these items. Within one year, the Federal Register swelled to 3,450 pages, which caused Congress to amend the law to require a codification

20 US Const. art. II, §3.

by subject matter. Today we have nearly 100,000 pages included in the Federal Register (see figure 3.1). Although some would argue that this huge quantity evidences excessive regulation, others would rightfully point out that the Federal Register includes much material other than actual final regulations themselves. Further, even changes to regulations to simplify or eliminate them would require additional pages. Still, many would agree that sound regulatory policy could dramatically improve the efficiency and effectiveness of regulations.[21]

And how many regulatory agencies exist today? That depends on who you ask:

FOIA.gov	252[22]
US Government Manual	316[23]
Federal Register Agency List	445[24]

21 The number of Federal Register pages is a rough but imperfect indicator of the amount of regulatory activity (as well as other activities of government). The Federal Register also includes presidential documents; notices of requests for public comment on proposed regulations; notices of changes in the schedules for consideration of new regulations; and prefatory material to actual final regulations, including discussions of public comment. Maeve P. Carey, *Counting Regulations: An Overview of Rulemaking, Types of Federal Regulations, and Pages in the Federal Register*, Congressional Research Service, October 4, 2016.

22 David E. Lewis, *Sourcebook of United States Executive Agencies*, Nashville, TN: Administrative Conference of the United States, 2012; accessible at https://bookstore.gpo.gov/products/sourcebook-united-states-executive-agencies-december-2012.

23 *Sourcebook of United States Executive Agencies.*

24 Federal Register.

FIGURE 3.1 **Number of pages in the federal register by year**

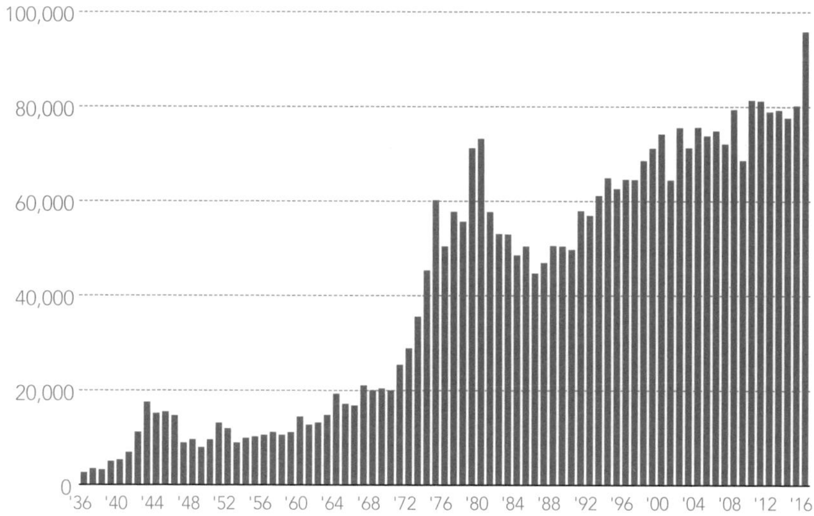

Source:
https://regulatorystudies.columbian.gwu.edu/sites/g/files/zaxdzs1866/f/downloads/Pages%20in%20the%20Federal%20Register.JPG

Notes: Comparisons between the numbers of pages in early years' issues and those issued since the 1970s are complicated by several factors. Proposed rules were not required to be published until the enactment of the Administrative Procedure Act of 1946. The issue of January 1, 1947 was the first to have a Proposed Rule category. Extensive preambles explaining rule documents were not common until the mid-1960s. The issues from the years 1936-1975 are not broken down by category and are not adjusted for blank or skipped pages.

Regulation now touches all aspects of our daily lives, and the total cost of regulation—administration, compliance, and so on—imposes an economic burden on our nation. Economists provide widely differing estimates of the annual burden of regulation, ranging between several hundred billion dollars and $2 trillion (National Association of Manufacturers).[25] The high-end estimate equates to 10 percent of our entire GDP[26] and exceeds the total amount of income tax collected by the federal government.[27] Other estimates, including by the Office

25 National Association of Manufacturers, "Regulatory Reform."

26 US Bureau of Economic Analysis (BEA), "National Data."

27 Office of Management and Budget (OMB), "Historical Tables."

of Information and Regulatory Affairs (OIRA), part of the Office of Management and Budget of the Executive Office of the President, are significantly smaller.[28] Whatever the size, this hidden tax burden ultimately falls on consumers, because businesses ultimately must pass on much of the taxes they pay to consumers (including in consumers' capacity as owners of businesses) if they are to survive. As large corporations continue to seek acceptable rates of return on their investments while balancing supply and demand, any incremental costs (whether labor, rent, taxes, or the cost of regulatory compliance) likely result in incremental price increases to the consumer, making corporations the unwitting accomplice to this hidden taxation. Further, these incremental costs are largely embedded in consumer pricing. As incremental consumer-price increases are disproportionately borne by low-income consumers, it is a highly regressive form of taxation.

Regulators must therefore do their best to impose regulation in the most efficient possible way, and to ensure that the benefits of regulation fully justify the costs.

At the same time, and if the regulatory system is working, those regulations also will generate benefits in excess of their costs. OIRA estimates both the benefits as well as the costs of major regulations (greater than $100 million of impact, or raising important policy issues) each year.[29] In its most recent estimate, OIRA found benefits of between $219 billion and $695 billion, with costs of between $78 billion

28 OMB, OIRA, *2017 Draft Report to Congress on the Benefits and Costs of Federal Regulations and Agency Compliance with the Unfunded Mandates Reform Act*, February 23, 2018 (available at https://www.whitehouse.gov/omb/information-regulatory-affairs/reports/). There are fundamental differences between the two types of estimates of the costs of regulation provided by NAM and OMB; see Maeve P. Carey, "Methods of Estimating the Total Cost of Federal Regulations," Congressional Research Service Report R44348, January 21, 2016. The larger, NAM estimate is called a "top-down" estimate, which starts with an estimate of the cost of all regulations in terms of total economic output. This is a monumental task methodologically, and its nature does not allow for a corresponding estimate of the benefits of all regulation. It therefore provides no guidance as to the evaluation of any particular regulation (including a proposed new regulation), only an assessment of the cost of all regulations together. The smaller, OMB estimate is based on separate estimates of the costs and benefits of individual regulations considered one at a time. It is helpful for considering the merits of a single regulation, but it presents its own methodological challenges (see Chapter 9 on "Social Regulation" below for the issues in assessing the benefits of protection of life or prevention of injury or disease), and it does not consider possible interactions among multiple regulations.

29 As defined in Executive Order 12866—Regulatory Planning and Review.

and $115 billion.[30] Thus, although all regulations entail costs, a well-functioning regulatory system should yield regulations based on a favorable balance of benefits to costs. These estimates of benefits are subject to challenge, however. Critics point out that OIRA must accept estimates from individual agencies that proposed the regulations, and question the objectivity of those estimates. Those critics also observe that more than two-thirds of estimated benefits come from regulations of the Environmental Protection Agency, which necessarily entail measurement complexities relating to the valuation of human life, uncertainties of developments in the distant future, and difficulties of valuing those future benefits in current dollars. In addition, the benefits of a regulation are not necessarily available to other actors in the economy to help them to pay their costs. And finally, we will advise that regulators consider the potential for a large number of regulations to create a cumulative cost of complexity and confusion.

For all of this uncertainty, probably all analysts would agree that considerable economic and social value could be achieved through the best possible analysis of each regulation, both existing and proposed. It is not helpful to observe that existing regulations have costs, and therefore to conclude that there should be no future regulation. It is equally unhelpful to claim that because existing regulations are estimated to have greater benefits than costs, issuing more regulations in the future must therefore be beneficial. The hard work of careful and sound analysis, case by case, is essential.

30 Office of Management and Budget, Office of Information and Regulatory Affairs, *2017 Draft Report to Congress on the Benefits and Costs of Federal Regulations and Agency Compliance with the Unfunded Mandates Reform Act*, February 23, 2018 (available at https://www.whitehouse.gov/omb/information-regulatory-affairs/reports/).

NONPARTISANSHIP OF REGULATION

FIGURE 3.2 **Number of economically significant final rules published**

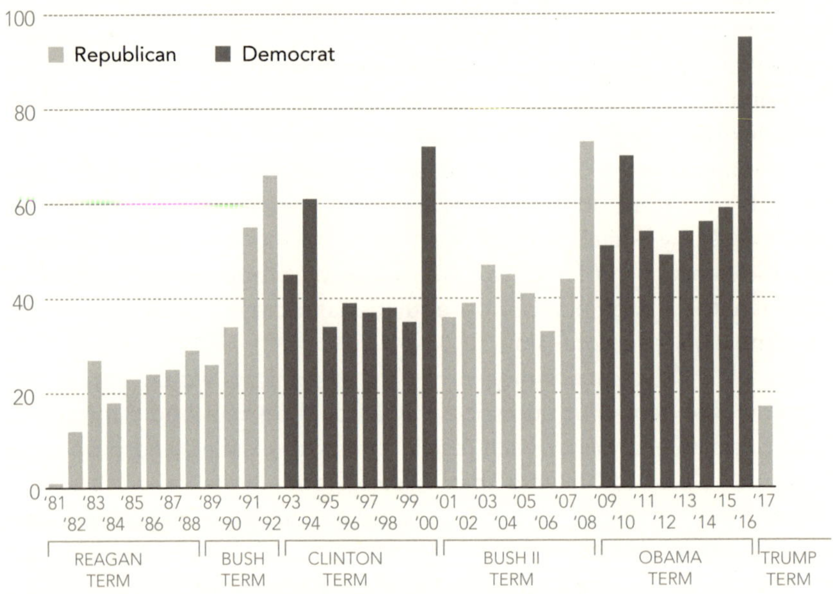

Source: https://regulatorystudies.columbian.gwu.edu/sites/g/files/zaxdzs1866/f/downloads/Economically%20Significant%20Final%20Rules%20chart.JPG

As evident in the chart above (figure 3.2), Democrats and Republicans alike have contributed to this burgeoning of regulation. In fact, it is worth noting that the most significant years seem to be the last year of each presidential term. Perhaps that is what Dylan Thomas had in mind when he wrote:

> Though wise men at their end know dark is right,
> Because their words had forked no lightning they
> Do not go gentle into that good night.

THE NECESSITY OF REGULATION

Following up on the previous chapter, it is important to answer the question "why" we have regulation. The easiest and most common answer to this question is that a regulation is written because a law called for it. While factually true, our forefathers were far more insightful in this regard. In the preamble to the Constitution, they offered us this prescriptive reason:

> . . . in Order to form a more perfect Union, establish Justice, insure domestic Tranquility, provide for the common defence, promote the general Welfare, and secure the Blessings of Liberty to ourselves and our Posterity...

It is highly doubtful that each of those 100,000 pages of regulations lives up to the lofty ideals of forming "a more perfect union." While this goal may at times seem ethereal, we should consider these words from the founding fathers as both inspirational and aspirational, guiding and challenging every action (or inaction) we take. As this portion of the preamble should be the standard for regulations, it seems appropriate to hold ourselves to this same standard as we set out in this book to provide meaningful recommendations for improvement in the regulatory ecosystem.

More specifically, in pursuing the Founding Fathers' global and aspirational goals, the major economic justifications for and role of regulation are fairly clear cut:[31]

- To address market failures where true costs and benefits are not reflected correctly in market prices;
- To reduce entry barriers, "level the playing field," encourage greater competition and innovation, and combat short-sightedness— all to increase economic growth; and
- To ensure consumer, worker and investor safety, transparency in information about products and services, and a fair distribution of net benefits. This category is often labeled "social regulation," but these policies also have economic justifications and implications.

---

31 Committee for Economic Development, *Regulation & the Economy: The Relationship & How to Improve It* (Washington, DC: September 17, 2017).

These objectives are of course highly conceptual. Taking such language to the operational level, and to the text of a regulation, is a serious challenge. For example, the fair distribution of benefits will be highly subjective. At one and the same time, innovators and risk takers deserve a return on their contributions, and the best-off should contribute to the maintenance of the society, including the rule of law, that allowed them to succeed. But operationalizing this broad principle will require negotiations among all stakeholders through the political process. More philosophically, we would cite John Rawls' *Theory of Justice*, in which he recommends that people should implicitly say what system they would accept if they did not know ahead of time what their life outcomes would be – which he called a "veil of ignorance." Many adults already know with at least some degree of precision what their lifetimes and careers will bring, and would be tempted to argue for a tax and public benefit system that would favor them. However, as close as experts can come to sampling opinion, citizens at large placing themselves behind this "veil of ignorance" would want a safety net for those who fall behind along with mildly progressive tax rates for those who succeed – in other words, a system approximating what we have today.

HOW A LAW BECOMES A REGULATION: ROLES OF THE LEGISLATIVE, EXECUTIVE, AND JUDICIAL BRANCHES

"Schoolhouse Rock," the Saturday morning children's educational television show, has given generations of Americans a basic understanding of the roles of the three branches of government, likening it to a three-ring circus.[32] In a similar vein, many Americans of a certain age well remember publications entitled *How A Bill Becomes A Law* from their early government (or even civics) instruction.[33] It is perhaps an indicator of the public's general regard for regulation that the children's book *How A Regulation Is Made* seems not yet to have been written. However, for those who still remember their elementary school classes, at least the

32 We borrow this image from Elizabeth H. Slattery, "Who Will Regulate the Regulators? Administrative Agencies, the Separation of Powers, and Chevron Deference," Heritage Foundation Legal Memorandum no. 153, May 7, 2015.

33 Several publications by this title still exist, including by John Hamilton, Abdo Publishing, September 1, 2004; Kyla Steinkraus, Rourke Educational Media, August 1, 2014; and Nancy Van Wie, MAX's Publications, March 8, 2012.

path of a regulation through the federal government is quite similar to that of a law. The roles of our three branches might seem very simple and discrete when viewed through this lens, but the reality is somewhat more complicated.

Legislative

The legislative branch has some authority in the regulatory process. Congress cannot write regulations narrowly defined. However, in the laws it passes it can either explicitly mandate the creation of regulations, or implicitly require regulation for the implementation of those laws (and therefore trigger the creation of regulations).[34] (In either case, it is the executive branch or the independent agencies that write the regulations.) Furthermore, Congress has the authority to repeal regulations by law. Its legislative activity in this realm, of course, has a political dimension as well.

There is real concern whether Congress has sufficient targeted resources (funds to hire staff with appropriate skills and experience) either to mandate or to review sound regulations. One specific worry is that Congress might specify infeasible requirements for regulation—that once all of the terms are met, it might be impossible for the regulation to achieve benefits that exceed the costs of implementation and compliance. There are questions as to whether Congress can replicate the "street-level" understanding of an agency that actually implements and enforces regulations. There are, of course, contrary concerns whether an executive agency can have the sensitivity to citizen problems that is instinctive at the level of the elected legislature.

And given that Congress's instinct is to write new laws, there is a question as to whether it in its current configuration it can or will devote sufficient resources to regulatory review. Congress does have a structural tendency toward inaction, given the routine requirement for 60 Senate votes to close potentially unlimited debate (a "filibuster") in order to enact any law. However, Congress does have an expedited process for review of new regulations without the possibility of a filibuster through the Congressional Review Act (CRA). (A congressional resolution of disapproval of a new regulation could be vetoed by a President, and then would require a two-thirds vote of both chambers of Congress

---

34 Nancy Beck, "Regulatory Policy: The United States Perspective," Organisation for Economic Cooperation and Development.

to override the veto.)[35] An extension of the CRA's authority has been suggested, in that the Act allows Congress a 60-day review period that begins when an agency files a report from the issuing agency. In some historical instances, agencies did not file such reports. This can allow a new Administration hostile to such regulations to file those reports, and thereby to open the review window during which Congress can file resolutions of disapproval—potentially years after the regulations were originally issued.[36] Some have thought that an agency could re-propose an unwanted but legally valid regulation so that Congress could vote against it using the CRS.

Another question is how Congress writes its laws that either mandate or implicitly require regulation. Some, perhaps many or most, scholars of regulation would recommend that legislators seek to achieve regulations based on principles sufficient to ensure that they are executed and enforced on the basis of their intent. However, many laws are passed with vague or ambiguous language perhaps as a matter of political expediency. If the law is ultimately perceived as successful, the legislature can take credit for its success. Conversely, if the law is perceived as a failure, the regulators can be blamed. It is said that victory has a hundred fathers (or in this case as many as 535 legislators), while defeat is an orphan.

Although reduced ambiguity in legislation would be helpful, the intent cannot be to expand the laws and regulations to cover absolutely every contingency. For one thing, such a web of rules would virtually invite businesses to find and exploit the loopholes. A key part of creating a level competitive playing field for business is closing loopholes through which bad actors can profit. The vast majority of ethical business leaders would behave well. But they (and consumers) would be the losers when the opportunities to profit from bad behavior inevitably pull all of the few unethical people out of the woodwork, and create incentives for a "race to the bottom."

---

35 Morton Rosenberg, "Congressional Review of Agency Rulemaking: An Update and Assessment of The Congressional Review Act after a Decade," Congressional Research Service Report for Congress RL30116, May 8, 2008; Maeve P. Carey, Alissa M. Dolan, and Christopher M. Davis, "The Congressional Review Act: Frequently Asked Questions," Congressional Research Service Report R43992, November 17, 2016.

36 Daren Bakst and James L. Gattuso, "Stars Align for the Congressional Review Act," Heritage Foundation Issue Brief No. 4640, December 16, 2016 (available at https://www.heritage.org/government-regulation/report/stars-align-the-congressional-review-act).

For another, the more detailed the rules, the sooner the inevitable changes in technology and the economy will render them obsolete. Even with all of the will in the world, regulators could easily fall behind in the process of revising regulations to keep them up to date. And even to the extent that the regulators were successful, such frequent changes in detailed rules could make compliance by businesses difficult and expensive—if it is even possible. And finally, highly detailed and prescriptive rules naturally entail greater compliance costs.

One of the ideas to be discussed in this book is the potential for "principles-based" versus "rules-based" regulations. In general, we believe that "principles-based" regulation is superior. But careful judgment and regulatory design is essential.

Different market situations create different opportunities, and impose different constraints. We discuss elsewhere that financial institutions must be required to use specific formulas for the "annualized percentage rate" (APR) that they charge for their loans and pay on their deposits. Allowing variations in the formula would enable bad business actors to exploit the public, and would confuse most consumers. So in such a situation, a detailed, prescriptive rule is necessary.

Too far to the other extreme would be a rule based on a principle so broad and general that it is, at the end of the day, meaningless and useless. An example would be a principle that business leaders should "behave ethically." We all could endorse such a principle. But it would be entirely subjective, and could alternatively lead regulators to throw up their hands in frustration and do nothing, or allow regulators to impose their own definitions and standards. In the latter instance, businesses would not be able to predict or understand what they must do to comply with even an ultimately justifiable regulation. The ultimate enforcement of many such regulations would inevitably wind up in court.

Under the right circumstances, we believe that principles-based regulation would achieve better results at lower cost. This would be particularly true where regulations can be based on achievement of targets that can be expressed in performance- or market-based measurements. A regulated firm that could demonstrate that it had met the target of the regulation—for example, a particular reduced level of pollution—would by definition be in compliance and would be protected by the law itself. This would be far superior to regulations that define ***how*** the firm should comply with the target, rather than that it should meet the target itself. Past examples of rules-based regulation—such as requirements to use a particular technology to reduce pollution, or to cover a particular device or pharmaceutical in a health-insurance policy, have failed on two grounds. First, they can fall behind the best practice to achieve the goal of the regulation, and can inhibit efforts to improve the best practice. And second, they can become open invitations to "crony capitalism," whereby incumbent interests entice regulators to mandate the use of their own particular technologies to achieve compliance.

Reducing the degree of prescriptiveness of each individual regulation in this way would most likely free up critical resources of the regulatory agencies to focus on accomplishing the objectives set out in the law rather than attempting to account for every possible circumstance in an increasingly complex world. Such an approach would also free the private sector to find better, less costly ways to achieve the regulatory objectives—especially important when advancing technology might allow such innovations.

Finally, principles-based regulations, as mandated by Congress, could be more comprehensive, and so might eliminate or reduce the executive branch's ability or incentive to issue new regulations in the waning days of an administration. Such regulations might be construed as an attempt to batten down the hatches against the wave of a new administration.

A change to principles-based regulation would best be promulgated through the laws themselves. Legislation instructing regulators to create regulations that are based on principles with performance- or market-based measurements would have the power of law, thus making the regulations subject to judicial review.

Executive

Once Congress mandates or de facto requires new regulation to enforce a law, the Executive branch must create it. This is a multi-step process.[37] The relevant agency drafts a proposed rule, which, if the rule is judged to be "significant," must be reviewed by OMB.[38] The agency publishes a notice of its proposed rulemaking, and the public is permitted to comment to the agency. The agency reviews the public comments and develops the proposed rule into a draft final form. OMB again reviews "significant" rules at this stage. Once it is published, the rule is reviewed

37 Nancy Beck, "Regulatory Policy: The United States Perspective."

38 As defined in Exec. Order No. 12866 (September 30, 1993) ("Regulatory Planning and Review").

by Congress under the CRA, and Congress can pass a disapproval resolution if it chooses. Alternatively, the rule may be challenged in court, and the court may "vacate" all or part of the rule. If the rule passes all of these hurdles, it goes into effect.

In the larger context, this brings us back to the Constitution. While history shows there may have been little discussion of the "Take Care Clause" at the Constitutional Convention, since that time we have not stopped talking about it. A google search of "Take Care Clause" comes up with 18 million results. As it turns out, this clause is a double-edged sword and is often cited for the President's *obligation* to execute the laws, and *discretion* in enforcing the laws.[39] There have been a number of court cases recognizing the *obligation* of the President to execute the laws, which would arguably require the President to create and enforce regulations.

Marbury v. Madison

Some will recognize *Marbury* as the landmark case in which Chief Justice John Marshall affirmed the legal principle of judicial review (the power of the Supreme Court to limit Congressional power by declaring legislation unconstitutional). However, it also had an impact on the President's obligation to execute the laws.

In the waning days of the Adams Administration, William Marbury was appointed by President John Adams as Justice of the Peace for the District of Columbia, and his appointment was approved by the Senate. When newly elected President Jefferson took office, Marbury's commission had yet to be delivered. So President Jefferson instructed then-Secretary of State James Madison not to deliver the commission and, in so doing, held that Marbury could not hold the office. Marbury petitioned the Supreme Court to force Madison to deliver the commission. The Court found the withholding of the commission to be illegal and stated that when an Executive fails a "specific duty assigned by law," the courts may enforce the law through a writ of mandamus. Curiously, the Court was ultimately unable to find in favor of Marbury because it ruled that the provisions of the Judiciary Act of 1789 under which the Court was petitioned were unconstitutional (hence the landmark ruling).

39 Todd Garvey, *The Take Care Clause and Executive Discretion in the Enforcement of Law*, Congressional Research Service Report to Congress R43708, September 4, 2014.

Kendall v. U.S.

In *Kendall*, the law provided unambiguous instruction to provide specific back pay to mail carriers. However, the Postmaster General (on instruction from President Jackson) refused to do so. In reviewing the case, the Supreme Court found "the duty and responsibility grow out of and are subject to the control of the law, and not to the direction of the President."[40]

Thus, Congress appears to have chosen to pass laws with or without a level of specificity, alternatively providing the President with direction or discretion. Perhaps this was best stated in *Ameron v. US Army Corps of Engineers*, "If Congress gives the President only a few general instructions, and allows the executive 'to fill up the details,'. . . then the scope of the executive power is great. If, on the other hand, Congress chooses to specify a great number of details concerning how it wants the executive to proceed, such as specifying what it wants the executive to procure, the legislature is entirely free to take that course."[41] And so decisions by Congress can either expand or contract the President's obligation to regulate.

Judicial

Several key rulings mentioned herein have highlighted the limits and obligations of the President and the Executive branch. Simply stated, the President cannot proscribe what the law prescribes, nor can the President prescribe what the law proscribes. In general, these rulings ensure that *if* a law is written with a degree of specificity, the courts generally require that the President and the Executive branch must execute the law as written. Conversely, if Congress provides only general principles, the Executive is free to determine how best to achieve those principles.

In addition to allowing the president to "fill in the blanks," the courts have shown great judicial restraint with regard to prosecutorial discretion by the Executive branch.

In 1971, the prisoners of Attica Correctional Facility rioted. While the riot was ultimately suppressed, 43 people died in the riots (including 33 inmates). The inmates of Attica Correctional Facility sought to compel the US Attorney to prosecute officials involved in the suppression of the Attica prison riot. The Second Circuit Court of Appeals rejected their

---

40 *Kendall v. United States ex Rel. Stokes*, **37 US 12 Pet. 524 524 (1838)**

41 *Ameron, Inc. et al v. US Army Corps of Engineers*, 809 F2d 979 (3d Cir. 1987)

petition. Not only did the court follow the tradition of judicial restraint, but cited the reasons why:

> . . . . [T]he manifold imponderables which enter into the prosecutor's decision to prosecute or not to prosecute make the choice not readily amendable to judicial supervision.[42]

The Clean Air Act addresses "sources" of pollution. Under the Carter administration, these were defined as any device in a manufacturing plant that produced pollution. In 1981, the Reagan administration adopted a new definition that allowed an existing plant to acquire permits for new equipment that did not meet standards so long as the total emissions from the plant itself did not increase. This was contested by an environmental protection group by challenging the EPA in federal court. Ultimately, the Supreme Court ruled in favor of the EPA:

> First, always, is the question whether Congress has directly spoken to the precise question at issue. If the intent of Congress is clear, that is the end of the matter; for the court, as well as the agency, must give effect to the unambiguously expressed intent of Congress. If, however, the court determines Congress has not directly addressed the precise question at issue, the court does not simply impose its own construction on the statute. . . . Rather, if the statute is silent or ambiguous with respect to the specific issue, the question for the court is whether the agency's answer is based on a permissible construction of the statute.[43]

Thus, it would seem that absent specific instructions in the law, the agencies are relatively free to interpret *and* enforce the law as they see fit, generally without the threat of judicial activism—a concept known to this day as "Chevron deference," in recognition of the Court decision in this case. Further, the executive agencies are free to re-interpret such laws provided that interpretation of an ambiguously worded law is permissible. Yet regulators consistently attempt to contemplate every permutation and combination of events, which results in labyrinthine regulations, favoring those with the ability to navigate the maze (typically large corporations) or to influence the maze makers (crony capitalists).

---

42 477 F. 2d 380 (2nd Cir 1973)

43 *Chevron U.S.A. v. NRDC, 467 U.S. 837, 842-43 (1984)*

Still, in the broad context of the making of regulations, the courts can have important influence. The current Administration has sought to curtail or eliminate regulation in many respects, and it has taken the steps available to it on numerous fronts. However, the prospect remains open that existing law (which cannot be repealed without 60 votes in the Senate) mandates regulation on some of these fronts, and that the Executive's current forbearance may be challenged in court as a failure to comply with those mandates. The ultimate filing and disposition of such challenges is of course unknowable at this time, but it is clear that the Executive may not have the certain and final word on every regulatory issue.

That coin has a second side, however. When we discuss the history of US regulation, we will note that the bipartisan wave of deregulation and reform in the late 1970s and early 1980s arose from the Executive and proceeded through Congress. The reason was that the law mandated forms of regulation over transportation, communications, and other issues, and that even though those regulations had become obsolete and economically inefficient, it was (and still is) not the remit of the Judiciary to say so. The Judiciary enforces the law as it is written. So in that historical instance, the court exerted its power by inaction, forcing the Executive and the Congress to act.

Within that constraint, the courts may still play an important role in making regulatory policy. In a nation so evenly divided politically, or perhaps with split political control between the Executive and Congress, substantive legislation can be difficult to pass. So if the Executive and the Legislative branches are deadlocked, and even though the regulatory power of the courts may be limited, they may be making what new regulatory policy is being made, when circumstances give them leeway.

THE FOURTH BRANCH . . . REGULATORS

Our next logical focus will be to address the executive agencies themselves. Given the latitude afforded the agencies by legislative ambiguity and judicial restraint, these regulators often are referred to as the fourth branch of government . . . one that effectively has the power of all three of the other branches in formulating the regulation, passing judgment on it (in company with OIRA—in theory subject to judicial review, but with that review restrained by "Chevron deference"), and enforcing it. This characterization applies to regulators in virtually all executive agencies.

Given the complexities of our economy, regulators certainly need subject-matter experts to best execute their assigned duties. Of necessity, these experts often come from the very industry subject to the regulation, thus creating a potential conflict of interest. Further, industry participants are often consulted in the process of drafting regulations, which warrants a natural skepticism due to the potential self-serving advice and conflicts of interest.

> To widen the market and to narrow the competition, is always the interest of the dealers. . . . The proposal of any new law or regulation of commerce which comes from this order, ought always to be listened to with great precaution, and ought never to be adopted till after having been long and carefully examined, not only with the most scrupulous, but with the most suspicious attention. It comes from an order of men, whose interest is never exactly the same with that of the public, who have generally an interest to deceive and even oppress the public, and who accordingly have, upon many occasions, both deceived and oppressed it.[44]

Potentially as risky as the dealer's, the regulator's motives also must be viewed with caution. As warned by Adam Smith, even the virtuous regulator may be swayed by the desire to continue his virtuous work:

> Virtue is more to be feared than vice, because its excesses are not subject to the regulation of conscience.

Approximately 240 years ago, Adam Smith cautioned the readers of his *Wealth of Nations* that policy actions touted by businesses and politicians as being in the public interest might actually be positions promoting their own, particular and very special interests. Fast forward to modern times and crony capitalism: the pursuit of private gain through influence in the public sector, which is a frequent topic of discussion and debate among the citizenry.[45] In the field of regulation, such manipulation can have a serious cost. Influence over the regulatory process could be

---

44 Adam Smith, *The Wealth of Nations*. London: Methuen & Co, 1776, book I, chapter 11, p. 267, para. 10.

45 CED, *Crony Capitalism: Unhealthy Relations Between Business and Government* (Washington, DC: October 14, 2015).

used to stifle competition, allowing existing businesses to charge higher prices. Even worse, and to a degree perhaps beyond even what Adam Smith appreciated, regulations could also be used to preclude innovation that would challenge incumbent businesses' entire business models. Stifling innovation could, in the longer run, slow US productivity growth and advantage other nations, which would allow the same innovation to achieve greater economic dynamism and challenge our economic standing. For these reasons, building regulatory governance structures that maintain a level playing field, encourage competition, and increase economic growth is essential.

Such an attempted manipulation of the regulatory process could be a straightforward one-on-one struggle between a particular private interest and the relevant governmental authorities. However, there have been occasional alliances between seemingly unlikely private collaborators in attempts to compound their political influence on regulation. Economist Bruce Yandle has dubbed such phenomena a "Bootleggers and Baptists" manipulation of regulatory policy. He first introduced the concept in a short paper in *Regulation* magazine in 1983[46] and revisited it in 1999.[47] His latest, more extensive take is in a 2014 book with the same title, coauthored with his economist grandson named, by the most extreme coincidence, Adam Smith.[48] As the two authors explain in the book's preface:

> The [Bootleggers and Baptists] theory takes its name from the classic example of laws requiring liquor stores to close on Sundays, which were supported by both alcohol bootleggers and anti-alcohol Baptists—with both groups willing to spend valuable resources in pursuit of such laws. The happy bootleggers eliminated competition one day a week, and the devoted Baptists could feel better knowing that demon rum would not be sold openly on their Sabbath day. Of course, no one will ever see bootleggers carrying signs in front of a

46 Bruce Yandle, "Bootleggers and Baptists—The Education of a Regulatory Economist," *AEI Journal on Government and Society*, May 1, 1983, pp. 12-16.

47 Bruce Yandle, "Bootleggers and Baptists in Retrospect," *Regulation* 22, no. 3, 1999, pp. 5-7.

48 Adam Smith and Bruce Yandle, *Bootleggers and Baptists: How Economic Forces and Moral Persuasion Interact to Shape Regulatory Politics* (Washington, DC: Cato Institute, 2014).

> state house seeking political support when closing laws are up for reauthorization. The point of the theory is precisely that they don't have to: the Baptists lobby state house members for them. For success to occur, according to the theory, a respectable public-spirited group seeking the same result must wrap a self-interested lobbying effort in a cloak of respectability. Both members of the politicking coalition are necessary to win. The Baptists enable accommodating politicians to say the action is the "right" thing to do and have folks believe them. The bootleggers laugh all the way to the bank—and may occasionally share their gains with helpful politicians.[49]

These "Bootleggers" and "Baptists" are indeed strange bedfellows, but the problem for society is not the oddity of these relationships, but rather the disparate and perverse motivations that are thus brought together to shape regulatory policy. Instead of the partnership allowing policymakers to better account for a broad and diverse set of viewpoints in their making of government regulations as good public policy, this collaboration between Bootlegger- and Baptist-types produces economic outcomes that are, ironically, bad for society and the public interest. Instead of appropriately correcting or improving situations in which the private market on its own would fail to generate an efficient and strong economy, regulatory policies that are tailored to "bootlegger" special interests (but cloaked in public-interest "Baptist" costumes) and end up distorting markets even farther away from what would best benefit society as a whole.[50]

Smith and Yandle explain:

> . . . [W]e are convinced that the rising tide of crony capitalism, or what we would call Bootlegger/Baptist capitalism, is drawing some seriously critical attention to capitalism itself. Capitalism has taken lots of hits recently. Everything from bailed-out banks and auto companies to subsidized solar product firms that fail spectacularly leaves the public with

49 Adam Smith and Bruce Yandle, *Bootleggers and Baptists*, p. viii.

50 Diane Lim, "Bootleggers and Baptists—How Crony Capitalism Has Captured Regulatory Policy for Centuries," CED, August 25, 2015.

> the feeling that the marketplace is seriously flawed. Anti-capitalism messages seem ubiquitous. Yet the proposed remedies for the system's failings all seem to involve more government regulation, which means more opportunities for Bootleggers and Baptists to line their purses with transferred rather than newly produced wealth.[51]

Enter OIRA . . . Once More into the Breach

The past six presidents each have attempted to address excessive and inefficient regulation, usually to little avail.[52] In retrospect, however, it is striking how closely aligned the stated objectives of presidents of different political parties and apparent ideological orientations really were.

In an effort to regulate the regulators, the ironically titled Paperwork Reduction Act of 1980 was signed by President Carter. It established the Office of Information and Regulatory Affairs (OIRA) as part of the Office of Management and Budget (OMB).

In 1981, President Ronald Reagan issued Executive Order #12291 which stated OIRA's mission as follows[53]:

a) Administrative decisions shall be based on adequate information concerning the need for and consequences of proposed government action;

b) Regulatory action shall not be undertaken unless the potential benefits to society from the regulation outweigh the potential costs to society;

c) Regulatory objectives shall be chosen to maximize the net benefits to society;

d) Among alternative approaches to any given regulatory objective, the alternative involving the least net cost to society shall be chosen; and

---

51 Smith and Yandle, *Bootleggers and Baptists*, p. x.

52 See Chapter 4 for some happy exceptions.

53 Executive Order No. 12291 (February 17, 1981) ("Federal Regulation").

e) Agencies shall set regulatory priorities with the aim of maximizing the aggregate net benefits to society, taking into account the condition of the particular industries affected by regulations, the condition of the national economy, and other regulatory actions contemplated for the future.

That sounds consistent with forming "a more perfect union." However, it would appear that President Reagan did not adhere to the doctrine of his Secretary of Defense, Caspar Weinberger. The Weinberger Doctrine delineates the need for "clearly defined . . . objectives and with the capacity to accomplish those objectives."[54] In this instance, the capacity to accomplish the objective was missing. OIRA is composed of approximately 50 individuals. This small platoon now seeks to rein in more than 300,000 regulators (seemingly insurmountable odds at 6,000 to 1).

To reduce the workload and improve the odds, President Clinton issued EO 12866 which limited OIRA review to "significant" regulations (those with an estimated economic impact greater than $100 million, or important policy implications).[55] This resulted in a reduction in the number of regulations reviewed from greater than 700 in 2003 to 415 in 2015, but still resulted in an undesirably long average of 88 days for a review.[56]

Generally, major new regulations (defined as those imposing costs on the private sector in excess of $100 million) require a cost/benefit analysis. The Mercatus Center analyzed 130 major regulations from 2008 through 2013 on five critical measures. On a scale of 1 to 5 (5 being compliant), the average rating under none of the criteria exceeded 2.8 (see below, figure 3.3).

54 *Washington Post*, "The Weinberger Doctrine," November 30, 1984. Exec. Order No. 13563 (January 18, 2011) ("Improving Regulation and Regulatory Review").

55 Exec. Order No. 12866 (September 30, 1993) ("Regulatory Planning and Review").

56 Maeve P. Carey, *Counting Regulations: An Overview of Rulemaking, Types of Federal Regulations, and Pages in the Federal Register*, Congressional Research Service 7-5700, R43056, October 4, 2016.

FIGURE 3.3 **Evaluation of key attributes of federal regulations, 2008-13**

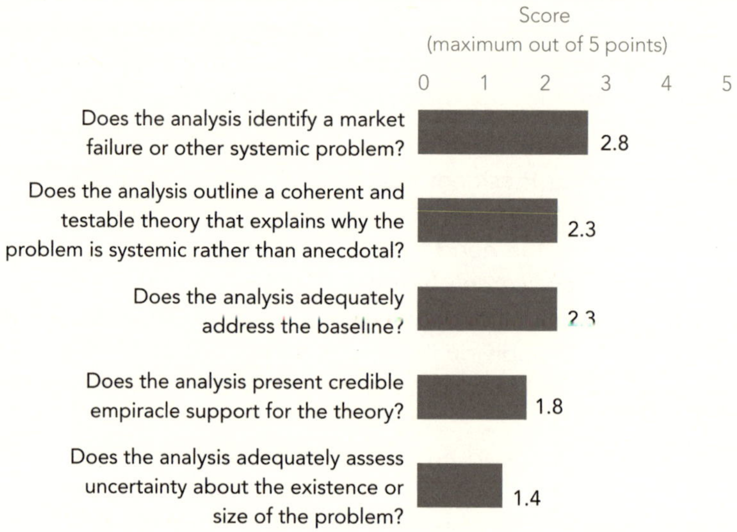

Source: "Regulatory Report Card," Mercatus Center at George Mason University.

As noted earlier, the cost-and-benefit comparisons reported by OIRA tend to be more favorable. But this evidence indicates that we need to do better. Much of the direction provided for cost-benefit analysis comes from a series of Presidential executive orders that are of course subject to Presidential fiat. Further, when faced with challenges from OIRA, a regulator is likely to "complain to Dad" (or in this case, the President). OMB has issued a series of best practices and standards (OMB Circular A-4) which, while good, lack the weight of law and are therefore subject to change.

This task is daunting. As we explain in greater detail in Chapter 5, "Techniques for Building (and Maintaining) Better Regulation," the economic effects of regulations, the fruits of which are often intangible, are more difficult to assess than the effects of other types of government policies that are measured directly in dollars.[57] Furthermore, every regulation is unique in a sense in which many other economic policies are not. Regulatory evaluation is inferential, whereas assessment of other economic policies can be just counting.

To judge whether a regulation will be good or bad for the economy and the society, first one must identify the purpose or goal of the regulation. Is it to achieve a more optimal outcome for the economy and society that the private market cannot deliver on its own because of a fundamental "market failure?" If so, what is the nature of the failure, and is a regulatory approach (and if so, what type) the best way to address (correct or adjust for) the failure, considering both the benefits and costs of the strategy? What kinds of evidence can and should be gathered and considered to evaluate the likelihood of success before a regulation is established?

Dudley and Brito's regulation primer suggests the following steps in describing "How to Analyze a Regulation" (chapter 8):

1. Identify a significant market failure or systemic problem;
2. Identify alternative approaches;
3. Choose the regulatory action that maximizes net benefits;
4. Base the proposal on strong scientific or technical grounds;
5. Understand the effects of the regulation on different populations;
6. Respect individual choice and property rights.[58]

In other words, justify a role for government, find the approach (regulatory or otherwise, and including not regulating) most likely to yield the best achievable economic outcome and maximize *net* benefit to society, and then consider (and address and adjust if needed) any undesirable distributional effects. These would be the steps an impartial economist would take in building a smart regulation, but of course, impartial economists are not the ones who propose, vote on,

57 Kevin A Hassett and Robert J. Shapiro, "Regulation and Investment: A Note on Policy Evaluation under Uncertainty with Application to FCC Title II Regulation of the Internet," Washington, DC: McDonough School of Business Center for Business and Public Policy at Georgetown University, July 2015.

58 Susan E. Dudley and Jerry Brito, *Regulation: A Primer*, 2nd ed. (Arlington, VA: Mercatus Center, George Mason University; and Washington, DC: George Washington University, 2012), pp. 89-103.

or implement regulations. Economists are on the sidelines, ready to analyze (when asked) the economic effects of regulations already in motion or in place.

RECOMMENDED SOLUTIONS

This review of the regulatory process highlights the need for several of the recommendations included in this book. Among them are:

- *Implement Principles-Based Regulations.* Improving the wording of legislation to include instructions to utilize principles-based regulations based on performance- and market-based measurements could significantly lessen the regulatory burden. Compliance would be a question of verifiable fact, not arbitrary judgment. At times, this will require that Congress also settle upon a perspective of the impact of the regulation, and consider the appropriate performance- and market-based measurements.
- *Establish Independent Analytical Expertise in Support of Congress.* Currently, Congress must rely on OIRA or the regulatory agencies themselves. To exercise independent judgment, Congress will need analytical capability that could reside within the Congressional Budget Office (CBO), which was established by Congress. The administrative costs should be offset by reductions elsewhere in the government, particularly in the regulated agencies.
- *Require a Regulatory Assessment of Significant Laws Prior to a Vote.* This step is akin to the process currently used for CBO estimates of dollar costs of bills. Such assessment would be a primary charge for the CBO to accomplish with its additional analytical expertise. The process will be difficult, because typically a law requires the enforcing agency to write the implementing regulation, to be completed after the law is passed. But Congress needs better guidance to help it call for regulations that have a real chance to succeed.
- *Continue to Utilize the Resolutions of Disapproval.* This step will reduce regulatory burden. The Congressional Review Act of 1996 provides for a fast-track vote on any such measures. From its enactment in 1996 through the end of 2016, this provision had been used only once. In 2017, this clause was used 15 times through November 10, 2017, a

clear message from Congress that it seeks to pull back on regulatory overreach beyond the intention of the law. Congress, not regulators, should make the laws. But note that predictability for the private sector would not be served by a regulatory pendulum swinging wildly back and forth with the shifting of the political winds. That is why establishment of and adherence to sound regulatory principles are essential. And with ex-post review performed diligently by OIRA and the executive agencies, Congress should not need to intervene often.

- *Increase Resources at OIRA.* Increased capital and professional resources at OIRA are necessary. As the only independent reviewer of regulations in the Executive, OIRA is woefully understaffed. Appropriate staffing will provide for more-timely responses. Additionally, we believe that the breadth of responsibility of OIRA should also be increased. As OIRA continues to develop more and improved methods of assessment, amendments to OMB Circular A-4 will be warranted. Again, any increases in the budget for OIRA should be offset with reductions in other agencies' budgets wherever possible.
- *Require Retrospective Evaluation of Existing Regulations and Regulators.* With additional resources, responsibility for retrospective evaluation rather than the current "set-it-and-forget-it" mentality could be an ongoing responsibility of OIRA.

4

A FOCUSED HISTORY OF REGULATION

In the late nineteenth century, after the end of the Civil War, the United States began to flex its economic muscle. Advancements of technology that had been accelerated by the necessity of the war were turned to civilian commercial use. As some would allege has occurred in recent decades, however, those new technologies conferred great favors on those who mastered them early. "First mover" advantages led to the creation of great fortunes—leading to what history has called the Gilded Age. Prominent among the fortunes of that era were those derived from railroads, which monopolized the long-distance transportation of goods from farms to cities, and from factories to towns and farms. Once the technological miracle of railroad freight hauling was perceived to have turned into an abuse of market power, public reaction drove the beginnings of modern-day regulation.[59]

However, with time, technology advanced further, and what had been natural monopoly came to be threatened by potential cleansing competition. By that stage, what had been regulation to protect the public interest naturally but unfortunately aged to become regulation to protect the first-mover advantages of the figurative heirs—several generations advanced—of those first movers. It took new thinking to recognize that the old order, though it had become a comfortable habit, need not—and in fact should not—go on forever. The new thinkers had

59 Martin, Albro, "The Troubled Subject of Railroad Regulation in the Gilded Age—A Reappraisal," *Journal of American History*, vol. 61, no. 2, 1974, pp. 339–71. Accessible at JSTOR, www.jstor.org/stable/1903953.

to work hard to capture the attention of policymakers who had many other things on their minds, but capture those minds they did.[60] Though many regulations were pulled out by the roots, the results might be thought of as **smart** regulation, with fewer and slimmer rules, but rules nonetheless, to keep economic activity advancing between the guardrails toward the public interest.

This focused history on the earliest of regulation—primarily regulation of transportation—has several important lessons to tell. Those lessons would guide us well in the regulatory challenges of the current age.

THE ORIGINS

During the 1860s and the 1870s, a groundswell of discontent arose among farmers, primarily in the Midwest.[61] They believed that the railroads were operating in a monopolistic way and were charging exorbitant rates both for the relatively short hauls that the farmers needed, and for grain storage (which was often controlled by the railroads). The farmers organized into a group, officially known as The National Grange of the Order of Patrons of Husbandry. The Grangers campaigned for state laws that allowed for the regulation of rates charged by the railroads. Several midwestern states passed Granger laws, including Illinois (1871), Wisconsin (1874), and Iowa (1874).[62]

This striking expansion of government's role in business and society elicited sharp reactions and was quickly tested.

Enter the Supreme Court: *Munn v. Illinois*

In 1872, a Chicago firm (Munn & Scott) was found guilty of violating the recently enacted Illinois Granger law. This resulted in appeals up to the Supreme Court, which found that "[u]nder the powers inherent in every sovereignty, a government may regulate the conduct of its citizens toward each other, and, when necessary for the public good,

---

60 This is a central theme of Martha Derthick and Paul J. Quirk, *The Politics of Deregulation*, Brookings, 1985, summarized on pp. 238-39.

61 Clark, Cynthia L. *The American Economy: A Historical Encyclopedia*, 2nd ed. (2 vols.) (Santa Barbara, CA: ABC-CLIO, 2011).

62 Clark, *The American Economy: A Historical Encyclopedia*.

the manner in which each shall use his own property."[63] This, for a short time, bolstered the state Granger laws.

Supreme Court Redux: *Wabash, St. Louis & Pacific Railway Company v. Illinois*

However, in 1886 the Supreme Court heard a case arising from a railroad company engaged in intra- and inter-state railroad transportation. The Court ruled the Illinois Granger law unconstitutional because it attempted to regulate interstate commerce, which was set aside by the Constitution[64] as the sole responsibility of the federal government.[65]

Still, the public support for restraint on the railroad monopoly was strong. The Supreme Court setback was followed quickly by the passage at the federal level of the Interstate Commerce Act of 1887.

The act[66]:

- provided that "all charges . . . shall be reasonable and just" (an admirable albeit undefined standard);
- prohibited rate differences based on like and contemporaneous services;
- prohibited discrimination based on long-haul versus short-haul shipping;
- prohibited carriers from pooling freight (seen to be an occasion for rate gouging);
- required the printing and retention of rate schedules; and
- established a commission, the Interstate Commerce Commission, or ICC, "which shall be composed of five Commissioners, who shall be appointed by the President, by and with the advice and consent of the Senate," to implement and enforce the act.

Thus was born the first regulator.

63 Legal Information Institute, *Munn v. Illinois*.

64 One of the "enumerated powers," set forth in Article I, Section 8, Clause 3.

65 History Matters, "The Supreme Court Strikes Down Railroad Regulation."

66 Interstate Commerce Act of 1887, PL 49-41 (February 4, 1887).

REGULATOR . . . THE FIRST OF ITS NAME . . . INTERSTATE COMMERCE COMMISSION

A Troubled Beginning

As the first independent regulator, the ICC had broad powers to review and rule on rates, require testimony, and compel attendance at hearings, thus empowered with aspects of the Executive, Legislative, and Judicial branches of government. Thus was born what some would call the *fourth* branch of government. And therefore, starting from the most basic rationale of remedying abuses by monopoly, regulation picked up a broad range of tools involving pricing and business practices that range from the common to the arcane.

The ICC did not initially set freight rates. Its early rulings were generally perceived as favoring the industry. But the ICC eventually established maximum rates railroads could charge.[67] When a challenge again rose to the level of the Supreme Court, the Court significantly limited the commission's power. It found that "Congress has not conferred upon the Interstate Commerce Commission the legislative power of prescribing rates either maximum or minimum or absolute." This significant setback to the ICC resulted in several additional pieces of legislation to clarify and enhance the authority of the commission.[68]

As the ICC strengthened its authority and expanded responsibility, it is also considered the first US regulator to become subject to "regulatory capture," where the regulators become responsive not to the public interest, but rather to the interest the regulators were hired to regulate. Many today would call this "crony capitalism." In fact, Richard Olney, as attorney general under the Grover Cleveland administration, reportedly commented:

> The Commission . . . is, or can be made, of great use to the railroads. It satisfies the popular clamor for a government supervision of the railroads, at the same time that supervision is almost entirely nominal. Further, the older such a commission

---

67 "Economic Regulation of Transportation: Surface Freight and Airlines," in W. Kip Viscusi et al., *Economics of Regulation and Antitrust* (Cambridge, MA: MIT Press, 1995), pp. 551–55.

68 Railroad Safety Appliance Act (1893); Hepburn Act (1906); Mann-Elkins Act (1910); Valuation Act (1913); and Adamson Act (1916).

> gets to be, the more inclined it will be found to take the business and railroad view of things. . . . The part of wisdom is not to destroy the Commission, but to utilize it.[69]

A Tumultuous Middle

After new laws reestablished its authority in response to rebukes from the Supreme Court, the ICC met with criticism that it was again overstepping its bounds. The Mann-Elkins Act of 1910 established a Commerce Court to review the decisions of the ICC, perhaps making it the first regulator to be subject to ex-post review.[70] By 1911, the Commerce Court had overturned many previous decisions of the ICC, only to be followed by the abolition of the court in 1913. President Woodrow Wilson nationalized the entire railroad industry in 1917 as a part of the war effort, but federal control was ceded in 1920 and the uncomfortable dance of the regulators, the regulated, and the courts resumed.[71]

An Inglorious, Yet Triumphant, Bipartisan End

Over time, the world changed. At the end of World War II, when again the pressure of conflict pushed the development of revolutionary new technologies, the nation spurted forward with growth. And among those new technologies were, again, revolutionary improvements in transportation. The nation built an interstate highway system, which facilitated long-distance hauling by road and truck. Flying advanced from an emergency activity undertaken by risk-takers and warriors to a routine means of transportation for people and cargo. The notion of freight hauling as a necessity controlled by railroads as natural monopolies aged from reality to history to forgotten. And yet, for years, even decades, the brand of regulation created by the Interstate Commerce Act and shaped by the courts, with incumbent business interests maneuvering to co-opt the regulators set up as their adversaries, persisted. Inertia and self-interest maintained the status quo.

The inertia was not surprising. There was very little Congressional oversight of regulation. Congress did review agency budgets, to be sure; and it wrote new legislation on occasion. But there was no regular, institutional review of existing legislation. In fact, there was

69 Thomas Frank, "Obama and Regulatory Capture," *Wall Street Journal*, June 24, 2009.

70 "Mann-Elkins Act," *Legis Works*, Congressional Data Coalition.

71 "Transportation Act of 1920," *Legis Works*, Congressional Data Coalition.

no requirement for cost-benefit analysis of new regulations (much less old ones) until 1981. Any serious effort to modernize regulation would require leadership from the Executive.[72]

Following those decades of inaction, the ICC became the target of a number of regulatory reform legislative efforts during the 1970s and 1980s. The way in which these efforts formed was a combination of circumstance, technological innovation, politics, and hard scholarly work.

In the late 1960s and the early 1970s, the United States began to experience accelerating inflation. Responding to the resulting popular outcry, President Richard Nixon embarked on one of the most intrusive bursts of regulation in modern US history, imposing wage and price controls on the entire economy.[73] And in 1973, when war in the Middle East triggered an OPEC oil embargo that sent gasoline prices soaring, petroleum and gasoline prices were explicitly regulated, as well.[74]

As inflation continued, it aroused growing concern. President Gerald R. Ford sought a solution to inflation in microeconomic rigidities that inhibited competition, and therefore prevented prices from falling and resources from moving to more-efficient uses in the economy. Ranking high among the sources of those rigidities, in the minds of the President and his advisers, was regulation. President Ford announced his reform campaign in Chicago in late 1974, declaring that his objective was to "take the shackles off American businessmen" and "get the federal government as far out of your business, out of your lives, out of your pocketbooks and out of your hair as far as I possibly can."[75]

With the help of both academic thinkers and business disrupters, President Ford came to understand that the regulatory system endorsed enormous waste. In the previous century, railroads were prohibited from combining loads because of fear that this would facilitate overcharging both customers. But by the 1970s, with railroads struggling to compete against truck haulers, those rules only prevented railroads from achieving efficiency savings that they would pass on to their customers in the

72 Robert E. Litan and William D. Nordhaus, *Reforming Federal Regulation* (Yale University Press, 1983).

73 "Address to the Nation Announcing Price Control Measures," *The American Presidency Project* (The White House, Washington, DC, June 13, 1973).

74 "Emergency Petroleum Allocation," *United States Code*, Office of the Law Revision Counsel.

75 Roderick M. Hills, obituary for President Gerald R. Ford, *Forbes*, December 27, 2006.

hope of keeping their business. Trucks, in an analogous restriction, were prohibited from finding loads that they could carry on the return trips after one-way hauls.[76] Again, in an increasingly competitive freight-hauling market, the savings were denied not to monopolies but rather to customers of competitive firms. Meanwhile, air carriers were restricted from pursuing new routes and adding new flights in markets that might be underserved by incumbents, and their ticket prices were held above technologically obsolete minimum levels.[77]

But this endeavor ran afoul of the politics of a captured regulatory structure. As is often the case in regulation, the benefits of better policy are spread thinly across the population as a whole. No individual would receive sufficient benefit to be roused to support better policy, and for that matter, many might be frightened off by the uncertainty of change. But direct market participants, including regulated business and even labor, have so much at stake that they engage continuously in influencing the regulations and their implementation. Often their struggles aim to achieve advantage in the marketplace through the major provisions and details of regulation. Once a firm or a union achieves a relative advantage through regulation, it becomes an opponent of regulatory reform. Thus, business can become pro-regulation, and pro-status quo.

What began to swing the balance was a combination of technology, scholarship, and communications[78] The power of a modernized transportation industry to deliver for consumers was fundamental. But more was needed to achieve such seismic change. Policy experts demonstrated that regulation protected producers from effective competition and raised prices for consumers. And the media of that era, even though agonizingly slow by today's standards, helped reach the public with that new knowledge and build acceptance for even such a seemingly radical change in industries that are fundamental to everyday life. So President Ford began a near-decade-long campaign to lift these

---

76 Clifford Winston, "US Industry Adjustment to Economic Deregulation," *Journal of Economic Perspectives*, vol. 12, no. 6, Summer 1998, p. 94; Agis Salpukas, "Railroad's Freight Comeback," *New York Times*, June 16, 1982.

77 United States Government Accountability Office, *AIRLINE DEREGULATION: Reregulating the Airline Industry Would Likely Reverse Consumer Benefits and Not Save Airline Pensions*, report to Congressional Committees, GAO No. 06-630 (June 2006).

78 Martha Derthick and Paul J. Quirk, *The Politics of Deregulation* (Washington, DC: Brookings Institution, 1985).

restrictive regulations, to enable the freight industry to innovate and provide better service.[79] Senator Edward (Ted) Kennedy (D-MA) was an early and steady collaborator.

Trucking deregulation moved forward with the bipartisan cooperation of Howard Cannon (D-NV) and Robert Packwood (R-OR).[80] Even more radical was the reshaping of the passenger air travel industry. The Civil Aeronautics Board, which had controlled routes and prices, was abolished outright. The result has been an enormous improvement in access to air transportation. Since 1978, airfares have dropped more than 40 percent (in inflation-adjusted dollars).[81] In 1971, only 49 percent of the US adult population had ever flown on an aircraft. By 2016, 81 percent had flown; 45 percent had flown in the past year.[82] Deregulation legislation was notably bipartisan, especially in the Senate, where Howard Cannon (D-NV) collaborated with James B. Pierson (R-KS).[83] In the House, there was somewhat uneasy cooperation between Glenn M. Anderson (D-CA, an aggressive deregulator) and Gene Snyder (R-KY, described as more cautious on the issue, but by no means obstructive).

Meanwhile, the courts attacked AT&T's monopoly over telecommunications, breaking up that monopoly into regional companies, and allowing an enormous wave of innovation that continues to this day. Notable bipartisan cooperation on the necessary implementing legislation for reform involved Senators Ernest Hollings (D-SC), Barry Goldwater (R-AZ), Harrison Schmitt (R-NM), and Cannon and Packwood. Noted House advocates included Lionel van Deerlin (D-CA), Tim Wirth (D-CO), Louis Frey (R-FL), and James M. Collins (R-TX).[84]

---

79 In a speech to The National Federation of Independent Businesses in mid-1975, President Ford outlined his views of excessive regulation: "Although most of today's regulations affecting business are well-intentioned, their effect, whether designed to protect the environment or the consumer, often does more harm than good. They can stifle growth in our standard of living and contribute to inflation." Gerald R. Ford, "President's Address to the National Federation of Independent Businesses " *Ford Library Museum*, Gerald Ford Presidential Foundation, box 19, folder no. 6/17/75, Ann Arbor, MI.

80 Cannon, Howard, "S.2245—96th Congress (1979-1980): An Act to Amend Subtitle IV of Title 49, United States Code, to Provide for More Effective Regulation of Motor Carriers of Property, and for Other Purposes," Library of Congress, July 1, 1980.

81 Airlines for America.

82 Airlines for America.

83 Cannon, Howard, "S.2493 - 95th Congress (1977-1978): Airline Deregulation Act," Library of Congress, October 1, 1978.

84 Derthick and Quirk, *Politics of Deregulation*, pp. 104-5.

President Jimmy Carter continued the effort of transportation deregulation. He began to dismantle the regulation of petroleum as well. In addition, an often-forgotten achievement of the Carter years was the deregulation of the beer industry. In 1978, the United States had only 44 domestic breweries. At the end of 2017, there were 6,372, of which 6,266 are characterized as smaller "craft" breweries.[85] Because the larger breweries of bygone decades were constrained to produce their product for a mass audience, perhaps uncharitably thought to be the "least common denominator," today's smaller breweries can produce an arguably higher-quality product that can satisfy more eclectic tastes.

President Reagan saw this round of regulatory streamlining through to its completion, including accelerating the deregulation of oil and gas.[86] And one of the most important legislative-branch leaders in the effort was Senator Ted Kennedy. Thus, these efforts were truly bipartisan, with a result that the public was better and more efficiently served, with faster shipping at lower costs.

And that takes us back to where we started: the Interstate Commerce Commission was truly no longer needed. The ICC Termination Act of 1995 was initially approved in the House by a vote of 417-8 (voice votes carried the final votes in both the House and Senate, indicating agreement so broad that there was no interest in a formal tally of support and opposition).[87]

The Legacy of the Interstate Commerce Commission—A Template for Future Regulators

While the legacy of the ICC might be seen as tarnished because of the fits and starts at its beginning or the resounding support for its termination, it is also recognized for its contribution to the structure of regulation broadly. The commissioners were appointed by the President and approved by the Senate. The commissioners and their staff were

85 Brewers Association. Factors other than federal regulation include changing excise taxation and changing state regulation of brewery-restaurants.

86 Peter Behr and John M. Berry, "Reagan Decontrols Gasoline, Crude in Deregulation Debut," *Washington Post*, January 29, 1981.

87 "ICC Termination Act of 1995," Library of Congress, December 29, 1995.

full-time regulators who were not permitted any economic ties to the industry. Some of the federal agencies following this model established by the ICC include:

- Securities & Exchange Commission
- Federal Reserve
- Federal Trade Commission
- Federal Communications Commission
- Federal Energy Regulatory Commission

The tale of the railroad industry is not the only example of the challenges associated with regulation. As was apparent at the ICC's demise, regulation of the airline and trucking industries has undergone a similar rise and fall, as has regulation of many other industries.[88]

LESSONS FROM THIS FOCUSED HISTORY OF REGULATION

This story of regulation began a century and a half ago. It traveled from the "wild west" of early modern capitalism, through a period of counterproductive regulation, to a victory of policy improvement. It left some important lessons along the way. We would highlight these five:

1. *Competition is better than regulation of market abuse.* Competition cannot solve all market failures. For example, in the instance of market "bads" like pollution, even competing firms would be unlikely to stop polluting on their own. (Unless you believe that idealistic consumers can and will undertake the research to learn that some firms are polluting and identify them, and then will be willing to pay more to firms that undertake the expense not to pollute. Especially if society's costs from the pollution are great, relying on socially active consumers would seem to us to be a risky bet.) Likewise, competition is unlikely to solve the underproduction of social "goods." (Thus, competing firms will be unlikely to invest in risky, "basic" research that, if successful, will reduce their competitors' prices as much as their own.)

---

88 Some of these processes are described elsewhere in this book: see the discussions of financial institutions and health care in Chapters 6 and 8, and of potential dramatic changes for regulation of cyberspace and electric power generation in Chapters 7 and 9.

However, competition did improve on regulation in freight transportation. Railroads once exploited their monopoly advantages vis-à-vis farmers who had no choice but to ship their goods over the nearest railway line, and it would have been unprofitable for a competitor to build a second line just to share half of the reduced (by competition) total revenues. Regulation probably achieved a better outcome, but it was rife with conflict, it was subject to industry capture, and policy swung between uncertain extremes because of periodic intervention by the courts. What really served consumer interests was the emergence of alternatives to the railroads through highway hauling and air transportation. At that point, all freight haulers had to serve consumer interests, or they would lose market share to their competitors.

2. *Even bad regulation can perpetuate itself, because it serves some interests.* Still, the world did not rush to a better deregulated freight market at the earliest opportunity. It took scholarship, business innovation, and advocacy to win the day. The major beneficiaries of such regulatory reform are often rank-and-file consumers, who are not expert, and whose individual shares of the efficiency gains may seem small, which means that they are unlikely to either recognize the effort or, if they do, to rise en masse in its support. But that does not mean that regulatory reform is bad public policy; it just means that it will be difficult to achieve.

   In particular, business and labor develop naturally to pursue profit within an existing regulatory system. That is what business is supposed to do. But it can mean that some parts of business that have obtained competitive advantage can be displaced if regulation changes to take advantage of technological improvement. It will be natural for business interests to resist such regulatory change, even if it carries advantages for the rest of society. Public policy must change to maximize the well-being of society as a whole—which does not necessarily improve the standing of every person and every interest within society. It must not be "captured" by incumbent interests that have reason to resist beneficial change. If public policy is reviewed and improved on a continuing basis, however, all business and labor interests will recognize that they must keep their eyes to the horizon, because policy will change when need be. That implicit warning will lead every enterprise to expect socially beneficial technological change, and to prepare for it.

3. *The world changes.* As the Greek philosopher Heraclitus notably said, you cannot step into the same stream twice because the flow of the water changes the stream constantly. It would have been easy to assume that regulation of the railroads would be necessary forever, and in the same form, because the freight market could be expected to continue unchanged. But entrepreneurs in our capitalist system are constantly pursuing profit opportunities, and in so doing are constantly developing new technologies. If for that reason alone, and there are others (like opportunities to improve on past public policy), we need to review regulation continuously, to see if new technologies will allow the removal of some regulations to allow the market to achieve still better outcomes.

4. *Smart regulation is better than under- or over-regulation.* Too much regulation, the legacy of a century-ago concern about railroad monopolies, could have shackled competition as technology advanced in the second half of the twentieth century. However, total deregulation could have allowed new interests to monopolize the freight business or could have removed safety protections. Regulation can maintain a level playing field so that the fruits of competition and innovation do materialize and are shared by business and consumer alike. Furthermore, it can prevent a "race to the bottom" that can reduce standards and erode consumer well-being. Some would emphasize the role of either under-regulation or inept regulation in the 2008 financial crisis, which carried enormous costs for our society as a whole.

   Smart regulation is grounded in principles rather than detailed step-by-step instructions that can be circumvented or can age in place while technology changes. Smart regulation is outcome-based, whenever possible with market-based measurements. And finally, smart regulation is supported by experts in analytics and carefully collected data. Smart regulation is not cheap; nothing is cheaper than unconscious lethargy and inaction once a regulation is put in place. But smart regulation is worth its cost.

5. *Good regulatory policy can achieve bipartisan support.* Much has changed in Washington since the heyday of deregulation in the 1970s and 1980s. Among the most regretted changes has been a rise in instinctive partisanship. It often seems as though one political party will block a potential policy improvement to perpetuate an issue for future elections—"Whatever they are for, we are against."

But the 1970s and the 1980s do show us that good regulatory policymaking can achieve the values of both political parties. The efforts of Ford and Reagan, and of Carter and Kennedy, were seen to be good for both sides, and for the American people as a whole. This should lead us to seek opportunities, as in the case of the obsolete restrictions of the ICC, to improve the circumstances of the American people, to the political advantage of both sides. Improvements of regulatory policy could be the chisel that cuts through the restraints and frees the political policymaking process to move again, for the benefit of all Americans.

In fact, a survey of the ex-post accounts of these regulatory improvements finds something of a dispute between advocates of the two partisan sides. Some commentators emphasize the role of Gerald Ford, others that of Jimmy Carter, and still others that of Ronald Reagan. Still others note that Richard Nixon, in his Quality of Life review process, took the first tentative steps toward cost-benefit analysis. And those who focus on the regulatory process more than the specific deregulation of transportation and telecommunications will point out that all of these presidents took similar steps toward process reform (and that each enjoyed some, but limited, success).[89]

But this only proves our point: Presidents and legislators of both parties valued these improvements in regulatory policy. In this sense, regulatory reform was truly bipartisan. It perhaps reflects a sentiment that is attributed to one of the actors in our drama, Ronald Reagan: "There is no limit to the amount of good you can do if you don't care who gets the credit." (Although, in a bipartisan twist to this story, a very similar statement is also attributed to Harry Truman.)

As much as some see regulation as a source of contention, the history of regulation is one part of Washington's heritage that has at least some good news to tell. We must try to make that happy history repeat itself.

89 Litan and Nordhaus, *Reforming Federal Regulation*; Murray Weidenbaum, "Regulatory Process Reform: From Ford to Clinton," Cato Institute, 1991; Andrew Downer Crain, "Ford, Carter, and Deregulation in the 1970s," *Journal on Telecommunications and High Technology Law*, no. 2, Winter 2007, pp. 413-48; James E. Anderson, "The Struggle to Reform Regulatory Procedures, 1978-1998," *Policy Studies Journal*, vol. 26, no. 3, 1998, pp. 482-98.

5

TECHNIQUES FOR BETTER REGULATIONS

Although many existing government interventions in the marketplace are justified, the results do not always live up to the "first-best" textbook ideal.

It is of vital importance for policymakers and regulators to apply regulation judiciously where markets fail, and where it can improve market outcomes and avoid any possible pitfalls. There is a role for government where markets fail to price goods and services to reflect economic and social values, for one of many potential reasons. Government intervention to correct prices, whether through regulations or fiscal (tax and spending) policies, can improve economic and social outcomes.

But this is not a blanket endorsement of government intervention. There is an elegant efficiency in the market-price system, allowing resources to flow naturally to their highest-valued uses as signaled by suppliers and demanders. Public policies are often imperfect fixes that can worsen rather than improve market outcomes. The free market still may be superior to government in getting most of the prices and flows of resources mostly right. The possibility of effective intervention does not mean we should hand over full control of markets to the government.

Government decisions are more susceptible to bias through the influence of special-interest money and politics, whereas free market outcomes are impartial to all the different participants in the marketplace who clearly signal values through the prices they are willing to pay or receive. Therefore, where there is a well-justified approach to government policy, private market prices are still the primary signal to steer resources, but regulations or other public policies supplement or correct the signals to more completely reflect public costs and benefits. And because "capture" (special interests or "cronyism") theories compete well with the public interest rationale to explain why and how the government actually regulates, policymakers in practice must be aware that regulated outcomes do not always improve on an even imperfect free-market result.

In this chapter, we will first survey the current thinking on how regulations should be formulated and governed. This will lead us to three ways in which US regulation can, through comparison of principle with actual practice, be improved. One way entails regulation through broad principles rather than detailed rules. The second way involves reviewing regulations periodically after they are promulgated, to ensure that they continue to fulfill their objectives at the least possible cost to the economy. The third way is better utilization of input from stakeholders in the outcome of any particular regulation.

OPERATING PRINCIPLES FOR SUCCESSFUL REGULATION

Many researchers and research organizations (US and international) have formulated guidelines for better regulatory policy. These can be categorized to focus on the following broad, general facets of regulatory practice: (i) *better information*, that is, improving the data and economic analysis, the "tools" in the regulatory tool box, that are used in the planning and evaluation of regulations; (ii) *better oversight and monitoring* of the regulatory policy process and the institutions and people involved—the regulators, or the "carpenters" who build and maintain the regulations; (iii) *better collaboration* between and input from regulators and all stakeholders (including businesses and the general public); and (iv) *better incentives* for actors in the private sector to cooperate in the most economically efficient way.

The Organisation for Economic Cooperation and Development (OECD) has long observed regulation in its member countries and has drawn inferences about the operating principles and the best practices for successful regulation.[90, 91] We find their ideas to be helpful, and particularly would cite the following overarching recommendations on how to improve the quality of regulatory policy (quoting):[92]

1. Commit at the highest political level to an explicit whole-of-government policy for regulatory quality. The policy should have clear objectives and frameworks for implementation to ensure that, if regulation is used, the economic, social and environmental benefits justify the costs, distributional effects are considered and the net benefits are maximised.
2. Adhere to principles of open government, including transparency and participation in the regulatory process to ensure that regulation serves the public interest and is informed by the legitimate needs of those interested in and affected by regulation. This includes providing meaningful opportunities (including online) for the public to contribute to the process of preparing draft regulatory proposals and to the quality of the supporting analysis. Governments should ensure that regulations are comprehensible and clear and that parties can easily understand their rights and obligations.
3. Establish mechanisms and institutions to actively provide oversight of regulatory policy procedures and goals, support and implement regulatory policy, and thereby foster regulatory quality.
4. Integrate Regulatory Impact Assessment (RIA) into the early stages of the policy process for the formulation of new regulatory proposals. Clearly identify policy goals, and evaluate if regulation is necessary and how it can be most effective and efficient in achieving those goals. Consider means other than regulation and identify the tradeoffs of the different approaches analysed to identify the best approach.
5. Conduct systematic programme reviews of the stock of significant regulation against clearly defined policy goals, including consideration of costs and benefits, to ensure that regulations remain up to date, cost-justified, cost-effective and consistent and [deliver] the intended policy objectives.

---

90 OECD, *Recommendation of the Council on Regulatory Policy and Governance*, OECD, 2012.

91 OECD, *Guiding Principles for Regulatory Quality and Performance*, OECD, 2005.

92 OECD, *Recommendation of the Council on Regulatory Policy and Governance*, pp. 4-5.

6. Regularly publish reports on the performance of regulatory policy and reform programmes and the public authorities applying the regulations. Such reports should also include information on how regulatory tools such as Regulatory Impact Assessment (RIA), public consultation practices and reviews of existing regulations are functioning in practice.
7. Develop a consistent policy covering the role and functions of regulatory agencies in order to provide greater confidence that regulatory decisions are made on an objective, impartial and consistent basis, without conflict of interest, bias or improper influence.
8. Ensure the effectiveness of systems for the review of the legality and procedural fairness of regulations, and of decisions made by bodies empowered to issue regulatory sanctions. Ensure that citizens and businesses have access to these systems of review at reasonable cost and receive decisions in a timely manner.
9. As appropriate apply risk assessment, risk management, and risk communication strategies to the design and implementation of regulations to ensure that regulation is targeted and effective. Regulators should assess how regulations will be given effect and should design responsive implementation and enforcement strategies.
10. Where appropriate promote regulatory coherence through co-ordination mechanisms between the supra national, the national and sub-national levels of government. Identify cross cutting regulatory issues at all levels of government, to promote coherence between regulatory approaches and avoid duplication or conflict of regulations.
11. Foster the development of regulatory management capacity and performance at subnational levels of government.
12. In developing regulatory measures, give consideration to all relevant international standards and frameworks for co-operation in the same field and, where appropriate, their likely effects on parties outside the jurisdiction.

THE IMPORTANCE OF "GOOD GOVERNANCE" OF REGULATORS

Meanwhile, fulfilling these operating principles requires good regulators and good regulatory practice. "Regulation policy" refers to the ways in which regulations in practice are made, maintained, and evaluated. Worldwide regulation policy over the past few decades has progressed from concepts of regulatory reform or deregulation, to regulation management, and most recently to regulatory governance—signaling a subtle change in state-of-the-art techniques of regulation, and a sense that the objective is neither more nor less regulation, but rather better regulation. In a 2011 report entitled *Regulatory Policy and Governance*, the OECD describes this progression of concerns and goals[93]:

> The OECD model of regulatory policy is founded on the view that ensuring the quality of the regulatory structure is a dynamic and permanent role of government. Governments must be actively engaged in assuring the quality of regulation, not reactively responding to failures in regulation. In advanced countries this concept is evolving into regulatory governance. Regulatory governance is grounded in the principles of democratic governance and engages a wider domain of players including the legislature, the judiciary, sub national and supra national levels of government and standard setting activities of the private sector. The integration of evidence based impact assessment of new and existing regulation, building strong institutions for regulatory management and placing a greater focus on users of regulation are all critical elements.

A common business perspective on regulatory policy is that regulations can often be helpful to the economy in encouraging competition, leveling the playing field, and promoting vibrant and dynamic markets that can be more responsive to evolving public interests. On the other hand, businesses also complain about regulations being overly burdensome,

93 OECD, *Regulatory Policy and Governance: Supporting Economic Growth and Serving the Public Interest* (Paris: OECD Publishing, 2011, p. 98), available at http://www.oecd.org/gov/regulatory-policy/regulatorypolicyandgovernancesupportingeconomicgrowthandservingthepublicinterest.htm.

inefficient, and sometimes inappropriate and unjustified. Of course, individual businesses can find much to complain about in specific regulations that impose new costs on them specifically, and may even seek regulations that give their business competitive advantages over others. Ironically, to promote a business-friendly regulatory climate—one that is hospitable to the public interest—large, powerful companies sometimes lobby for what are effectively special-interest regulations that keep potential new, innovative competitors out of the market and thus remove much of the incentive for their own companies to continue to innovate.

Who is responsible for designing and implementing regulations, and can that person or entity be trusted to pursue and enforce economically beneficial regulatory policy? Can we better avoid "regulatory capture" and cronyism? Regulation policy experts including former OIRA Administrator Susan Dudley (such as in her 2015 Case Western Law Review article and the OECD have published recommendations on improving regulatory process to keep it impartial, transparent to stakeholders and the public, comprehensive (that is, broadly applicable, without special exemptions), and free of "cronyism" or "capture" of regulators by special interests.[94]

The OECD's (2014) *The Governance of Regulators: OECD Best Practice Principles for Regulatory Policy* established "seven principles for the governance of regulators"[95]:

1. **Role clarity**: An effective regulator must have clear objectives, with clear and linked functions and the mechanisms to coordinate with other relevant bodies to achieve the desired regulatory outcomes;
2. **Preventing undue influence and maintaining trust**: It is important that regulatory decisions and functions are conducted with the utmost integrity to ensure that there is confidence in the regulatory regime. This is even more important for ensuring the rule of law, encouraging investment and having an enabling environment for inclusive growth built on trust;

94 Susan E. Dudley, "Improving Regulatory Accountability: Lessons from the Past and Prospects for the Future," *Case Western Law Review*, vol. 65, no. 4, 2015, pp. 1027-57.

95 OECD, *The Governance of Regulators: OECD Best Practice Principles for Regulatory Policy*, OECD, 2014.

3. **Decision making and governing body structure for independent regulators:** Regulators require governance arrangements that ensure their effective functioning, preserve [their] regulatory integrity and deliver the regulatory objectives of [their] mandate;
4. **Accountability and transparency**: Businesses and citizens expect the delivery of regulatory outcomes from government and regulatory agencies, and the proper use of public authority and resources to achieve them. Regulators are generally accountable to three groups of stakeholders: (i) ministers and the legislature; (ii) regulated entities; and (iii) the public;
5. **Engagement**: Good regulators have established mechanisms for engagement with stakeholders as part of achieving their objectives. The knowledge of regulated sectors and [of] the businesses and citizens affected by regulatory schemes assists to regulate effectively;
6. **Funding**: The amount and source of funding for a regulator will determine its organization and operations. It should not influence the regulatory decisions and the regulator should be enabled to be impartial and efficient to achieve its objectives;
7. **Performance evaluation**: It is important that regulators are aware of the impacts of their regulatory actions and decisions. This helps drive improvements and enhance systems and processes internally. It [the performance evaluation] also demonstrates the effectiveness of the regulator to whom [the regulators are] accountable and helps to build confidence in the regulatory system.

CURRENT US REGULATORY POLICY RULES AND GUIDANCE

So how well are current US regulatory practice and policy shaped, according to the standards set by the OECD and other authorities?[96]

To take a basic snapshot of the system today: The federal government guidance on US regulation policy writ large comes mostly from the US Office of Management and Budget's Office of Information and Regulatory

96 The scope of current US regulatory policy rules and guidance, and recent and current proposals for regulatory process reform, are described in Maeve P. Carey, *Cost-Benefit and Other Analysis Requirements in the Rulemaking Process*, Congressional Research Service Report R41974, December 9, 2014.

Affairs (OIRA).[97] Several executive orders and other circulars from OIRA shape the current US regulatory process:

- Executive Order 12866,[98] issued by President Bill Clinton in 1993, echoes many of the principles laid down by the OECD, and expresses the philosophy that regulations should:

1. address a "compelling public need, such as material failures of private markets";
2. be based on an assessment of "all costs and benefits of available regulatory alternatives, including the alternative of not regulating"; and
3. "maximize net benefits" to society unless otherwise constrained by law.

    - This guidance requires that regulatory analysis be performed on all rules deemed to be of "significant economic impact" of $100 million or more in a year, and that agencies submit such significant regulations for review by OIRA before publication in the Federal Register in proposed or final form. This in turn establishes the need for observation of central principles of regulation beyond the focused perspective of a particular agency. Assessing the option of not regulating recognizes the potential cost of the total weight of regulation, and the possibility that the remedy of a small distortion might occasion excessive costs for that reason. Maximizing net benefits emphasizes the principle that cost-benefit analysis is the central tenet of regulation.
    - OMB Circular A-4,[99] whose most recent version was issued in October 2003 (during the George W. Bush administration), is essentially OMB's and OIRA's guidebook for federal agencies on how to do regulatory analysis, i.e., what are "best practices." The 2003 version refined a prior guide developed in 1996 and published in 2000.

---

97 OIRA, The White House, 2016.

98 William Justin, *Regulatory Planning and Review*, Fed. Reg. 58, no. 190, October 4, 1993.

99 *Circular a-4: Regulatory Analysis*, The White House, October 9, 2003.

- The Obama Administration's E.O. 13563[100] ("Improving Regulation and Regulatory Review," January 18, 2011), E.O. 13579[101] ("Regulation and Independent Regulatory Agencies," July 11, 2011), and latest E.O. 13610[102] ("Identifying and Reducing Regulatory Burdens," May 10, 2012) all placed heavy emphasis on ex-post (retrospective) analyses, but only requested that regulatory agencies (starting in 2011) develop a preliminary plan and then (in 2012) take further steps to institutionalize regular assessments and promote public participation in retrospective review. Unfortunately, this process has not advanced beyond that admonition.
- The Trump Administration's E.O. 13771[103] ("Reducing Regulation and Controlling Regulatory Costs," January 30, 2017) specifies that to manage the costs associated with regulation, at least two regulations must be eliminated for every one that is imposed. For the then-current fiscal year (2017), each agency recommending a new regulation must identify at least two to be repealed. Furthermore, the total incremental cost of all new regulations for that fiscal year must be no more than zero (including the reduction of cost from regulations that are repealed), as determined by guidance issued by the Director of OMB. Beginning the next fiscal year (2018), the OMB director shall create a regulatory cost budget to limit each agency's incremental net cost (again taking into account regulations that are eliminated). The Executive Order makes no reference to the benefits that accrue from any regulations, including those that are recommended for imposition or repeal. Logically, if only costs are considered, then every existing regulation should be eliminated, and no new regulations should be imposed. Presumably, this logical inconsistency will somehow be dealt with in the guidance issued by the OMB director.

---

100 Barack Obama, Exec. Order No. 13563 (January 18, 2011), ("Improving Regulation and Regulatory Review").

101 Barack Obama, Exec. Order No. 13579 (July 11, 2011) ("Regulation and Independent Regulatory Agencies").

102 Barack Obama, Exec. Order No. 13610 (May 10, 2012) ("Identifying and Reducing Regulatory Burdens").

103 Donald J. Trump, Exec. Order No. 13771 (January 30, 2017) ("Reducing Regulation and Controlling Regulatory Costs").

Beyond executive orders and other such directives, legislation relating to oversight of regulatory policy (as described on pages 46-47 in the Dudley primer[104]) that has passed since 1998 (when CED issued its most recent report on regulation) includes the following:

1. The ***Congressional Review Act of 1996*** (CRA, contained in the Small Business Regulatory Enforcement Fairness Act of 1996) allows Congress to overturn regulations within a specified time through a resolution of disapproval. Because such a resolution would be subject to a presidential veto, and with a presumption that a president would support his own regulation with a veto, the CRA garnered little attention. However, the CRA also requires each agency issuing a regulation to submit a report to Congress, and the deadline for a resolution of disapproval occurs after the report is filed. Because the requirement for a report may have been ignored for some regulations created since the CRA's 1996 enactment, a new administration hostile to any such regulation could file a report on a regulation issued at any time after the CRA was enacted, and thereby empower Congress to pass a resolution of disapproval.
2. ***The Omnibus Consolidated and Emergency Supplemental Appropriations Act of 1999*** (section 638(a)) requires OMB to report to Congress yearly on the costs and benefits of regulations and to provide recommendations for reform;
3. The ***Truth in Regulating Act of 2000*** gives Congress authority to request that GAO conduct an independent evaluation of economically significant rules at the proposed or final stages; and
4. The ***Information Quality Act of 2000*** requires OMB to develop government-wide standards for ensuring and maximizing the quality of information disseminated by federal agencies.

In sum, the US executive and statutory directives toward regulators and the regulatory process echo many of the principles set forth by the OECD. However, one apparent key to good regulatory performance is the ability to assess ex post the success of individual regulations.

---

104 Susan E. Dudley and Jerry Brito, *Regulation: A Primer*, 2nd ed. (Arlington, VA: Mercatus Center; and Washington, DC: George Washington University, 2012).

The United States has paid fervent lip service to that objective, but in practice has done little to deliver. And pledges to remove any number of existing regulations without assessment of the success of those regulations is pointless.

CHALLENGES TO EVALUATION OF US REGULATORY POLICY

Within those principles of regulation and regulatory governance, how can our nation do a better job of constructing and implementing sound regulation policies and avoiding cronyism and otherwise unwise or misguided policies? This turns out to be a most difficult question.

In asking, "How could regulatory policy do better for the economy?" we must first acknowledge the current resource constraints, which impose challenges on the evaluation of all of the economic effects of regulations. There are both data and analytical limitations. Federal agencies currently are not adept at monitoring and measuring the effects of regulations and collecting data along the way for later analyses. Comparing effects at different points in time (involving discount rates), placing values on human lives, and dealing with uncertain outcomes are all technically complicated. Robert Hahn has argued that not enough progress has been made in the actual, evolving practice of regulatory assessment in terms of the rigor and quality of economic analysis and its potential to improve regulatory policy.[105] Yet Hahn also acknowledges the understandable and persistent political obstacles to strengthening the role of economic assessments in regulatory decision making.

Although all regulations must at least implicitly pass a society-wide cost-benefit test, measurement (especially of benefits and especially in the case of social regulations) can be extremely difficult. Given the limits of available knowledge, benefits can be highly uncertain. Furthermore, many regulations by nature require investment-type activities, which provide their uncertain payoffs years in the future.

Thus, even if those benefits were known with certainty (which they are not), decision makers still could disagree over how many future dollars

105 Robert W. Hahn and Paul C. Tetlock, "Has Economic Analysis Improved Regulatory Decisions?" *Journal of Economic Perspectives* 22, winter 2008, pp. 67-84; and Robert W. Hahn, "An Evaluation of Government Efforts to Improve Regulatory Decision Making," *International Review of Environmental and Resource Economics* 3, no. 4, May 2010, pp. 245-98.

of benefit are required to justify one dollar of current cost. Still further, because those remote and uncertain benefits often include claims of saving human lives, those decision-makers are caught in the analytical and ethical quagmire of valuing a human life, under various combinations of controversial circumstances (such as people of different ages, and different work histories and prospects; the same of course can be true of valuing the avoidance of injury or illness). Environmental regulation is a good (and large) example: the economic costs of environmentally motivated regulatory policies in terms of reduced economic output (activities that explicitly enter GDP) are much easier to price financially (in dollar values) than are the environmental benefits. Thus, although approving or rejecting a proposed regulation inevitably and implicitly passes judgment on a cost-benefit test, in many instances that judgment will of necessity be highly controversial.

Furthermore, as Hassett and Shapiro explain, the economic effects of regulations are fundamentally more challenging to evaluate than the effects of other types of government policies that are more easily "parameterized" (such as tax policy's effects depending on the breadth and uniformity of the tax base and level of marginal and average tax rates).[106] Regulations are varied and hard to generalize because every case is unique and it is difficult to find directly relevant empirical evidence. Hassett and Shapiro conclude that "policymakers must draw inferences concerning the likely impact of regulations from analogies"—and based on international comparisons reflecting differences in regulatory climates and stringency. (Note that this also supports a "principles-based" approach to regulation, as broader economic principles typically are applicable and relevant across countries, whereas specific rules usually are not.)

To evaluate the effectiveness of particular regulations on the particular (more specific) activities of particular businesses and households, we need more "*micro*-level" data. Here the case for more adequate funding for statistical agencies and programs must be made: All stakeholders in regulatory policy should collect adequately detailed data to measure these *micro* effects so that regulations do what they are supposed to do,

---

106 Kevin A. Hassett and Robert J. Shapiro, *Regulation and Investment: A Note on Policy Evaluation under Uncertainty with Application to FCC Title II Regulation of the Internet* (Washington, DC: McDonough School of Business Center for Business and Public Policy at Georgetown University, 2015).

in economically sensible, efficient ways. Assessing the economic costs and benefits of particular types of regulations cannot be done using "*macro*-level" data. Given that aggregate or average, economy-wide effects are typically very small, the most significant effects are the allocative and distributional effects (across geographies, industries, companies within industries, and different types of people), which require micro-level data to measure.[107] Moreover, regulatory policies are not imposed in a vacuum, so without the more detailed data it is extremely problematic to attribute changes in business or household behavior entirely to any one cause, such as the regulatory policy. Micro-level data are needed to control for other factors affecting decisions and outcomes.

A great example of the kind of microdata needed to study the effects of regulations on the very activities that are being regulated (and hence whether regulations are achieving their public interest goals) is found in a paper by economists Joseph Shapiro and Reed Walker, which uses factory-level records from the Census Bureau and the Environmental Protection Agency (EPA) to isolate the effects of environmental regulations from other factors that affect pollution emissions (trade, productivity, and consumer preferences).[108] Using a "model-driven decomposition" of the causes of the observed pollution changes, the researchers find that environmental regulation explains 75 percent or more of the observed reduction in pollution emissions from US manufacturing over the period of 1990-2008.

Considering all of these measurement challenges, some international arbiters have expressed their opinions of the US regulatory system. For example, in its most recent reports on regulatory policy (*Regulatory Policy in Perspective*,[109] *Regulatory Policy Outlook 2015*,[110] and *Framework for Regulatory Policy Evaluation*[111]), the OECD concludes that the

---

107 Cary Coglianese, Adam M. Finkel, and Christopher Carrigan, *Does Regulation Kill Jobs?* (Philadelphia: University of Pennsylvania Press, 2014); and Daniel E. Walters, "Analyzing the Job Impacts of Regulation," *RegBlog*, April 15, 2014.

108 Joseph S. Shapiro and Reed Walker, *Why Is Pollution from US Manufacturing Declining? The Roles of Trade, Regulation, Productivity, and Preferences*, Washington, DC: US Census Bureau Center for Economic Studies, 2015.

109 OECD, *Regulatory Policy in Perspective: A Reader's Companion to the OECD Regulatory Policy Outlook*, 2015.

110 OECD, *Regulatory Policy Outlook 2015.*

111 OECD, *Framework for Regulatory Policy Evaluation 2014.*

evaluation of regulatory costs and benefits is well developed in the United States, with the degree of evaluation efforts proportional to the anticipated impacts of the regulatory proposals. The OECD also notes that the United States has institutionalized ex-post evaluation via executive order (discussed later in this chapter), but in terms of stakeholder engagement, there is "no mandatory requirement . . . for consultation with the general public in the development or maintenance of primary laws [i.e., laws that call for regulations] initiated by Congress." (A deeper discussion of the issues associated with retrospective review is presented below. The OECD indicators distinguish between "primary laws" and "subordinate regulations"—only the latter being subject to OMB OIRA [executive] review and a required public comment process.) Chapter 1 of OECD's *Regulatory Policy in Perspective* volume,[112] written by Martin Lodge of the London School of Economics, identifies four main "deficits" in the current state of regulatory policy in OECD nations: oversight, participation, incentive, and adaptation.

We agree in broad generality with the OECD assessment and will provide our own interpretation and recommendations in each of these four categories of constructive criticism.

"Regulatory Overload"

From the perspective of any one business dealing with any one issue, regulation can be relatively simple. However, it can become much more complex under real-world conditions.

In particular, regulation can impose a burden that is heavier than the sum of its parts. A business can perceive a body of regulation from which it must extract those regulations that are most important to it. That may require sorting through a number of regulations that do not apply to it, because failure to address regulations that turn out to be relevant may have adverse consequences. Thus, some significant part of the total volume of regulation, rather than only those regulations that directly apply to a particular business, may be the more accurate measure of the regulatory burden. The typical citizen may find an analog in the formidable individual income tax instruction book that used to accompany the tax forms (but now merely lurks online). The typical taxpayer does not know what parts of the book apply to him or her,

---

112 Martin Lodge, "Trends and Challenges in Regulation and Regulatory Policy," in OECD, *Regulatory Policy in Perspective*, pp. 11-33.

and so must invest (or waste) time understanding, at least to some level, some parts that in the end are not pertinent.

This concern applies especially to new and smaller businesses. Large firms can have the economies of scale to invest manpower in regulatory expertise (as they can, for example, in providing health insurance for their employees). The smallest firms obviously lack that capability. Because new firms, usually small, provide much of the innovation, market disruption, and job creation that drive the nation's economy forward, burdens that retard business formation and growth can be costly.

There are two important implications for regulatory policy and practice.

First, when draft regulations are subjected to cost-benefit analysis, the weight of the regulation in creating a larger and more complex overall body of regulation should be included in the cost. That would implicitly impose a de *minimis* threshold on regulatory benefit before a regulation would be imposed.

Second, a special effort is necessary to communicate regulations to small and new businesses. With an understanding that small businesses lack the economies of scale to dedicate resources to study the regulatory system, government needs to take the regulatory system to them. Such an effort could not only minimize the costs of compliance, but also improve compliance itself.[113]

INCENTIVES: USING MARKET-BASED MECHANISMS OF REGULATION

One of the "four broad principles" emphasized in CED's 1998 policy statement was that:

> Where feasible and effective, regulations should be applied with a "soft touch" that allows flexibility of response, including the use of market incentives, in lieu of command-and-control directives.[114]

---

113 OSHA has a "Compliance Assistance Quick Start" tool aimed especially at new and small businesses. OSHA also offers on-site, no-cost, confidential reviews with priority to high-hazard worksites. The EPA has "Compliance Assistance Centers," including plain-language materials and internet tools). These are clearly among the most important regulatory issues for typical US businesses, but there is much less evidence of such outreach from other agencies.

114 CED, *Modernizing Government Regulation: The Need for Action*, 1998, p. vii.

This statement next explained a continuum of regulatory policy approaches in terms of the degree of control the regulation attempts to impose on markets. The reporting of information lies at the minimum end, and traditional directive rulemaking at the maximum. The former might not actually remedy a market failure; the latter could easily impose a government failure even more serious than the problem it set out to solve.

But in the middle of this spectrum are a variety of mechanisms that affect economic incentives through the price system, such as (in the case of environmental policy) through pollution taxes or tradable permits. Economists of all political persuasions tend to favor regulation via market-based adjustment of prices (to account for differences between social costs or benefits and private costs or benefits) over regulation based on requiring changes to quantities of specific inputs or outputs (which would override rather than simply adjust the natural market-based price incentives). Using the price system allows markets to "self-correct" in response to government-adjusted social costs and benefits while preserving the market-fluctuating signals contained in the private component of prices, in contrast to the latter "command and control" approach, where the government essentially sets *quantities* and thus predetermines (full) prices in a hit-or-miss process—usually more miss than hit. The market-based forms of regulatory policy are also more consistent with a principles-based as opposed to a rules-based approach.

There are noteworthy examples of quantity-based rules that have had adverse consequences. In 1981, the United States imposed restrictions on imports of Japanese-manufactured automobiles through a quota (based on allegations of dumping and other unfair trade practices, which we do not evaluate here). Japanese manufacturers, recognizing that offering low prices would be of no value to them, because they could not sell as many vehicles anyway, raised prices. Therefore, the resulting additional revenues went to the Japanese manufacturers, rather than into the US Treasury. Had the restraints been imposed through an equivalent tariff, Japanese vehicle sales might have been reduced by the same amount, but the US taxpayers, rather than the Japanese manufacturers, would have reaped the benefit of the increment to prices.

Similarly, the US CAFE (corporate average fuel economy) fuel efficiency standards are an alternative to higher fuel prices in creating an incentive to economize. This quantity-oriented device has several adverse consequences, including low fuel prices incentivizing vehicle owners to drive more, rather than use public transportation or other means. But in addition, for a variety of reasons, the political system has dictated that there are separate and more lenient CAFE standards for trucks than for cars. Therefore, for large family vehicles that are close to the boundary line, there is an incentive for manufacturers to characterize their products as trucks rather than cars. This can lead to building bigger, heavier vehicles (which consume more fuel)—sometimes including truck frames, which threaten the safety of passengers in other vehicles involved in two-vehicle accidents—rather than lighter (and potentially safer) unit construction.[115]

Another prominent variation of quantity-based rules is the "best available control technology" standard that has been applied to pollution regulation. Such requirements may be interpreted to demand inflexibly that the cost of remedies far exceeds possible benefits. There has been a movement toward potentially far more efficient performance standards instead.[116]

Another advantage of using more market-based approaches to regulation is that they facilitate the collection of "real-time," objective information on the behavioral effects of these programs. Randall Lutter writes that the permit-trading approach to environmental regulation has several advantages. In addition to promoting the lowest-cost means of meeting a specified emissions target, environmental regulation also generates emissions permit prices, which are "unsurpassed at measuring one important aspect of the effects of regulations on regulated entities—the current marginal cost of controls, averaged across the industry." Also, futures markets for permits can "also provide information about current expectations of future control costs."[117]

Not all quota-based regulatory standards can be converted into price incentives. But at the very least, regulatory authorities should try to foresee unintended consequences, and to write standards that are related as clearly and directly as possible to the actual value that the regulation is to pursue. Those who are regulated understandably

115 See, for example, Robert P. Murphy, "5 Unintended Consequences of Regulation and Government Meddling," Atlanta, GA: Foundation for Economic Education, July 15, 2015.

116 United States Environmental Protection Agency, "Clean Air Act Overview: Setting Emissions Standards Based on Technology Performance."

117 Randall Lutter, *The Role of Retrospective Analysis and Review in Regulatory Policy*, Arlington, VA: Mercatus Center, George Mason University, 2012.

seek to achieve compliance at the lowest cost to themselves; and if regulations are written with excessive complexity in exceptions and different standards for different parties, the result can be manipulation rather than performance.

We believe that there is enormous potential in the conversion of micro-managing rules into price-based incentives. While the cynical or the opportunistic might portray these price incentives as "taxes," business leaders can explain that overly prescriptive rules are taxes, just as surely as are corrective prices, and distorting rules cause more-costly economic distortions. Business leaders can see through the smokescreens that may be deployed for political gain and explain why the economy would function better with more efficient price-based incentives.

ADAPTATION: RULES- VS. PRINCIPLES-BASED REGULATION

We believe that regulations should facilitate but not necessarily subsidize business activity in ways that maximize the net benefits to society as a whole. This is why we favor a more principles-based regulatory strategy. Regulations are more likely to promote the public interest over the long term (with less need for review and revision) if they are based on broad principles rather than narrow rules. Broad economic principles last forever, but narrow legalistic rules, particularly those that are heavily prescriptive with respect to remedies, can become stale over time. Broad principles do not favor specific companies over others, whereas narrow rules easily can and sometimes do.

To be sure, regulation based on broad principles is not always attainable and can conceivably be abused.

The argument for a highly specific rules-based regulatory system is that in our litigious society, laws and rules must fully cover every contingency, lest the clever manipulate the system to take unfair advantage of it. Even sound and well-intended rules, this perspective would contend, could leave enormous and debilitating uncertainty until all of those contingencies were resolved—perhaps even in court. James Surowiecki wrote skeptically about regulating by principles when it was advocated in April 2008 by Henry Paulson, then Treasury Secretary, with Surowiecki sniffing, "But the best principles in the world won't help much if those in charge aren't willing to enforce them."

Principles should have clear meaning. They cannot be vague, as in the United Kingdom, where one finds principles like "A firm must observe proper standards of market conduct" or "A firm must conduct its business with integrity." To me, those are not principles. They are just glittering generalities.

There are many regulatory problems that are better addressed with bright-line regulation. For example, the algorithm for calculating the APR of interest should be standardized and clearly specified by regulators.[118]

Surowiecki's example is important. Some regulatory situations require specific rules. Allowing discretion in the formulation of the annual percentage rate (APR) reported to customers on their deposits and loans would invite financial institutions to profit by distorting information to present more favorable numbers to potential customers. That could force institutions to race to the bottom, lest they lose out in an unfair marketplace. It would create the opposite of a level playing field for competition. In this and similar situations, there is no alternative to explicit rules.

There is, moreover, a potential obverse problem. Regulators might use vague statements of principles to render arbitrary judgments against confused, ill-informed businesses. Or, for that matter, manipulative regulatees might seek a defense in vague principles for a failure to achieve the spirit of a regulation. Neither outcome is acceptable.

However, we maintain that broad principles are superior when they can express the true intent of a regulation, and especially when the goals of the regulation can be set in market-driven and performance-based quantitative terms. As Surowiecki put it, "But in an increasingly complex and fast-paced market environment, there are likely to be many regulatory issues where principles-based regulation will prove to be more robust."[119]

Arnold Kling has described principles-based regulation in the following way:

> [L]egislation would lay out broad but well-defined principles that businesses are expected to follow. Administrative agencies would audit businesses to identify strengths and weaknesses in their systems for applying those principles,

---

118 James Surowiecki, "Parsing Paulson: Paulson Plan to Regulate Financial Markets," *The New Yorker*, April 28, 2008.

119 Surowiecki, "Parsing Paulson."

> and they would punish weaknesses by imposing fines. Finally, the Department of Justice would prosecute corporate leaders who flagrantly violate principles or who are negligent in ensuring compliance with those principles.[120]

We believe that government regulations are more likely to improve rather than impede the performance of the economy when they adhere to broad economic principles rather than impose narrow legalistic rules. Principles-based regulatory approaches have the advantage of greater adaptability to changes in economic conditions and economic opportunities, as new markets and technologies develop in the economy and particular businesses rise or fall in response to appropriate price signals.

In our litigious culture, which has relied on judicial processes that parse down to the last semicolon, the lack of specificity in principles-based regulations can cause several alternative problems. Principles-based regulation may allow unintended behavior to be characterized as "compliant."

On the other hand, whereas a highly prescriptive rules-based approach makes it harder for businesses and regulators to "fudge" compliance, such brighter-line regulations can become so specific and tailored to the situation of the moment that they can easily become obsolete or even counter-productive—particularly from a public-interest or societal perspective—as the economy evolves. They can also be specifically designed to favor incumbent businesses as well (supporting "cronyism"), to the detriment of new-business formation and the innovation and productivity growth of the overall economy. Analysts also question the ultimate power of even a mass of complex rules. For example, Arnold Kling argues that "The banks will always be savvier than the consumers and nimbler than the regulators, so bright-line regulation is bound to fail."[121] Harlan Loeb has blogged that detailed rules can be either over- or under-inclusive[122]; presumably, either failing could be fatal for a regulation.

---

120 Arnold Kling, "Why We Need Principles-Based Regulation," *The American*, American Enterprise Institute, May 22, 2012.

121 Kling, "Why We Need Principles-Based Regulation."

122 Harlan Loeb, "Principles-Based Regulation and Compliance: A Framework for Sustainable Integrity," Huffington Post, May 4, 2016.

Ultimately, we believe that the benefits of a more concise principles-based approach are substantial enough that the nation should change its collective mentality, including perhaps developing a dispute-resolution system that could deliver timely judgments, perhaps with penalties for attempts at manipulation that are fairly determined as frivolous.

OVERSIGHT: RETROSPECTIVE REVIEW—THE CARE AND FEEDING OF A REGULATION AFTER BIRTH

Many regulatory policy experts across the political spectrum call for better review of regulations after they are put in place to facilitate eliminating or improving stale, outdated, and inefficient regulations. The findings from ex-post, retrospective reviews could also serve to validate ex-ante assessments of subsequent new regulations. Susan Dudley provides a concise "retrospective review of retrospective review" in a May 2013 brief for George Washington University's Regulatory Studies Center, with an overview of the history and current status of the practice, as well as arguments for greater effort in this direction.[123]

Despite this consensus in the academic and practitioner communities, we conclude that there remains too little effort toward expanding the practice of retrospective review (and too little recognition that regulations may be suboptimal in a variety of ways and a variety of cases that evolve over time). There may be greater institutional rewards for turning out new regulations than for improving old ones. And for that matter, new regulatory requirements in new laws carry deadlines, whereas improving old regulations can always be put off until tomorrow. In a world of scarce resources and manpower, procrastination on ex-post review might often seem to be the better choice.

But as the world changes (including but not limited to advances in technology), regulations, even those based on principles rather than narrow, specific rules, can become obsolete and even counterproductive. It is not surprising that scholars of regulation around the world have cited retrospective review as one of the areas where other nations have made advances, and the United States, while still a world leader, has lost some of its comparative edge. We believe that our nation must invest more in continuing review of its stock of regulations, and in the data and other resources to support it.

---

123 Susan E. Dudley, "A Retrospective Review of Retrospective Review," Washington, DC: George Washington University Regulatory Studies Center, May 7, 2013.

That does not determine precisely what organization should perform such review. We are skeptical that an analytical body of a sufficient size and strength could be created within Congress. Retrospective review must rely heavily on the street-level body of knowledge and information already resident within the executive agencies, and with the associated leadership resources in OIRA. However, we also are concerned that the instincts of self-justification within those agencies—the reflex to defend the judgments taken by those same executive offices in the past—could prevent objective retrospective review. Still, the success of self-review at the National Highway Traffic Safety Administration (documented below) demonstrates that open-minded self-criticism can be achieved (even more so with the expertise and leadership at OIRA), with the President's own authority (and the persuasive power of his budget office) behind it.

One way to circumvent any tendencies of agencies to be close-minded and defensive about their own regulations in any review process would be to expand the resources of OIRA so that it could have a separate unit that focuses on retrospective review. Alternatively, a new and independent office could take on that responsibility. What would not work is requiring existing staff at OIRA or the agencies, already required to assure the quality of new regulations, also to take on the responsibility for retrospective review, perhaps somehow to be performed during their lunch hours. Both functions would suffer, beyond any self-protective instinct in the retrospective review function.

The office charged with retrospective review could select existing regulations for the earliest review, guided by priorities set by Congress. Those priorities could include the "significance" of the regulations as measured by the cost impact in dollar terms, and the length of time that the regulations have been in force, as well as the degree of public demand expressed through the current comment process. We also note that the experience of the regulated should be incorporated into these reviews. The public comment process should be used to identify substantive reactions based on operational experience (regulated entities are already invited to submit comments), and OIRA should take advantage of constructive, practical suggestions in re-molding regulations to be more successful in achieving their objectives.

In particular, we see this function as an ongoing challenge of regulation, so we do not see the government institution to fulfill the function as a one-time, temporary "commission" with unpaid citizen members. A primary cause of inefficient regulations is changing technology and market conditions. The best one-time review cannot foresee the future. Retrospective review must be a continuing responsibility, not a one-time quick fix achieved on the cheap by volunteer commissioners.

Congress must play a stronger role in regulation. There is always the potential for a costly Catch-22 dilemma for the executive, should a less-than-fully informed Congress mandate the creation of a new regulation that must pass a cost-benefit test, while imposing conditions that make the creation of such a regulation impossible. Congress does need more expertise to ensure that the legal foundations that it builds for future regulations are sound.

Better creation and ex-post review of regulation will thus cost money. It is important that the nation not swallow whole the fallacy that more resources for regulators means more regulation. More resources must equal better regulation—better data to facilitate stronger and more frequent review—and therefore the cleaning out or improvement of obsolete or deficient regulations that otherwise would evade scrutiny. To achieve that, leadership and understanding are the only prerequisites; a dynamic, prosperous economy will surely follow.

There is considerable support for this perspective. Michael Mandel and Diana Carew of the Progressive Policy Institute, in a May 2013 report, wrote of the adverse effects of "regulatory accumulation" ("the natural buildup of regulations over time") on economic growth and its disproportionate burden on small businesses caused by its hurdles to business formation, hiring of workers, and expansion of product markets. They describe three types of regulatory accumulation: (i) "pebbles in a stream," where too many regulations in the aggregate cause a blockage effect that increases costs and slows innovation; (ii) interaction between small numbers of existing regulations (intended or not, obvious or not) that raise costs for businesses; and (iii) "behavioral overload" that forces management to prioritize compliance with regulations over growth and innovation.[124]

Multiple presidents (from both parties and with increasing emphasis over time) have pushed via executive orders for greater retrospective review of regulations. Recently, several legislative proposals for regulatory reform have been introduced, as discussed in Susan Dudley's testimony before the Senate Homeland Security and Governmental Affairs

124 Michael Mandel and Diana G. Carew, "Regulatory Improvement Commission: A Politically-Viable Approach to US Regulatory Reform," Washington, DC: Progressive Policy Institute, May 2013.

Committee.[125] Yet "retrospective review" of the "cumulative effects" of regulation is not commonly practiced because it is time consuming,

---

125 Susan E. Dudley, "A Review of Regulatory Reform Proposals," testimony before the United States Senate Homeland Security & Government Affairs Committee, September 17, 2015. Dudley listed the following proposed legislation: S. 708, the "Regulatory Improvement Act of 2015" (sponsored by Sen. Angus King, I-ME), would establish a Regulatory Improvement Commission responsible for evaluating regulations that have been in effect for at least 10 years and for making recommendations for their "modification, consolidation, or repeal." Congress would vote up or down on a full package of recommendations, and federal agencies would have 180 days to implement the approved set of actions.

S. 1683, the "SCRUB (Searching for and Cutting Regulations That Are Unnecessarily Burdensome) Act of 2015" (sponsored by Sen. Orrin Hatch, R-UT) would establish a Retrospective Regulatory Review Commission to review and make recommendations to repeal rules or sets of rules that have been in effect more than 15 years. Congress would approve the full package of recommendations via joint resolution. The commission's report would include estimated costs of the reviewed rules and would sort the most burdensome rules into two categories (cut immediately or save for later cuts). Agencies would be required to repeal rules in the first category within 60 days of the joint resolution's approval, and as new regulations are issued, agencies would be required to "cut as they go" (or "cut-go") and repeal rules in the second category to offset the costs of new regulations.

S. 1817, the "Smarter Regulations through Advance Planning and Review Act of 2015" (sponsored by Sen. Heidi Heitkamp, D-ND) would promote "an evaluation mindset" and require agencies to be forward looking and include in proposed major regulations a framework for measuring effectiveness, benefits and costs, and plans for gathering the information necessary to do so. The act would require assessment to take place within 10 years of a rule's promulgation, to measure benefits and costs, evaluate how well the rule accomplishes its objectives, and determine whether the rule could be modified to achieve better outcomes.

These proposals are explicitly supported by former OIRA Administrator Susan Dudley and implicitly achieve policy goals laid out by many other regulatory policy experts. The regulatory commission idea is modeled by Mandel & Carew, "Regulatory Improvement Commission," after the Base Realignment and Closing (BRAC) Commission. Their conception is that:

The [Regulatory Improvement] [C]ommission would consist of eight members appointed by the President and Congress who, after a formal regulatory review, would submit a list of 15-20 regulatory changes to Congress for an up or down vote. Congressional approval would be required for the changes to take effect, but Congress would only be able to vote on the package as a whole without making any adjustments.

The current practice for retrospective review is regulatory agency "self-review," which Mandel and Carew state is problematic because it is costly and time consuming for the agencies to review regulations already in place, and agencies have little incentive to be self-critical.

analytically challenging, expensive (both staff- and data-intensive), and difficult to operationalize in an effective and impartial manner.

In a working paper for George Mason University's Mercatus Center ("The Role of Retrospective Analysis and Review in Regulatory Policy"), Randall Lutter (2012) observed that the "most prominent practitioner of retrospective analyses is apparently the National Highway Traffic Safety Administration (NHTSA), which has completed (at the time of his writing) 92 separate evaluations of the costs and the effectiveness of various facets of its regulatory program since 1973."[126] He describes examples of specific retrospective analyses and the insights that were gained. Lutter praises the NHTSA for the "unusual" rigor of their analyses and their "apparent comfort with self-criticism" that "sets the agency apart." He speculates that this may stem from the NHTSA's "engineering culture" and "unparalleled access" to timely and high-quality data—both not the case in most other regulatory agencies—which encourage the practice of data-driven decision making (rather than ex-post data-supported policy advocacy).

Lutter's paper also describes how the data-driven NHTSA practices the most rigorous forms of analyses of their own regulations, both prospectively and retrospectively. He mentions a 1998 detailed reappraisal (a quintessential retrospective review) of the cost and effectiveness of the 1983 rule mandating center high-mounted stop lamps on cars and light trucks, and the original prospective study that had randomly assigned vehicles to have the special stop lamps under consideration. Such use of "randomized controlled trials" as a means of informing regulatory policymaking and retrospective review is championed by former OIRA Administrator Cass Sunstein in a 2014 paper on "The Regulatory Lookback."[127] But for the vast majority of regulatory agencies that aren't naturally so "data-driven" in the development and administration of their regulations, further efforts to emphasize and institutionalize retrospective review are needed.

There is enormous potential for improving data availability and quality for retrospective review. "Big data" arising from the tracking of consumer transactions would be one possible source. Traffic flows and the use of public transportation can be measured and monitored. Social media

126 Randall Lutter, "The Role of Retrospective Analysis and Review in Regulatory Policy," Arlington, VA: Mercatus Center, George Mason University, April 18, 2012.

127 Cass R. Sunstein, "The Regulatory Lookback," *Boston University Law Review*, vol. 94, 2014, p. 579.

could provide helpful information. But many other opportunities exist. Advances in the processing of such data expand the potential even more. There are important challenges to the protection of individual privacy, which must be respected. Regulators should work conscientiously to see how they can assess the performance of regulatory systems and improve regulation as a result.

The Government Accountability Office (GAO) in April 2014 (GAO-14-268) reported on the progress of agency retrospective reviews (conducted over the 2011-13 period).[128] GAO found that agencies had made some progress in the practice of retrospective review, and that the reviews often made a difference in bringing about improvements to the clarity and effectiveness of regulations, and in reducing the "burden" on regulated entities (probably taken as referring to compliance costs). This is illustrated in figure 5.1. But GAO also concluded that more guidance from OIRA was needed to improve the transparency and usefulness of the information to policymakers and the general public, and to strengthen the links between retrospective analyses and the regulatory agencies' performance and priority goals.

FIGURE 5.1 **Breakdown of the types of reported retrospective analysis outcomes for executive agencies that implemented the final actions from January 2011 through August 2013**

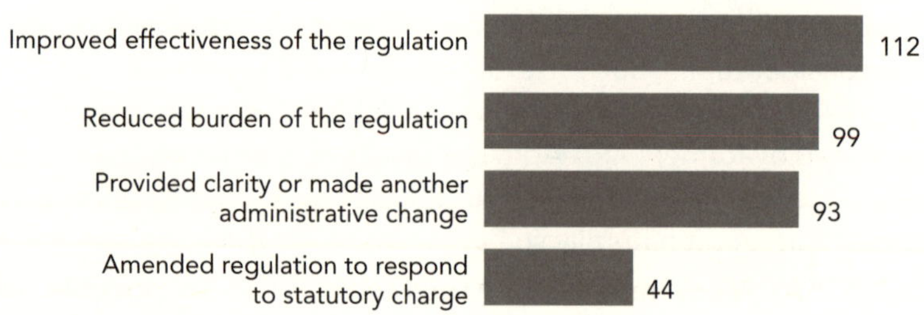

Results represent 19 agencies and 246 completed retrospective analyses. The outcome categories are not mutually exclusive. Agencies reported outcomes in multiple categories for 76 of the completed analyses.

Source: http://www.gao.gov/assets/670/662517.pdf

128 Government Accountability Office, *Reexamining Regulations: Agencies Often Made Regulatory Changes, but Could Strengthen Linkages to Performance Goals*, April 11, 2014 (GAO 14-268).

The GAO report identified the major strategies and barriers that affect agency implementation of retrospective analyses:

Strategies: (i) establish a centrally coordinated review process to develop review plans; (ii) leverage existing regulatory activities to identify needed changes; (iii) use existing feedback mechanisms to identify and evaluate regulatory reforms; and (iv) facilitate tracking of reviews and interagency discussion and collaboration on best practices.

Barriers: (i) competing priorities hinder agencies' ability to conduct retrospective analyses; (ii) agencies reported difficulty obtaining sufficient data to identify improvements attributed to regulations; and (iii) deciphering and analyzing data to be able to attribute effects to regulations vs. other factors are difficult.

In his testimony that dissents from Susan Dudley's positions on the merits of current legislative proposals for retrospective review, Sidney Shapiro of the Wake Forest University School of Law states that "the regulatory system has become out of balance" with a hugely cumbersome and time-consuming rulemaking process (taking five years or longer), and that the "one-size-fits-all requirements that would be imposed by the proposed bills discussed threaten to exacerbate the problem." He argues that what is needed to make the regulatory policy process function more efficiently is to provide more resources and legal authority to the regulatory agencies themselves and to free them from "unnecessary analytical requirements."[129]

Therefore, some approaches that would help put retrospective review into better practice follow:

- Perhaps most important, and perhaps most difficult, regulations must be designed to facilitate retrospective review. This might even include creating opportunities for randomized trials (such as what was included in the regulatory mandates for center high-mounted brake signal lights by NHTSA). Many variations of such trials would be possible, with various techniques being compared with an unaffected control group, or different techniques being tried in different geographical areas.
- Data must be collected as regulations go along, not long after the fact;
- Agencies must be forced to or more strongly encouraged to analyze data at regular intervals and in an impartial manner; and

129 Sidney A. Shapiro, "A Review of Regulatory Reform Proposals," hearing before the US Senate Committee on Homeland Security and Government Affairs, September 16, 2015.

- The regulatory system must better provide and align resources and incentives to undertake and enforce retrospective review.

PARTICIPATION: STAKEHOLDER ENGAGEMENT IN THE REGULATORY PROCESS

Stakeholder engagement is an important ingredient in the good governance of regulators. Steven J. Balla and Susan E. Dudley (2014), in a report for the OECD on "Stakeholder Participation and Regulatory Policymaking in the United States"[130] (a summary brief is provided in figure 5.2[131]), identify the different ways stakeholders can participate in the regulatory policymaking process:

FIGURE 5.2 **U.S. Rulemaking Process**

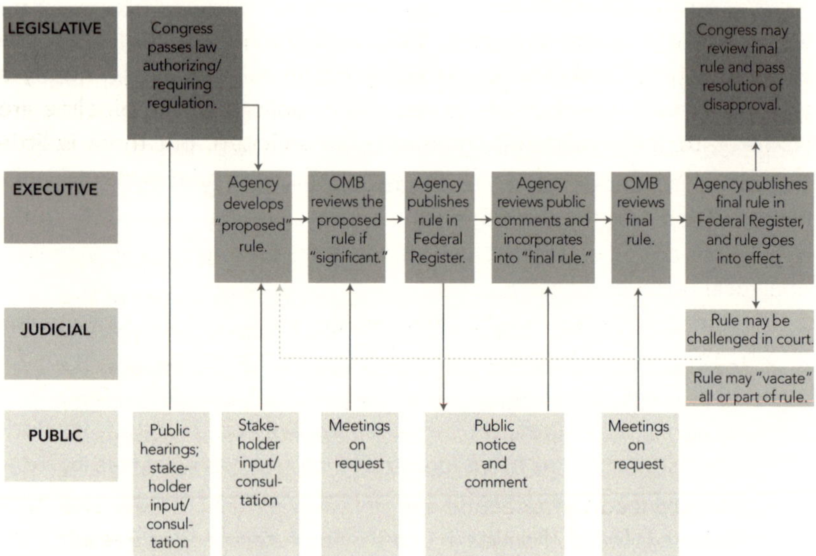

Source:
https://regulatorystudies.columbian.gwu.edu/sites/regulatorystudies.columbian.gwu.edu/files/downloads/Balla-Dudley-USStakeholder-Reg-Process-11-2014.pdf

130 Steven J. Balla and Susan E Dudley, "Stakeholder Participation and Regulatory Policymaking in the United States," prepared for the Organisation for Economic Co-operation and Development (OECD), Washington, DC: George Washington University Regulatory Studies Center, 2014.

131 Susan E. Dudley, "Opportunities for Stakeholder Participation in US Regulation," Washington, DC: George Washington University Regulatory Studies Center, September 23, 2014.

Online technology has certainly allowed more of the general public to become aware of regulations (both proposed and in place) and to submit comments about them, via the "regulations.gov" website. Managed by the "eRulemaking Program Management Office" (in partnership with regulatory agencies and the OMB):

> Regulations.gov is your source for information on the development of Federal regulations and other related documents issued by the US government. Through this site, you can find, read, and comment on regulatory issues that are important to you.[132]

Balla and Dudley also describe how Internet access has inspired some nonprofit and academic institutions to develop their own innovative approaches to interfacing with stakeholders and the general public regarding regulatory policy.

Despite the recent progress, Balla and Dudley conclude that the current state of stakeholder participation in rulemaking is mostly a one-way street. Descriptions of regulatory policies in the pipeline are provided to the public and comments are solicited, but there is little evidence that feedback collected via public comment systematically figures into actual decision making:

> Our review demonstrates that there are extensive opportunities for stakeholder participation at all stages of the regulatory process. These opportunities, however, are typically oriented toward facilitating the provision of information on the part of stakeholders. Instruments of participation, in other words, do not generally advance stakeholder engagement in deliberative decision making, where deliberation is characterized by reflection on positions held by others and the possibility of changes in one's own preferences as a result of such reflection.[133]

---

132 https://www.regulations.gov/.

133 Balla and Dudley, "Stakeholder Participation and Regulatory Policymaking in the United States.

The Administrative Conference of the United States's (ACUS) "Petitions for Rulemaking" "identifies agency procedures and best practices for accepting, processing, and responding to petitions for rulemaking.[134] It seeks to ensure that the public's right to petition is meaningful, while still respecting the need for agencies to retain decisional autonomy. Building upon ACUS's previous work on the subject, it provides additional guidance that may make the petitioning process more useful for agencies, petitioners, and the public." The ACUS made these final recommendations[135] on improving communication and engagement between regulatory policymakers and general-public stakeholders, informed by New York University's Institute for Policy Integrity's recommendations to the ACUS, which included "the enhanced use of online platforms to educate the public; the facilitation of consultations with petitioners before and after submission; the creation of public comment periods for all petitions; the collection of statistics on agency petitions; and the establishment of default timelines for responses."[136]

We conclude that the regulatory process could indeed make far better use of the expertise and experience of those actually affected

134 79 Fed. Reg. 75114, 75117 (Dec. 17, 2014).

135 Administrative Conference of the United States, "Administrative Conference Recommentation 2014-6: Petitions for Rulemaking," December 5, 2014.

136 Institute for Policy Integrity, New York School of Law, "Policy Integrity Helps Reform Federal Rulemaking Petition Process," December 8, 2014.

by regulations. Given the lower cost of collecting and processing such input, this would seem to be one of the greatest wasted opportunities for improvement in US regulation.[137]

---

137 Several recent legislative proposals (from the 114th Congress, calendar years 2015 and 2016) have pursued better regulatory policy practice in other respects—particularly in improving analysis for decision-making *before* regulations are issued:

S. 1818, the "Principled Rulemaking Act," would codify the language of President Clinton's Executive Order 12866 and President Obama's Executive Order 13563. This would give congressional support to the EO's nonpartisan principles, could be applied to independent agencies, and would make compliance with legislative requirements subject to judicial review.

S. 1820, the "Early Participation in Regulation Act of 2015," would require agencies to publish an advance notice of proposed rulemaking (ANPR) at least 90 days before publishing a proposed major rule, which would be valuable to solicit input from stakeholders *before* decisions are made.

S. 1607, the "Independent Agency Regulatory Analysis Act," would explicitly authorize the president to require that independent regulatory agencies (such as the Securities and Exchange Commission, the Federal Communications Commission, and the Consumer Product Safety Commission) comply with regulatory analysis requirements. Currently, the analyses supporting regulations issued by independent agencies tend to be less robust. The Administrative Conference of the United States recommended in 2013 a Cost-Benefit Analysis at Independent Regulatory Agencies (78 Fed. Reg. 41352, 41355 (July 10, 2013): that independent regulatory agencies adopt more transparent and rigorous regulatory analysis practices for major rules; according to government data cited in the Dudley testimony, "more than 40 percent of the rules developed by independent agencies over the past 10 years provided no information on either the costs or the benefits expected from their implementation."

Additionally, the recently House-passed (pending in Senate) H.R. 427, "Regulations from the Executive in Need of Scrutiny (REINS) Act," also focuses on documenting and considering the economic costs of regulations before they are put in place. The legislation:

Revises provisions relating to congressional review of agency rulemaking to require a federal agency promulgating a rule to publish information about the rule in the Federal Register and include in its report to Congress and to the Government Accountability Office (GAO) a classification of the rule as a major or non-major rule and a complete copy of the cost-benefit analysis of the rule, including an analysis of any jobs added or lost, differentiating between public and private sector jobs. Defines "major rule" as any rule that is made under the Patient Protection and Affordable Care Act or that the Office of Information and Regulatory Affairs of the Office of Management and Budget finds has resulted in or is likely to result in: (1) an annual effect on the economy of $100 million or more; (2) a major increase in costs or prices for consumers; individual industries; and federal, state, or local government agencies, or geographic regions; or (3) significant adverse effects on competition, employment, investment, productivity, innovation, or the ability of US-based enterprises to compete with foreign-based enterprises.

CONCLUSIONS

US regulatory practice still is cited as among the best in the world.[138] However, the consensus among the scholarly and practitioner communities is that the US edge is slipping. And given the growing need for faster economic growth to address our federal fiscal shortfalls, as well as to raise sagging standards of living, there is no reason to ignore the opportunity to aid our economy through more efficient regulation.

We particularly cite the failure to achieve the oft-called-for retrospective review and the intricacies of rules-based regulation as key shortcomings. We also believe that the input of regulated entities, particularly the businesses that must attempt to function under the regulations, is a key wasted resource in the regulatory process. And we would urge policymakers to allow the market to work by using corrective prices in a free-market concept, rather than prescribing technologies or output caps to attempt to resolve our market failures.

We believe that these steps would allow our economy to work more efficiently and would foster innovation and improve the growth of living standards for all Americans, without losing any of the values now pursued by US regulation.

138 World Bank, *Doing Business 2017: Equal Opportunity for All; Comparing Business Regulation for Domestic Firms in 190 Economies* (Washington, DC: World Bank, 2017).

6

The Financial Services Industry

The financial services industry plays an important role in the US economy, for corporations as well as individuals. The times of economic strength in the last few decades, and the financial crisis and recession of 2008-9, in turn bear eloquent witness to the beneficial and the destructive capabilities of our financial system.

There is broad acceptance of the need for financial regulation, but wildly varying opinions on the appropriate nature of that regulation. We focus here on the crucial issue of financial regulation at length, believing that it should prioritize some important principles, to avoid a replay of the recent crisis and to facilitate future economic growth. This chapter will consider current regulatory practice; what is working and what is not; and recommendations for a more effective and productive regulatory approach going forward.

A BRIEF HISTORY OF FINANCIAL SERVICE INDUSTRY REGULATION

Regulation of the US financial services industry has for a long time been complex. The founding of the first national bank in 1791, the First Bank of the United States, was one of the earliest policy battles. Treasury Secretary Alexander Hamilton strongly sponsored the bank, and President George Washington appears to have reluctantly cooperated, but Secretary of State Thomas Jefferson and Representative James Madison strongly opposed its creation. The contemporary arguments for both sides still echo in our modern times. According to Hamilton:

> The tendency of a national bank is to increase public and private credit. The former gives power to the state for the protection of its rights and interests, and the latter facilitates and extends the operations of commerce amongst individuals.[139]

While financial services are a recognized and necessary part of a functional modern economy, the role of individual financial institutions is still debated. The two extreme views result in conflicting legislative and regulatory approaches. One camp sees financial institutions as dynamic—providing not only an efficient means of sharing liquidity and capital between those who have it and those who need it, but also a vehicle for creative innovation and economic growth. However, others strongly believe that financial services are so fundamental to the economy that they should behave as utilities and provide safe havens for deposits, and at the same time also function as vehicles for the implementation of public and social policy. (The most obvious example is the use of the banking system to provide credit and loans to those with lower credit ratings, both corporate and individual. The most visible example of this mandated social policy role is the Community Reinvestment Act, or CRA, whose goal is to expand homeownership.)

This dilemma has played out over the past 30 years, as policymakers have attempted to use legislation and regulation to accomplish social policy, but with unfortunate results. In the 1980s, as a result of efforts to expand homeownership, the savings and loan industry received broader powers, which the regulators were encouraged to support. The unfortunate results were unbridled and undisciplined S&L expansion and massive losses for the taxpayers.

In the late 1990s, Congress again encouraged a social agenda to expand homeownership by lowering credit underwriting standards. For example, there was criticism from regulators who questioned Fannie Mae and Freddie Mac's expansion of their portfolios into subprime housing. Unfortunately again, this Congressional signaling was a major contributing factor to the financial crisis and economic collapse of 2008-10.

The natural reaction to each major crisis is to take steps to ensure that "this will never happen again." The unfortunate truth is that far too often the well-intentioned actions, usually unveiled with great pomp

139 Letter from Alexander Hamilton to Robert Morris, April 30, 1781.

and circumstance, address largely historical issues. They are not forward looking; they "fight the last war."

So let's review the fundamentals of financial services regulation, to find sound regulatory policies and practices for tomorrow, not yesterday.

SHOULD FINANCIAL SERVICES BE REGULATED?

Economists virtually unanimously believe that under ideal conditions, the unfettered market provides the best outcomes for both buyers and sellers of goods and services. Under such circumstances, regulation could only reduce and restrict the performance of the economy and the well-being of most participants in it.

However, circumstances are rarely ideal. The financial services industry might be a leading example of what economists would call the "imperfection" of a market.

Probably the leading source of that imperfection would be what economists (again) would call "asymmetrical information/understanding." Ideally, a buyer and a seller of a good or service would face off with the same total understanding of the subject of the contemplated transaction. The buyer then could know what he or she would be willing to pay for the good or service; the seller would know what amount he or she would need to accept the transaction; and the sale would occur or not, with both parties feeling that a fair bargain had been struck in the former case.

Financial transactions in an unregulated market often would fail to meet that standard. Imagine a loan as a simple and straightforward example. The "price" of the transaction is the rate of interest and the "structure" of the transaction (tenor; collateral; appropriateness/suitability). That price could be expressed in an enormous number of ways. In the absence of regulation, unscrupulous lenders could employ their greater understanding of the alternatives (they usually are financial professionals, whereas borrowers most often are not) to understate the true cost to the borrower. In particular, an unscrupulous lender could make an inferior offer look better to a non-expert than a more accurate characterization by an honest lender. The borrower could be harmed, and the pressures in the marketplace would push the honest lender to misrepresent his service just to remain competitive. To prevent such exploitation of the consumer and the resulting "race to the bottom" in lending practices, regulation requires that lenders adhere to a standardized definition of the "annual percentage rate" (APR) for each loan.

And this is just one example of the potentially damaging information asymmetries in financial services. In another example, sellers of corporate stock could inflate the perceived values of the underlying firms to a non-specialist public by omitting information or distorting the measurement of assets and liabilities in their representations to the public. Individual investors contemplating thousands of alternative securities could not possibly accurately assess even a small relevant subset of the alternative securities that are offered in the market. Accordingly, we have a Securities and Exchange Commission (among other regulators), which provides some oversight on the information presented by corporations to the investing public.

Furthermore, the financial services industries underlie virtually all of the commerce in every modern economy. Malfunctioning of financial services could lead to the most painful economic fallout (witness the Great Depression, and the financial crisis of 2008). Misreporting of information could distort economic decisions to exaggerate this effect. Thus, extreme imperfections in the market for financial services could harm so many people to such an extreme degree that the entire economy would be threatened. Regulation of financial services is therefore essential in the view of most scholars.

However, the near-consensus on the need to regulate the financial services industry has not yielded a universally preferred set of regulatory policies and practices. In fact, far from it.

Today the financial services industry is regulated by a hodge-podge of regulatory agencies at both the national and state levels. The overlaps create inconsistency in rules and regulations as well as in interpretation of all those overlapping—competing and conflicting—approaches. This inconsistency is compounded by a failure of congressional oversight to support the regulators in the face of often-differing political and public policy priorities. Such waffling can and has led to extremes in terms of regulatory behavior, lax when it should have been strong (e.g., housing in the 1980s and the 2000s) and excessive when it should be allowing some latitude (e.g., with new technology-based entities—"FinTechs" and "RegTechs" today, as discussed later in this chapter).

Legislation has been created far too often inexpertly by well-meaning individuals but based on shibboleths (false mythologies that are popular, but just simply "not so"). Badly designed and drafted legislation creating poor regulations not only hurts the economy but, also and even more important, puts critical stakeholders in danger. We will discuss below some of the legislation such as Dodd-Frank and its Volcker Amendment, and Glass-Steagall, to address these points.

One of the great ironies is that nearly 100 percent of the serious mistakes made by practitioners—despite common folklore—have embarrassingly not been generated by great complex models and unfathomable algorithms. Instead, the massive losses have been created by the most basic violations of simple fundamental truths (or, in the parlance of the street, shocking "rookie mistakes").

To use an industry shorthand, close to 100 percent of the major material mistakes can be attributed to shortcomings in addressing one of the five historic CAMEL principles. CAMEL is the acronym that regulators for years have used to evaluate financial institutions:

- Capital (adequacy)
- Asset (quality)
- Management (experience, integrity, capability, and capacity)
- Earnings (ability to generate profits)
- Liquidity (sufficient ready cash to meet all calls and demands)

Despite what the media and politicians discuss, it was liquidity—or rather, illiquidity, a failure to have sufficient cash accessible—that was the culprit in 2008. Industry subject-matter experts will always rank liquidity (often referred to as treasury management) as by far the most critical of the five CAMEL elements. Management experience, capability, and capacity would usually be seen as the second most important element. Asset quality (risk underwriting and structuring) would be the third element. Earnings (managing revenue generation and costs) would come next for most industry insiders. Ironically, capital would come last as insiders know that capital is really an accounting term, and while it might capture the amount of leverage undertaken by an institution, by itself it can be misleading.

Managing financial institutions frankly is not so complex as some consider it. However, the critical elements of risk are not widely appreciated outside the industry. One risk stands out among all others (first among everything): liquidity, the ability to deliver cash to meet obligations. Obligations could be depositors wanting their money back. Liquidity can be meeting debt maturity obligations. Liquidity can be the ability to deliver the appropriate currencies when they are due. These all require cash. The number one (actually number one through 99, out of

100) potential killer of financial institutions is a failure to have adequate cash to meet all obligations. The analogy often used is that liquidity is the equivalent of a tank of air for a scuba diver at 100 feet. Divers can lose everything they have from their diving knives to their masks to their flippers and be able to surface safely, but if they lose their air tank or run out of air at 100 feet, they will most frequently die. The same is true for financial institutions. Hence, as a key principle, regulations must start with liquidity management as the initial and key focus. *Any body of financial regulations that does not focus first and foremost on liquidity management has missed the existential issue for bank survivability.*

What comes next? Management. As referenced elsewhere, regulators for years have provided boards with a CAMEL rating to describe their assessments of the individual core components of a financial institution.

Most regulators will say when asked privately that it is hard to judge management, with the result that the management variable often receives less attention than the easier-to-discuss quantitative criteria. Even when regulators have had concerns, they have hesitated to express them until problems have emerged.

However, given the importance of management capability, competence, experience, and depth to the health and outcome of a financial institution, we strongly urge that regulators ensure that management receives not just equal attention to the non-liquidity components of CAMEL, but perhaps attention and documentation second only to liquidity when they do their reviews and provide their findings.

Management is not that hard for an experienced regulator to evaluate. It is fairly transparent whether the individuals in management have at a minimum been exposed to key issue areas that they are being asked to oversee. Even a world-class tennis player would rarely be the right overseer for an F-5 fighter jet.

Bank executives (and yes, regulators) should have experience of and exposure to a wide range of business cycles. Sailing on a calm lake is far simpler than taking a ship around the Cape of Good Hope in winter.

Turnover and depth of management (sufficient numbers of appropriate executives, stability of retention, and adequacy of informal and formal training) can and should be monitored and evaluated. In this age of cost cutting, it is incumbent on regulators to ensure that institutions have not cut corners on management adequacy and competence.

Regulators as a "best practice" in countries ranging from the UK, Hong Kong, and Singapore to Poland have included formal "fit and proper" evaluations in their approvals for management positions. In some countries there are even tests and degree requirements for individuals who aspire to assume positions in regulated financial institutions. We do not suggest that the United States take its management evaluations of "fit and proper" quite that far, but we do believe that management is too important for regulators to fall short of a full measure of attention.

Regulators should have the skills to judge whether individuals in management (and on the board) have appropriate subject matter expertise and business cycle exposure.

So is capital the next element of CAMEL to discuss? No, asset quality is next. The two great determinants of asset quality are the quality of the target-market client lists and the target-market products. The target market client list is a critical outline of the types of entities—for example, what lines of business—with which the institution should be doing business. Client selection is a critical determinant of a financial institution's long-term health. Clients should not only be selected carefully to align with the risk tolerances of management, but also to align with the skill sets of management (i.e., serving textile or clothing manufacturers requires a knowledge base and industry understanding significantly different from that of banking technology companies or agricultural companies). It would be fair to note that lax target-market client selection is not only unhealthy for the financial institution, but also for the customers, because the financial institution will not be able to provide appropriate advice and products; nor can it provide knowledgeable support in times of stress.

An inventory of appropriate target-market products that are suitable for the institution as well as the client base is also crucial to maintaining a sound and productive business.

So, finally, is the accounting term *capital* the next component of CAMEL to consider? The next one is actually good earning capability, which allows the institution to support its clients, to hire/train top staff, and refresh and incorporate new technologies into its business (and its ability to attract capital to grow and support clients).

Then comes capital, an element that allows third parties to judge the degree to which the balance sheet—particularly asset levels, long/short-term matches, and liquidity—are in harmony. It is not that capital isn't a useful frame of reference, it is just that its utility lags behind the other four CAMEL measures; and yet, politicians have placed it at the head of the list for regulators to use as the basis for overseeing their industry participants. Bad legislation has led to mistaken regulatory policies that have made banks less useful to society and less competitive and have not solved the underlying issues either. Well-intentioned legislation that restricted financial institutions from charging enough on high-risk individuals to cover their costs may have put the most vulnerable at far greater risk by forcing them to turn to shadow elements for their financial-service needs; these institutions reduced the ability of those most in need to get competitive financial products and exposed them to the most unscrupulous elements.

2008: FOCUSED ON BASICS, NOT EXOTIC PRODUCTS AND TRADING

There is a shibboleth that trading and exotic products were at the heart of the 2008 financial crisis, and that somehow the 1990s changes to the Glass-Steagall Act opened the door to the 2008 market meltdown. However, embarrassingly for the industry, the mistakes that were made —which were major, massive, and fundamental—were not rooted in sophisticated products whose dangerous toxicity escaped the control of the banks. No, instead, the grievous errors were of the most basic kind, mere replays of those made just a few years before: first in the 1980s in the savings and loan meltdown, and then shortly thereafter as commercial banks introduced toxic products of their own in terms of "low-doc, no-doc" mortgages, to disastrous impact.

In the 2000s, the affected banks' first major mistake was that managers, some of whom lacked appropriate business-cycle experience, thought there was a deep pool of inexhaustible liquidity (think of the word "cash") that would always be available. Borrowing (or as financial institutions call it, "funding") short term was much cheaper than borrowing long term; i.e., the interest rates for short-term borrowing in days, weeks, and months were much lower than for borrowing that reaches out years. This strategy required almost daily trips to the market to borrow new money to repay the maturing money. This was not prudent. Had the funding strategy matched the terms and conditions of the lending strategy, this approach would still not have been smart, but it would have been less dangerous. However, the new managers in place did not have the experience or the insight to recognize the possibility that someday people might get nervous and not agree to lend out new funds or roll over debt coming due; i.e., the liquidity would dry up (there would be no cash available at virtually any price). Members of management of some institutions were so naive as to even offer to be the "lender of last resort" to other institutions by committing to provide liquidity for literally just a few basis points in the event that those banks had trouble acquiring funding for some of their balance sheet activities (which meant that the guarantors were generally funding off-balance sheet securitizations).

The second egregious error was to ignore basic, truly recent market history. In the 1980s, a stunning poison pill of a product was created referred to colloquially as a "low-doc, no-doc mortgage." This product, which in theory was designed to help self-employed persons with highly variable incomes, badly damaged the then number-one ranked mortgage company in the United States. This was no small isolated incident in a small geographic corner of the market; rather, it was a major front-page-news explosion. It is hard to believe that some market participants failed to foresee the ugly consequences when this product was reintroduced.

In the run-up to the financial crisis, this same bank, and many others, then created the first cousin of "low-doc, no-doc mortgages"—the so-called sub-prime mortgages and Alt A mortgages. Coupled with this was the decision to take these very poor-quality mortgages, mismanage their documentation, and then create securitized bundles that were cut up further into smaller bundles and sold to investors and their advisors, who in turn failed to do the necessary analysis, instead relying on a rating agency for truly existential decisions. In 1992 and 1993, similar products called collateralized mortgage obligations (CMOs) exploded and did a great deal of damage to many.[140]

Neither of these two major failures should have been repeated. The issues were not complicated, and neither of these basic errors had anything to do with the changes related to the Glass-Steagall Act.[141] Such mistaken funding practices and poor-quality lending were fully available to badly managed financial institutions even prior to the changes in

140 Affected institutions included Kidder Peabody.

141 The Glass-Steagall Act of 1933 (passed in the wake of the 1929 stock market crash) separated the commercial banking and investment activities of banks. Some continue to maintain that the repeal of Glass-Steagall in 1999 set the stage for the financial crisis of 2008-9. However, as we maintain above, the issuance, securitization, and resale of unsound mortgage loans that was the root cause of the financial crisis would have been perfectly legal had Glass-Steagall not been repealed. See also Oonagh McDonald, *The Repeal of the Glass-Steagall Act*, Cato Institute, November 16, 2016.

Glass-Steagall; in fact, they were fundamental to the earlier savings and loan debacle, and so should have been understood by managements that availed themselves of any experienced personnel.

This last point illustrates why legislation and therefore regulations that are unartfully drafted by politicians, lawyers, and academics can unfortunately emphasize the wrong areas. Rather than making markets safer, they distract attention from the real issues and therefore actually make markets riskier.

The Risks Involved

Today, due to Dodd-Frank and the Volcker Rule, although banks may entail less inherent risk than before, the markets themselves are far riskier. No asset class today has more liquidity than it did before 2008. Most asset classes in fact have dramatically less liquidity (the amount of available assets on balance sheets and the number of market participants has shrunk in everything from the trading of US Treasury securities to foreign exchange). In addition, massive amounts of funding are now in asset classes that most people apart from the top seasoned market professionals do not understand to be highly illiquid in a crisis. Mutual funds and exchange-traded funds (ETFs) are classic examples of assets misunderstood by the average consumer: they are difficult to convert into cash in a market crisis in a timely manner and for anything approximating their pre-crisis values. In some cases, these assets may not attract any buyers at all.

Legislation and regulatory review have directed and forced trades and certain transfer activity that were formerly done in individual institutions to go to a very small number of consolidating organizations called clearinghouses. The risk now is much more concentrated, and in a crisis the clearinghouses may indeed lack the resources or ability to keep up with the pace of trading. Hopefully the technology of the clearinghouses is catching up, but this consolidation has created a well-intentioned new risk.[142]

142 Ideally it can be reasoned that today's financial institutions understand this clearinghouse risk far better than they did at the time of the massive and potentially lethal meltdown of the SIMEX Singapore exchange, when Barings Bank failed. At that point, few institutions understood how their various "clearinghouse" memberships often brought with them a variety of risks, including joint and several obligations to make good on the losses on a given exchange.

For industry players there is concern that this forced concentration of activity may have created massive new risk. In the next crisis, few of the clearinghouses appear to have the capacity to withstand a meltdown without significant government and therefore taxpayer support. The failures will be rare, but because there is a massive concentration of the exposure from a wide number of banks into just a small number of clearinghouses, any problem will be of gigantic scale. When one institution involved in the clearing of an enormous volume of securities fails, other institutions that hold those securities as collateral will not be able to sell their assets, leading potentially to a string of large defaults.

Although it is a fairly technical issue, one of the most serious problem areas is the so-called tri-party repo market, which has been a critical source of funding for the markets and is material in size.[143] In 2008 this market peaked at roughly $2.8 trillion of securities; at that time some participants had more than $400 billion of assets in this mostly overnight market. While the market shrank dramatically down to roughly $1.5-$1.6 billion after the market collapse, it is still of systemic importance. Again, the problem is that financial institutions rely on this market to realize their collateral holdings for rapid turnover, under potential market stress. If this market were to freeze, a chain of defaults could result.

With the departure of J. P. Morgan from the activity, there is only one provider of service for the entire market: The Bank of New York. This means that one of the cornerstones of funding for the US markets is at risk if this one institution would have an operating failure that its systems could not manage (natural disaster or man-made such as a cyberattack).

Why would (should) we care? Here are some reasons.

> The potential for the tri-party repo market to cease functioning, with impacts to securities firms, money market mutual funds, major banks involved in payment and settlements globally, and even to the liquidity of the US Treasury and Agency securities, has been cited by policy makers as a key concern behind aggressive interventions to contain the financial crisis.[144]

---

143 Adam Copeland, Darrell Duffie, Antoine Martin, and Susan McLaughlin, *Key Mechanics of the US Tri-Party Repo Market* (Federal Reserve Bank of New York, 2012).

144 Adam Copeland, Antoine Martin, and Michael Walker, The Tri-Party Repo Market before the 2010 Reforms, Federal Reserve Bank of New York Staff Reports, no. 477, November 2010, p. 1.

The problems noted above, particularly liquidity risk, are compounded by global public policies encouraging national "ringfencing"—legal restrictions on the ability of one financial entity to transfer funds to another. National public ringfencing policies mandate that financial institutions cannot transfer funds or honor certain obligations. Ringfencing might be imposed ostensibly to protect one nation from a financial spasm in another. However, global cooperation in the next crisis may be diminished even further as each country tries to protect itself at the cost and exclusion of other countries by pulling its proverbial drawbridges up around its financial systems. These ringfencing restrictions will restrict already-damaged global liquidity even further. Foreign exchange may not be transferred, letters of credit (LCs) may not be honored, money transfers may not occur, automated teller machines (ATMs) may not function, and credit cards may not be recognized. The consequence could be chaos.

And as discussed in sections below, focus on the wrong risks (capital vs. liquidity and management) creates new risks such as market risk concentrations. There has been too little attention to the real emerging risks involving technology (which can include cyber, crypto-currency, and third-party vendor risks). Technology needs enormous attention and focus.

MAJOR *MATERIAL* ISSUES THAT NEED / REQUIRE REGULATION

In many endeavors, less is more. That can certainly be true of regulation. Excessive regulation ends up being ineffective, or even counterproductive.

While the printed version of the Dodd-Frank bill itself is listed at 848 pages and several sources estimate that its addendums reach over 2000 pages, the law firm Davis Polk as recently as 2016 indicated that almost 20,000 pages of regulations had been generated from this bill and that there was yet more to come. While considerable focus has been on the direct cost of adding significant numbers of new regulators with their accompanying costs (offices, benefits, and the like), the real cost has been significant economic inefficiency in the markets due to regulation that:

1. does not focus sufficiently on the real areas of principal risk (liquidity, management, and so on) and instead directs excessive focus on an accounting item called capital;
2. loses focus in terms of failing to prioritize the analysis of the key risks that could "sink the ship," and instead by massive overkill literally loses the ability to see what is material versus what is trivial; and
3. has drawn significant and much-needed resources away from investments that would strengthen financial-services operations such as updates in existing technology; replacement of old technology with new technology; and training and hiring of staff (and instead has driven many financial institutions to reduce their number of skilled, experienced staff in order to pay for some of these unproductive regulatory requirements).

There is wide agreement that consumers, particularly the least wealthy and financially trained— the "widow and orphan" categories—need to be protected prudently and appropriately. The creation of the Consumer Financial Protection Bureau (CFPB), while well-intentioned, added yet another bureaucratic entity to the process of creating an overlapping competing player. As often is the case, simpler and clearer enables more-effective action. The consumer would have been better protected by combining the Federal Reserve and its regulators with those of the Office of the Comptroller of the Currency, and having one organization with a clear charter to oversee retail and consumer financial activity. More discipline and more focus would not only have been more cost effective for the American taxpayer, but also would have provided far more focused oversight that avoided creating more overlap and more inconsistency.

Rules and regulations are effective only if they are clear and understood, and sufficiently concise that those regulated can actually read them. Dodd-Frank created a malicious precedent in girth at 2000+ pages of new additive regulations, but it did not stop there.

The mandated "stress tests" and "living wills" could be argued by reasonable people to be necessary requirements. However, to be useful, those requirements must focus on material risks and avoid excessive volume, which can allow the real risks to get lost in the tsunami of paper generated.

Today the "stress tests" have become massive Maginot Lines of manufactured material that arguably can fail to distinguish between the trivial and the terminal. Rather than making senior managements and boards focus on the five to 10 critical risks that can sink the ship (returning to CAMEL), there are thousands upon thousands of items experimentally stressed. The consequence is that the regulators have even had to go to third parties to have stress tests analyzed, leading to an empty exercise.

But it gets worse.

The "living wills"—how you "resolve" or close up a failing bank—have become a massive industrial complex of activity that fails to meet its objectives.

The so-called "living wills" of the major banks have taken on annual volumes (with addendums) that reach 50,000 pages and in some banks are rumored to have touched 100,000 pages. Despite the fortunes spent, they are virtually useless. A mark of obfuscation and evasion in a university class is a paper that will bury the professor in detail and minutia. Professors defend themselves by requiring students to show that they understand the point of the class with brevity and clarity. To make these living wills effective, the regulators should forcefully encourage (or even require) brevity. Far less paper could capture the risks that could sink the institution and make it clear to all involved whether the management and the board have thought through the key risks and have a workable plan.

One supposed remedy of the paperwork burden has been to lift the requirements from smaller institutions. But both "stress tests" and "living wills" are, if executed properly, healthy and relevant exercises. Rather than excluding smaller financial institutions from participating, these tools should be made material and relevant to the size and scope of the risks facing the institution in question. This would benefit everyone and make the market safer for all stakeholders.

Principles vs. Rules-based Regulation: Changes Necessary

More prudent, protective, and effective regulatory coverage will require a number of changes of regulatory policy.

The regulatory system must follow the market's lead and move from prescriptive rules-based regulation toward principles-based regulation. As we note elsewhere, there are instances in finance (such as the calculation of an annual percentage rate, or APR) where bright-line regulatory rules are needed. But today's balance leans too far in that direction. Particularly with new technologies, a rules-based approach is not only too easy to game, but too rigid and unresponsive to keep up with a fast-moving and changing landscape. Principles-based regulation will require even more-talented, more-trained, and more-experienced regulators, plus a national policy to strengthen the quality of the US regulatory structure, rather than seeking to address new circumstances by heaping one more regulation on top of all the others.

Still further changes will be needed:

1. We need consolidation of the multiple conflicting and overlapping financial regulatory organizations into one clear, focused group.
2. The regulators must be able to hire and pay "subject matter experts" at market levels. Other countries such as Singapore (the Monetary Authority of Singapore, or MAS) and Hong Kong (the Hong Kong Monetary Authority, or HKMA) have already and successfully moved in this direction.
3. Technology and training must be available to enable regulators to remain current with the fast-moving markets and the environment in which they operate.
4. Regulators need strong congressional support to be sensitive to public policy priorities (like the CRA), and also ensure that prudential practices are in place. Where there is a conflict between policy preferences and prudent behavior, Congress must make it clear that stakeholders should be protected by prioritizing "safety and soundness." This balance has been lost at times, such as with Fannie and Freddie at the outset of the financial crisis.

Anticipating and Addressing Emerging Risks in Technology

Technology is changing and even reshaping the very nature of how individuals and institutions use financial services. Just as credit cards, ATMs, and various forms of online banking have changed our behavior (visits to banks to deposit and withdraw cash are a fraction of what they were even 30 years ago), so is today's advancing technology changing interactions with financial services as tools ever more rapidly. The number of new companies using technology either to substitute for old practices, or to introduce new products and services, is already large and still expanding. These newly formed and forming financial technology-focused companies are often referred to as FinTechs, and their close cousins that use technology to help deal with regulatory and legal requirements are referred to as RegTechs in shorthand. These are generic labels without a narrow definition.

Most focus on FinTechs (and RegTechs) has been around two areas: payments and blockchain (or, in its more technical name, distributed ledger technology). However, there are literally thousands of other FinTechs focusing on direct client activity (front office); supporting the areas of audit, legal, risk, compliance, and the like (middle office); and streamlining the operations and production areas (back office).

Some believe that this is a bit of a fad, noting how few of those technology companies survived and prospered in recent years (PayPal is a rare exception). Why is now different? There are two reasons why technology is becoming more impactful—why we are at a true inflection point:

1. Technology is increasingly capable today, and more widespread;
2. The cost of setting up and creating a new technology company is a fraction of what it was in 2000, allowing literally anyone to set up a technology company anywhere that can reach any place on the globe. Several technology-based consulting firms have estimated that what in 2000 might have taken $5-10 million to produce in a time span of 6-18 months can now be done for a small fraction of the price, perhaps for less than $10,000, and in fewer than 72 hours, thanks to tools such as application-programming interfaces (APIs) that are now available through the Internet.

As a result, the number of these FinTechs (and RegTechs) that have sprung up is enormous, and they literally are in almost every country of the world. Today there is almost always a form of emerging technology that compares and competes with nearly every existing legacy financial service. There are many valid reasons, from competence to confidence, why people may not choose to substitute a new financial technology-based service for their existing service from a bricks-and-mortar institution, but the groundwork for such a revolution is there.

The critical question for legislators and the regulatory bodies is how and to what extent they should involve themselves with these new FinTechs and RegTechs. As of 2019, there are no firmly established best practices, but some countries have taken a proactive approach with Singapore and

Hong Kong, and perhaps the UK in the early lead; they have gone so far as to set up funding operations to support financial technology entrants ("incubators" for new products) and some varying forms of safe harbors for the FinTechs and RegTechs to test their technologies, usually in a limited way, with actual customers (a so-called "sandbox" approach to regulation; these terms are defined more specifically in the Appendix to Chapter 7 on cyber regulation).

Again, much of the current wave of regulation was based on false understandings of what were the underlying drivers of the 2008-9 global financial crisis. Regulation misperceived how the financial services industry actually contributed to the problems; and, as important, the legislative and regulatory focus was backward looking. False assumptions that the problem was technology and complex financial instruments have led to arguably excessive regulation that can stifle productive (and inevitable) technological progress. The result could well be that the United States will fall behind the curve of global financial services advancement.

Fundamentals, particularly in terms of liquidity management and management competence, will remain critical to US leadership, and safety and soundness. However, keeping up with the phenomenal pace of growth in technology around the world will also be crucial.

Crucially also, many institutions have no liquidity through available earnings to pay for these new technologies, and therefore will need often to "rent" the technology from third-party providers. This raises many dangers. Leading the list is cybersecurity—a serious, potentially existential risk, but as outlined below it is just one of many technology matters that require oversight. Renting technology introduces additional fundamental risks to the market and requires heightened focus.

What are the principal elements of these emerging risks? EY (Ernest & Young Global Limited) in their annual study on banking provides an excellent working summary in Figure 6.1:

FIGURE 6.1 **Technology investment plans today and over the coming years**

In which of the following technologies are you investing now and in which do you plan to begin, reduce, or increase investing in over the next three years?

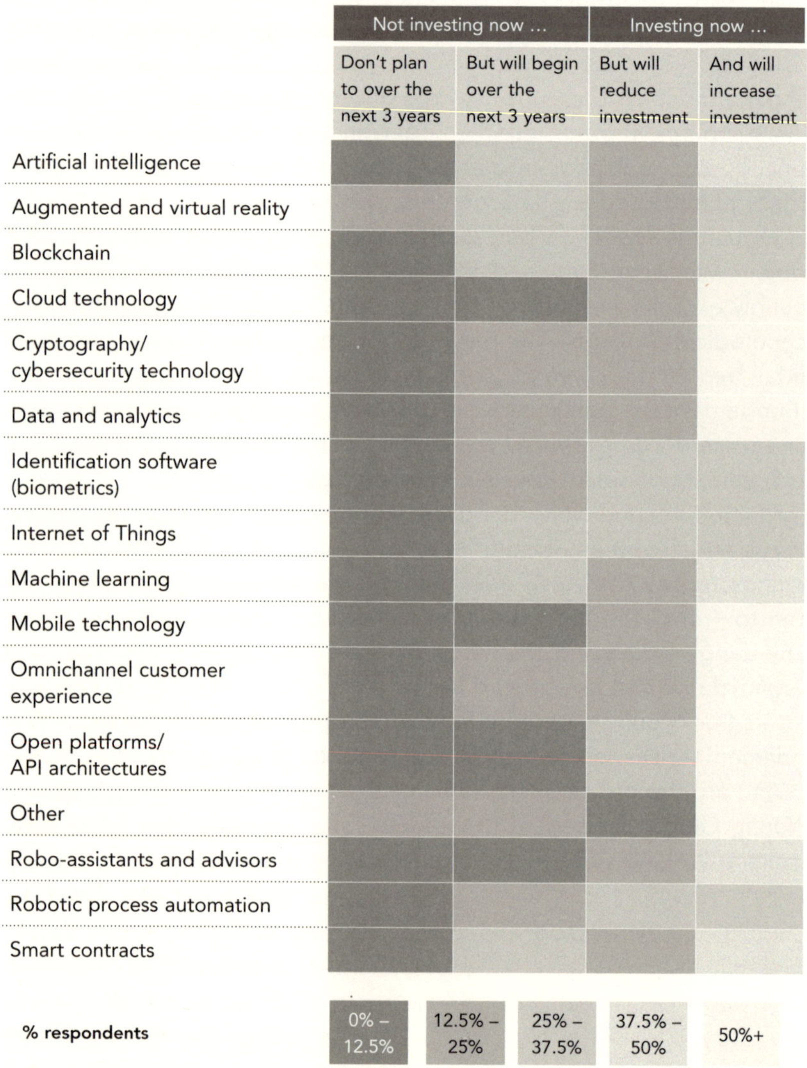

Source: EY, *Global Banking Outlook Survey 2018.*

Today, global regulators are struggling with how best to respond to this growth and evolution of technology. Challenges include long-standing fundamental questions, like their proper roles, which could range from traditional passive oversight to providing "safe harbors" or even funding innovation hubs. US regulators have been comparatively cautious, whereas some foreign regulators ranging from Singapore to the UK have already reached out to find ways to bring FinTechs and RegTechs under the regulatory umbrella without stifling progress.

If public policy and regulation view the financial services industry as merely a public utility, and therefore restrict activity to traditional ways of doing business, innovation could be driven outside of the legacy regulatory environment. Outside the regulatory purview, there is risk of a sudden failure (e.g., an "initial coin offering" [ICO] fails, and crypto-currencies such as Bitcoin lose all their investor monies). Extreme potential outcomes include systemic and liquidity failures if payment and control systems fail. New players may have less concern about appropriateness, suitability, and fairness; and thus the most vulnerable elements of society will not have the protections provided by established financial institutions and their accompanying regulatory overseers.

An ironic unintended consequence and risk of such excessive unproductive regulation is that, as these new technologies have drawn massive amounts of funding over recent years, the institutions that deploy them are under tremendous pressure to report "improved" operating performance ratios. How have they reported improved margins over this period of low margins in the market, surprisingly weak demand for banking products, and fierce new global entrants, while at the same time spending vast amounts on mandated regulatory compliance activity? An uncomfortable answer that highlights how risk reappears in unexpected places is that the institutions are being forced to take every cost-cutting opportunity—from looking to the cheapest third-party vendors, to reducing all middle management that is not mandated, to replacing experienced senior officers with hopefully bright but clearly inexperienced junior officers. When sports teams release their expensive senior players and add inexpensive farm team players and rookies, the activity is called a "rebuilding year," and the fans merely resign themselves to the prospect that their team will be in the cellar for a while. But when a financial institution drops experienced personnel for less expensive junior staff, the result can be painful failures and calls on the taxpayer. We argue that the financial crisis was caused by repetitions of relatively basic errors, including several directly from the savings and loan crisis of the 1980s. Arguably, a lack of experience and perspective was involved.

NECESSARY CHANGE: TOWARD IMPROVED AND EFFECTIVE REGULATION OF FINANCIAL SERVICES

Our basic assertion is that regulation in this society and economy is necessary to achieve efficiency, stability, and fairness. But regulation must be directed toward the appropriate issues and artfully crafted so that it does the most good and the least harm. Used carelessly and excessively, regulation hurts the economy, hurts society, and may even hurt the most vulnerable whom it was intended to support and protect.

All industries touch multiple stakeholders, and therefore regulation's reach is everywhere. However, the reach of financial services is among the broadest and deepest of all industries—and therefore financial regulation is virtually ubiquitous.

So, although appropriate financial regulation is essential, excessive financial regulation can not only fail to achieve its goals of prudential and constructive industry oversight, but also can actually hurt the very stakeholders it is intended to help.

Consolidation of Regulators

One of the major failings of the current financial services regulatory structure is that there are too many regulatory agencies dividing the turf among themselves. The result is multiple practices and standards, ambiguity, and "regulator shopping." Congress must recognize this failing and react to it. It can start at the national level and then encourage artful necessary state consolidation as well. As states fight increasing fiscal problems, perhaps the prospect of more-efficient state bureaucracies can overcome states' rights as a concern regarding federal influence.

Rather than creating the CFPB, Congress should have gone the other way and merged the regulatory activities of the Federal Reserve Board, the Office of the Comptroller of the Currency, and the Federal Deposit Insurance Corporation. Then Congress should have instructed through appropriate legislation that in addition to appropriateness, suitability, and fairness for consumers, the regulated institutions should train their customers in financial literacy. Although this is social policy, pure and simple, it aligns with the vested interests of all stakeholders—the financial institutions and the businesses and consumers they serve—and is a fitting quid pro quo in return for the benefits of a national charter.

This alternative would create far more consistency and focus in regulatory oversight, and generate cost savings.

A significant portion of the savings should be used to increase compensation and resources of the regulators. Increased wages would encourage highly skilled market participants to work at the regulator and to stay, a step that will provide heightened skills and increased continuity and institutional memory.

Move to Principles-Based Regulation and Oversight

As we noted earlier in this chapter in our discussion of regulatory policy, we believe that a move toward principles-based oversight is required given the continued rapid pace of change in the marketplace. Rules-based regulatory oversight is not sufficiently flexible to deal with the pace of change, and forces financial institutions (and regulators) either to respond to inefficient and outdated requirements, or to engage in "game-playing" to evade those rules.

A principles-based approach relies on regulators with greater skills and experience who can apply judgment as to whether the spirit of a regulation is being prudentially followed.

Rules-based approaches can be implemented in a "check-the-box" manner by a junior examiner. However, sad experience teaches that the criteria for checking boxes will become outdated, and institutions will be driven into a "race to the bottom" to satisfy the letter but not the spirit of the regulations.

Introduce Materiality Concept: An Economic Tracking

Congress needs to introduce the concept of materiality into regulation. This will give the regulators both the guidance and the authority to focus on the most important issues. Current legislation, and therefore regulatory oversight to implement that legislation, is being driven toward excessive volume and quantity and away from quality. In fact, as explained above, because of the quantity the quality is lost, and stakeholders are at more rather than less risk.

Regulators should be directed to produce only concise documents and documentation, and to see verbosity or excess volumes of data as a "red flag" signaling that senior management and board members do not know or understand the material risks of their franchises.

Regulatory policy and execution must achieve a balance between prudential oversight and flexibility. Excessive intrusion and micromanagement create inefficiency and hurt economic growth; neglect, even benign neglect, can create forms of "moral hazard." Regulatory absence in parts of the marketplace may tacitly and mistakenly suggest that participation is safe. Examples of this phenomenon today would include initial coin offerings (ICOs) and FinTech and crypto-currency trading. Not only might those directly involved suffer, but there could be knock-on effects or contagion to many other markets.

Appropriateness of Current Regulatory Requirements and Need for "Scaling"

Certain tools used by regulators to test for safety and soundness—in particular, living wills and stress tests—are potentially highly beneficial. The problem has been in the application. By ignoring standards of materiality, regulators have lost the utility of these tools and have not achieved the objectives of safety and soundness.

Because the tests have become far too detailed and onerous, legislators have sought to apply them only to large institutions.

Living wills and stress tests are constructive tools for senior managements and boards to review the health of their organizations. We recommend that they be kept and applied to all regulated institutions, but that they focus on and test only the most significant and material issues. An inability of an institution's management to identify the five to 10 most critical issues should be a major red flag for the regulators that management does not understand their business (remember again the CAMEL criteria).

For those who still suggest a small institution exemption as backdoor regulatory relief for the current excessive paperwork burden of living wills and stress tests, we suggest a note of caution. History has shown that small financial institutions with limited geographic footprints, limited products, and limited client sets are challenging (though not impossible) to oversee. They are inherently less diversified, and therefore potentially more risky. The easy-to-see historical precedent would be the savings and loan industry, which struggled to survive within these boundaries—and when these institutions tried to expand, many failed in a collective major financial crisis. Regulation can be successful if it is a national policy imperative, but politicians must know their history and be ready to make politically difficult decisions.

Need for Renewed Focus on CAMEL, Particularly Liquidity and Emerging Risks

Regulatory focus must be on the critical factors that affect a financial institution's health, such as liquidity, management capacity, experience, and the quality of its operations. Capital as an accounting term is a useful reference point, but lags behind the other four real economic drivers.

Regulators also need to increase their engagement with technology issues, whether they are the challenges of maintaining legacy systems or of keeping systems in step with real-world developments. (For years, most institutions used static credit lines for daylight and overnight controls to manage exposure while other market counterparts had real-time information. This was a major risk that regulators rarely if ever recognized).

Whether it is new technologies such as distributed ledger (blockchain), crypto-currencies (Tether, Ethereum, Bitcoin, and the like), or new mixes of technology such as Initial Coin Offerings, balanced regulatory engagement must keep new entrants working under the regulatory umbrella by applying the minimum necessary regulatory oversight. This will prudentially allow entrants into the markets, versus adding all the lead weights into the new saddles until the new players would drop to their proverbial knees. It is in everyone's interest to keep all market players under suitably coordinated regulation.

Need for a Focused Plan for Working with the Fintechs and Regtechs etc.

As discussed immediately above, the general "best practice" is to encourage the emerging FinTechs and RegTechs to work within the regulated environment, and as appropriate to partner and coordinate with legacy financial institutions. In some countries, including the United

States, there has been a tendency for regulators to either stay on the proverbial sidelines until they see how market innovations develop, or to apply all of today's onerous regulatory requirements to these start-ups. Understandably, the startups have usually resisted being pulled under the umbrella, because they don't want to carry that excess baggage, which they see as bringing little to no value and plenty of negative energy.

Best-practice tools used by regulators from Singapore to Japan to Hong Kong to the UK include introducing "sandbox" vehicles to allow safe-harbor new product introductions, and even some funding incubators (MAS) to encourage innovation and alignment with existing industry players.

It is critical to have policies, regulations, and behavior that encourage keeping new technologies and new entrants under the regulatory umbrella (i.e., the benefits to innovators outweigh the negatives) rather than outside of oversight and therefore creating new risks.

THE BURDEN OF THE MASS OF REGULATION

There must be fewer regulations, but to maintain adherence to and enforcement of those that remain on the books. It is critical to signal clearly, loudly, and frequently the nature of regulatory policy and enforcement behavior.

It is interesting that there are powerful tools on the books today—such as Regulation F, which oversees a bank's counterparties; and the Qualified Financial Contracts provision, which allows the regulators significant flexibility and capability to oversee professional markets, trades, and positions. If institutions believed that these were going to be strictly applied, they would directly influence the prudential behavior of how banks deal with risky counterparties. The failure to signal that these tools will be used has created a "moral hazard" of sorts, which has necessitated otherwise superfluous "Too Big to Fail" legislation and regulation. And Congress needs to allow the regulators the flexibility to make the best judgments that they can in the "fog of an economic crisis," rather than impose rigid restrictions that would hamper the ability of regulators to respond prudentially in the next crisis. This flexibility must include serving as a credible "lender of last resort" to calm the markets in times of trouble.

A sense of incremental materiality is essential: The weight of a single new regulation on top of the cumulative mass and complexity of existing regulation—the "sand in the gears" of the economy—must be compared with the marginal benefit of the new rule considered on its own. And in finance as in all regulation, the nation needs rigorous retrospective review to ensure that existing regulations continue to provide net benefit to society on these terms, and that all regulations that do not are eliminated or are revised so that they do. With additional resources, responsibility for retrospective evaluation rather than the current "set-it-and-forget-it" mentality could be an ongoing responsibility of the Office of Information and Regulatory Affairs (OIRA).

The Benefit of Improved and Streamlined "Living Wills"

Regulators and Congress must revisit the general concept of "Too Big to Fail." This construct really should have been "too big to fail in a disorderly and uncoordinated fashion." Markets can absorb failure if it occurs in an orderly, telegraphed, disciplined, and transparent manner; and failure must be an option in a market-based economy. Clearly, a single failure is less traumatic to the system than a group collapse. Clear policy communication in advance is critical.

Professionals can be disciplined if they know that there are consequences to their actions. The failure to have a clear policy and communicate it with candor, clarity, and conviction has led to waffling and uncertainty from the failures of Continental Illinois to Washington Mutual. Qualified Financial Contracts are still in the law, and if professionals know that there will be real consequences, they will make far better calculated-risk decisions.

CONCLUSION

Regulation, appropriate in nature and focus, is needed for something as integral to the economy as the financial services industry. A focused review of current regulation is necessary in order to prioritize what is truly material to the health of a financial services company. Fewer but more appropriate regulations focusing on areas such as liquidity and management would be productive. Quality of review should be emphasized over size, scale, and girth. Tighter, more-focused regulatory review will both reduce the risk of failures and allow for more productive servicing of the economy; further, it will help to keep regulations in step with innovation in the industry. The regulators need adequate financial support to hire, train, and retain the best and the brightest; and they need rhetorical support when they take the difficult steps to do their jobs. The regulators need tools to handle emergencies—and not lose them. Legislative action must support the regulators that take a more active role in helping to shape and align and incorporate FinTechs and RegTechs into the regulated economy. There must be recognition that regulation needs to fit the level of risk and therefore adopt and adapt coverage that is intense enough to avoid driving these companies outside the regulated sphere. Also, allowing these new activities to grow outside oversight (e.g., billions in Initial Coin Offerings and crypto-currency offerings) is in many ways through silence a new form of "moral hazard" that will impact both individuals and overall economy. As new technologies evolve, legislators and regulators have a responsibility to provide prudential levels of oversight.

In short, financial institutions need smart, lean regulation directed to the true material risks to consumers and to the economy as a whole.

7

REGULATING NEW TECHNOLOGIES: CYBERSPACE

New technologies—true breakthroughs, as opposed to even quantum leaps in existing ways of doing things—can pose enormous challenges to regulation. In the limit, a new technology can confront society with a range of possibilities that extends from enormous benefit to tremendous harm, with little or no precedent on how to judge the prospects. There can be significant costs both to over-reaction, and to failure to react at all. And given the pace of technological advancement today, the frequency of these challenges is likely to increase. Such new technologies, which emerge constantly, are rarely neatly addressed by existing laws and regulations. Recent examples include artificial intelligence (AI), nanotechnology, bio-engineering,[145] changes in banking and insurance, and self-driving cars.

There have been historical examples of the introduction of new technologies that have had radical social, economic, and political consequences, such as assembly lines, organ transplantation and harvesting, or advances in shipping or rockets that led to new international maritime and space regulations. These milestones required significant regulatory responses that can serve as guides for consideration of modern-day issues. This discussion uses two of those episodes, maritime commerce and outer space, as a historical basis on which to outline a potential best-practice framework to deal with emerging technologies.

145 Clustered regularly interspaced short palindromic repeats (CRISPR) provide a prominent example.

We use cyberspace as our primary example for that framework, but we believe that this framework can apply to a broader range of evolving regulatory needs.

DARNED IF YOU DO: REGULATING A NEW TECHNOLOGY

When new market activity or new technologies emerge, politicians and regulators have three potential, logically alternative approaches:

1. Do nothing, and leave the new activity unregulated until and if a need for regulation is clear; 2) Apply existing rules to the new activity; or 3) Act proactively and predictively, and adapt and adopt a new, specifically designed mode of regulation as soon as possible.

   In an environment of enormous uncertainty, each of these alternatives carries significant risks.

2. *Do nothing*:

   Policymakers and regulators could choose to wait until it becomes clear whether, and how, this new technology will impact stakeholders. This will mean taking no action, setting no policies, regulations, or guidelines until there is sufficient clarity to determine what if anything is required and warranted. The positive aspect of this alternative is that it allows the new activity to grow and develop relatively unimpeded. The negative is that there may be unprotected hazards that grow more quickly in size, scale, and scope than anyone anticipated; material harm may occur while the regulators wait.[146]

3. *Apply existing rules, regulations, and requirements*:

   The safest course for politicians and regulators might be to impose immediately the regulations and standards that would apply to the closest pre-existing analog to the innovation. Incumbents who might be affected adversely by the new competition are likely to favor this approach. But this alternative might also have negative effects in a variety of ways; in the worst case, it could kill US innovation. Applying regulations that do not fit the new technology (whether there is principles-based or rules-based regulation) can inhibit and impede

146 Some of the risks are explained in Government Accountability Office, *High-Risk Series: Urgent Actions Are Needed to Address Cybersecurity Challenges Facing the Nation*, GAO-18-622 (September 2018).

the development of a potentially beneficial activity (such as work on medicines, services, foodstuffs, energy, and the like). It can drive new activity outside of the regulated sphere, in that some implementors of the innovation would try to recharacterize it in a way that makes the existing rules inapplicable. That could make the innovation obscure and opaque and place the activity outside the oversight of a regulated environment. Alternatively, this approach could drive the new activity to other geographies where it will not be so restricted. In either event, it is likely that US consumers would not fully enjoy the benefits of the innovation. If the innovation were to be driven overseas, the US economy could suffer a competitive disadvantage.

4. *Adapt and adopt new policies and regulations as applicable*: Policymakers and regulators might choose instead to design new rules to fit the innovation from the outset. This scenario requires the policy actors to make early consequential judgments of when, how, and to what degree to apply oversight and constraints (usually through forms of regulations or financial requirements) to this new activity, at a time of ultimate uncertainty. (The distinction between this and the previous approach may be a matter of degree, as some tools from existing regulations may be borrowed to create the new regulatory regime.) A continuing process would be needed to keep in step with the development of the innovation. The degree to which the regulators directly engage will be a challenge, because the more explicit the involvement, the more accountability and risk the regulators will take on. One element of the design process will be to judge the materiality of issues that arise, and to choose the degree of oversight ranging from none to full. Objections will be raised by legacy incumbents who will claim favoritism if the new regulations are an iota less stringent than those already in force for the existing players.

One potential tool, close to the first alternative, will be to allow development and engagement through "incubators" and to allow degrees of testing through "sandbox" approaches. An extreme is a purely theoretical sandbox, all in the laboratory, whereas an incubator might allow limited testing in the open public (with safe harbors provisions granted). This alternative will require an appetite for risk from the regulators and significant public policy support from politicians. It would probably encourage new entrants and new activity (if innovators consider such testing to be less risky than a totally unregulated approach), and be most likely to involve critical activity that is conducted transparently and with a reasonable degree of regulatory and public policy oversight. This approach may bring the most favorable risk/reward return for the sum of stakeholders. (See the Appendix to this chapter for an explication of incubators, accelerators, and sandboxes.)

HOW INNOVATIONS TAKE ROOT AND EVOLVE: SOME HISTORICAL EXAMPLES

In the early stages of any new activity, the impact tends to be small and localized. But the pace with which the new technology evolves easily may outstrip any expectations, and the reach of the innovation may extend beyond pre-existing rules or guidelines. When society begins to take notice (through the volume of activity, and perhaps some adverse impact), an informal set of customary "rules of the road" can develop that help society to cope. If the new activity continues to grow, a call for more formal oversight, laws, and regulations usually follows.

History suggests that the sequence of the propagation of an innovation and the regulatory response tend to follow this prototype:

- The new activity develops.
- The activity reaches sufficient scale, scope, and size to warrant guidelines (if it ever does).
- Initial guidelines are based on customary practice and are driven by the major participants.
- The guidelines become effective if either i) the stakeholders find it necessary to honor them in order to participate in the activity, or ii) it is possible to enforce the guidelines, which therefore become "rules."
- An innovation may reach significantly beyond national boundaries. Nation-states will follow international customary practice, which may evolve into global rules— but only as long as those rules do not materially contravene local or national laws. In practice, stakeholders will defer to their own home country "laws."

One of the newest and most impactful of technologies, simultaneously evolutionary and revolutionary, is the Internet: the World Wide Web and its various features. For this discussion we will use the terms "cyber-realm" or "cyberspace" to capture its wide range of activity, from basic person-to-person email to massive AI-driven activity on the part of large businesses or nation-states. The cyber-realm clearly has reached a stage calling for formal establishment of "rules of the road" on the basis of all of the above standards, especially given its Malthusian pace of growth.

As a useful starting and simplifying approach in thinking about potential rules and regulations for cyberspace, we might ask if there are historical precedents that would provide some pertinent guidance. In doing so, we might note some of the cyber-realm's most striking, even unique characteristics:

- It has a stunning ease of entry for participation, across virtually every form of commerce.
- Its speed of entry is extremely fast (hours or days, versus months or years for many other technologies).
- It has shown the potential for extraordinarily fast rates of growth (geometric in some dimensions).
- Participation is uniquely opaque. Attribution of misbehavior (or any behavior) to any particular participant is extraordinarily difficult.

Cyberspace includes additional important characteristics that are more common to existing proxies:

- It is relatively borderless.
- It is global in scope. Some countries have dominant shares and positions, but the cyber-realm is open to all countries.
- Both public and private activity abound.

Two past examples seem most pertinent: maritime commerce and the use of outer space. Both seem to align with material aspects of the cyber-realm. We may be able to learn from these two historic developments how to create a thought framework about cyberspace and other emerging technologies.[147]

Both maritime commerce and outer space have fundamental characteristics whose regulatory development aligns well with the prospects for cyberspace. Both maritime and space activities occur in open territory that touches on multiple shores and is relatively seamless. In both maritime and space activity, both the public and private sectors

---

147 We also considered the American so-called Wild West, given how often that metaphor is used in describing cyberspace. There are some similarities—frontiers by definition are least established or stable— but we saw more limitations in using the Wild West as a reference point.

are significantly involved. The creation of customary rules from similar pragmatic processes has inevitably proved helpful to both commerce and safety in maritime and outer space activity. These rules have evolved through a fairly standard formula that created the regulatory foundation in each case, and we hope to apply this formula to developing a framework for cyber regulations. Thus, critically, they all seem to originate from customary practice.

There are certainly differences between maritime or outer space commerce and that of the cyber-realm, but enough points of common reference in their historical development provide a good starting ground for considering new technology guidelines, in cyberspace and perhaps in other new technologies.

Maritime Commerce

The rules for maritime commerce are the oldest uniform set of commercial and public global guidelines.[148]

Maritime transactions are usually international, or at least often involve individuals from different jurisdictions. The complex and challenging international aspect of maritime commerce involves both national laws and international rules of engagement. Courts of one country will often look to the precedents or statutes of another country for inspiration or guidance.

The Romans are the first to have provided robust documented maritime regulations (in the third century BC). But their rules refer to far earlier rules of the sea from the island of Rhodes (Rhodian laws and rules of roughly 900 BC), which were recognized in the Mediterranean world as a method of providing predictable treatment of merchants and their vessels. The complexity and attention to detail found in the Rhodian Sea Laws demonstrated the sophistication of commerce and trade of ancient Greece. Rhodes was the center of this world of commerce and so could dictate (and enforce) terms for trade. This ability to enforce rules is a recurring critical variable.

Although Rhodes declined and Rome replaced it, Rhodian law was recognized as essential to peaceful and profitable trade for more than 1,000 years. The Digest of Justinian, dated AD 533, references Rhodes:

148 We use "maritime" and "admiralty" laws synonymously. Also, for practical purposes, we include the so-called Law of the Sea, although the former and the latter cover different areas of the law. Legal scholars might find this terminology to be loose, i.e., that those distinctions are not material for the points being raised in this discussion.

"This matter must be decided by the maritime law of the Rhodians, provided that no law of ours is opposed to it."[149]

Thus, step one of the framework of maritime commerce was attracting sufficient activity to require rules regarding efficiency and dependability, which in turn entailed the development of "customary" practices or guidelines.

It was efficient for the various stakeholders, Rhodes's trading partners, to adapt and adopt their own rules to Rhodes's, because uniformity was in the best interests of all involved. Over many years, as the nature of maritime commerce expanded, permutations of the rules developed (a modern example of this phenomenon would be containerization). There were historic periods when certain nation-states created separate or differing rules. However, on the basis of necessity, the rules have tended to revert to the prior customary practice, because more standard uniform practices were preferable to all.

Roman law, evolved from the Rhodian law, formed the basis for the three core codes that have applied from the early Middle Ages, and on which much of today's maritime practice is based:

- *Consolate del Mare* (Regulation of the Sea), developed in the Mediterranean region;
- Laws of Oleron, developed in France and England; and
- Laws of Wisby, developed for the cities of the Baltic.

In this evolution over the centuries, countries and cities, even sometimes companies with the necessary expertise, formed the basis of maritime laws: for example, the Laws of Oleron (800 years ago a major commercial maritime center in France—but small today). Just as Bermuda and London became leaders in insurance, so cities and countries with particular expertise have tended to make lasting contributions to various legal and regulatory fields.

It is hard to overemphasize how important the breadth of the Roman Empire was to establishing standard principles. It established the concept that a wider-reaching law could take precedence over local laws. This was followed in Europe by Canon Law, which also superseded local laws. The driving fact was that in both these cases there was the ability

149 Quoted verbatim from the emperor Antoninus Pius (reigned AD 138-161) in a case of plunder following a shipwreck (reference Nicholas Joseph Healy, "Maritime Law: Historical Development," https://www.britannica.com/topic/maritime-law).

to enforce these over-arching laws. Furthermore, worldwide consistency was advantageous to all parties in international maritime commerce.

The challenge in such instances is a successful balance between nation-state interests and the utility of global policies. Some countries often want to participate in the development of global guidelines to pursue their own vested interests, without necessarily having the requisite technical expertise. Here consistency between the lobbyist and hobbyist interests with the subject matter experts is important. This issue is not new. There were global attempts at creating single maritime conventions in the past: the League of Nations; the 1958 Conventions on the Law of the Sea (four of them); and the 1982 Convention exemplify situations where complicated vested interests raised considerable controversy. One example, seabed mining—only a few countries have the capacity to do this, but every nation wants to expand its resources—is a clear example of this conflict of interests between capacity and self-interest. The United States found the multiplicity of conflicts among players (and an unacceptable approach to technology transfer) as grounds not to support the 1982 Convention.

Even maritime laws change as circumstances dictate. Certain historic maritime hazards are the same over the millennia, but other aspects of the business do change, and laws need to follow. For example, naval architecture and cargo handling have changed in significant ways. Crude-oil carriers as well as carriers of liquefied natural gas pose new hazards, raising questions of liability for oil pollution and damage to the marine and shoreline ecology. Modern maritime law thus consists of a combination of legacy laws and new laws.

Except to the extent that it may be obligated by international conventions, each country has the right to adopt maritime laws as it sees fit.

The current process for creating new maritime regulations may serve as a reference point. In maritime law, the International Maritime Committee (*Comité Maritime International*—CMI), composed of the maritime law associations of more than 30 nations, is often the source of new rules. The Comité principally drafts international conventions. Drafts are submitted to the Belgian government, which then convenes a diplomatic conference. If the revised draft is approved, it is then submitted to the national governments for official ratification. Many of these conventions have not been approved, while others have become established practice and have been highly successful.

Because the cyber-realm extends far beyond national boundaries, there may be a role for the model of maritime law in the evolution of regulation of cyberspace.

Outer Space

Outer space shares many similarities with cyberspace, as well as some clear differences. Space exploration has only 60 years of history, not the 3,000 years of maritime law. There is also only a fraction of the number of active participants in the use of outer space (at this stage) relative to those involved with the cyber-realm or even maritime shipping. Moreover, the private sector is only recently becoming an important player in space activity. Though both maritime and cyberspace operations entail significant commercial activity, space activity has been principally driven by national security concerns. But the fundamental foundation and framework for the development of outer-space-related regulations seem to parallel closely those for maritime commerce, and therefore the latter may be useful building blocks for cyberspace and other new technologies.

The inflection point for the need for space laws and regulations was reached with Sputnik in 1957. In fact, the initial and formal US response was indifference and to champion the concept of "freedom of space." But there was such a strong American popular interest in the launch that US politicians became engaged. Before Sputnik, all thinking was theoretical, and there was no pressure to formalize rules. Because the initial scale, scope, and cost of space was only feasible for nation-states, the default approach was to negotiate treaties between or among countries. After Sputnik, however, there was more of a sense that rules of the road for space were necessary.

A sufficient number of important players must agree if there is to be further support. Furthermore, any "best practices" must minimize the degree to which any individual player's self-interest trumps greater stakeholder benefits.

In both maritime commerce and outer space, laws came about to make activity more dependable and efficient, so that participants could reasonably anticipate the outcomes of various eventualities; and to ensure the safety of people and property. As previously noted, space law and regulatory oversight are very young phenomena compared to the 3,000-year history of maritime laws. However, the fundamental groundings of why and how laws and regulations sprang up and developed seem to follow a pattern very similar to that of the development of maritime laws. Where in maritime commerce the successful seafaring Rhodians, followed by the large and more homogenous Roman Empire, created the rules of the road, in space the United States and Russia (albeit with some input from other countries) have assumed this role.

At one stage there was an EU Code of Conduct, followed by the International Code of Conduct, but a lack of buy-in by other countries and an inability to enforce these rules have rendered them moot. The US direction is to favor "custom" as the driver for "rules" for space. As occurred in maritime law, accepting a set of rules promulgated external to the country creates concerns about sovereignty and protecting rights.

Geopolitical adversaries of this country may treat international guidelines as legally binding commitments and use them against our nation, while they ignore these agreements whenever it is more convenient. Monitoring and enforcing compliance guidelines are always the challenge. As the United States moves to establish custom and rules, does it want to do so through bilateral engagements, or rather defer to multilateral initiatives?

This dilemma strongly resembles the current controversies over standards of conduct in the cyber-realm.

Regulating a New Activity: Behind the Need for Cyber-Realm "Rules of the Road"

Today the cyber-realm is critical, and in many ways unique. Cyber communication has become embedded in the US economy, and in the economies of all our major trading partners. Contemporary commerce without a well-functioning Internet is virtually unimaginable. In terms of our historical overview, cyberspace has reached the stage where "rules of the road" are manifestly needed.

The cyber-realm began with the World Wide Web, which was created with an expectation and a vision of limited use. The "pipes" or "protocols" were designed to function in a closed environment. However, the inherent capacities of cyberspace allow for scale and scope with unprecedented reach; companies and entire industries have grown to globe-spanning size in a fraction of the time of any preceding entity (Amazon and Ant are easily identified examples). Available tools allow for not just minimal development costs, but also for far less technical knowledge than any previous activity. Stunningly, cyberspace is seen by many as a classic example and a complete fulfillment of Jonathan Haskell and Stian Westlake's vision in *Capitalism without Capital.*[150]

At the core of the cyber-realm is a remote addressing system. Just as a phone has a unique instrument and location associated with it, so cyberspace (the Internet and the World Wide Web) has unique identifiers called Internet Protocols (IPs). To communicate with each other, each PC (and PC network) must have its own individual address. These addresses are controlled and distributed by the *Internet Corporation of Assigned Names and Numbers* (ICANN). Every cyber device we use has such a unique IP address so that it can correspond with other members of the cyber-realm. Thus, cyberspace was capable of engaging virtually everyone's attention. And it is well on its way to doing so.

Cyber commerce, besides touching on so many aspects of daily personal and commercial activity, has the unique ability because of its scalability to create nearly instant de facto monopolies. Cyber commerce can also change industries almost overnight.

Cyber commerce is the proverbial iceberg with dramatically more activity below the surface of our lives, than visibly above it. Using financial services as an anecdotal reference point, much of the cyber activity is focused on flows of money: payments, lending, and blockchain (distributed ledger) recordkeeping, but there is also massive activity in less-visible middle- and back-office cyber technology.

The cyber-realm, with its digital technologies and Web-based activity, has already become ubiquitous, with every indication that it does or will shortly touch virtually every aspect of our daily lives. And there is even more growth ahead. AI abilities today are in comparative infancy. AI is evolving rapidly to ever greater capability that will lead to broader use. Cyberspace already influences us from communications, to our health care (including data mining), to our financial activity, to our very safety (from traffic lights to air-traffic control). It is commercial and it is public. Cyber activity ranges from relatively benign tracking of our Internet search activity to overt invasion of our lives and homes[151]—convincing many people that the intrusion of this new technology in our lives needs more formal "rules of engagement" (regulations).

150 Westlake and Haskell, *Capitalism without Capital: The Rise of the Intangible Economy* (Princeton, NJ: Princeton University Press, 2017).

151 An intercepted shipment of household goods from overseas showed that toasters, hair dryers, and coffee makers had embedded undisclosed radio frequency identification (RFID) chips.

In the absence of proactive implementation of regulation, cyberspace actors have expanded the scale of potentially troublesome activity to certainly impactful levels. For example, Initial Coin Offerings (ICOs) by the middle of 2018 had taken in billions of dollars from the general public. Regulatory "silence," in the absence of formal action, has created for some a tacit, implied approval, leading some of these investors to assume that these products have received some form of oversight. As losses on these investments mount, investors will question how this scale of inherently risky activity could be allowed without oversight.

As a further example, cyber data-gathering is contributing to a new frontier of medical advancement, leveraging AI to enable cutting-edge advancements. However, regulations lag behind technology. Unexpected and unintended consequences may arise from areas such as genome modification. Is this another instance of implied approval due to the absence of laws and regulatory oversight?

These elements of cyber commerce seem sufficient even now, so shortly after its creation, to warrant formal rules and regulations—like maritime and potential outer-space commerce before it. Commercial activity in cyberspace is more than material to our society's well-being, but some of that activity has led to harm, with the potential for more. The need for accepted "rules of the road," if not formal regulation, is clear. In fact, cyberspace's reach today is so broad that it exceeds recognized political boundaries, a potentially major challenge.

With the need for cyber "rules of the road" so clear and undeniable, what would be the best path for maximizing the benefit from cyber commerce, while minimizing the cost?

REGULATING CYBERSPACE: ADAPTATION OR INNOVATION?

The volume and growth of cyber activity in recent years might suggest that there is a sufficient volume of established customary practice to provide guidelines for comprehensive cyber regulations. But in dealing with any new activity or technology, an element of caution is necessary. These new activities may be exciting and powerful, but significant lessons are learned only through time and experience. For historical example, both X-rays (along with the uranium that enables them) and credit derivatives are powerful tools that have changed our lives for the better, but still proved deadly to their early practitioners.

Establishing customary behavior and therefore regulations requires thoughtful prudential implementation to reduce the incidence of such unexpected consequences. And for just one contemporary example, we don't yet know how big-data analytics (based on facial or retina or voice or fingerprint recognition, among other things) will affect our daily lives.

One question to ask in this instance and in others is: Why can't we just apply existing laws and regulations? Or to what partial extent might existing rules be usable?

Cyberspace presents three unusual, or even unique, challenges for oversight, which are likely to render existing regulatory regimes ineffective or irrelevant:

- *Attribution*
- *Mitigation*
- *Retribution*

Attribution. Unlike maritime and space commerce, attribution of cyberspace activities is exceptionally difficult. Sophisticated players (nation-states, global criminals, cyber vigilantes, and others) exerting robust efforts can make it exceptionally difficult for any authorities to have 100 percent surety of who is behind any activity.

Mitigation. Cyber threats and challenges come in many forms: One expert breaks them down into "vandals, burglars, thugs, spies, and saboteurs."[152] Cyber players can steal money, sensitive information such as on finance or health, or identities, or proprietary business information; monitor competitors and enemies remotely; damage reputations; manipulate or damage systems and machinery; or surreptitiously spread false disruptive information to the markets and the population ("fake news"). What is the remedy to such violations? Achieving effective mitigation will be a huge new challenge.

Retribution. In 1986, reportedly after watching the movie *War Games,* President Ronald Reagan pushed Congress to enact the Computer Fraud and Abuse Act, which is deemed to make hacking (entering a third

152 Christian Caryl, in "The United States: A Rich Cyber Target for Hackers That Fails to Protect Itself," *Washington Post,* August 2, 2018, presents this quotation without attribution (it may be from "Andy Ozment on Information Sharing and Cybersecurity, *Wall Street Journal,* February 10, 2016, accessible at https://www.wsj.com/articles/andy-ozment-on-information-sharing-and-cybersecurity-1455082611).

party's computer system) illegal.[153] This law has created behavioral gray areas. There is an understandable reluctance to allow cyber vigilantes to roam the cyber-realm, enforcing justice as they see it. But modern maritime piracy was sometimes allegedly reduced when civilian maritime ships began to arm themselves and "fire back." This reaction is not unanimously viewed as effective, legal, or moral. (How should the death of one of the pirates be viewed?) But attribution on the high seas is clear, and retribution is specifically targeted. As noted earlier, in the cyber-realm, accurate attribution and retribution is at best very difficult and uncertain, and at worst impossible (at 100 percent certainty). A variation on this question remains on the table: Should companies be allowed to even retrieve stolen documents, stolen research, and stolen information from the culprits? Most knowledgeable readers of the existing US Computer Fraud and Abuse Act would say that this could lead to a long jail sentence. Effective enforcement by appropriate and empowered authorities remains a prerequisite of successful regulation.

Yes, cyberspace is significantly different from other regulatory environments, but do these differences require a different mindset? Individuals and companies seem limited to playing defense versus offense both from a technical and a legal perspective, at least so far. But can that change? Perhaps the question should be raised differently: Is cyberspace sufficiently different that the regulatory approach must also be different, perhaps *sui generis*?

Two derivative questions must be addressed: i) Who is impacted? Who are the stakeholders? and ii) What is the degree of impact on these stakeholders—from benign or mere nuisance, to draconian or catastrophic or existential?

The answer to both questions in terms of degree of impact is the classic "It depends."

Cyber technology echoes maritime and outer-space innovations in the global (or beyond) reach of the technology. But where the cyber-realm clearly differs from either maritime or space commerce is in the scale and scope of the stakeholders. While there are large nation-state participants and large industrial players in all three activities, the individual participants in cyberspace are legion in number, extending beyond all borders.

---

153 Fred Kaplan, *Dark Territory: The Secret History of Cyber War* (New York: Simon & Schuster, 2016).

Cyberspace sets itself apart from other new activities and technologies also by the minimal cost to enter for either an individual or a nation-state; and the minimal end-to-end technical skills required.

What in 1980 cyberspace was massively expensive and in 2000 was relatively expensive is nearly 20 years later indubitably cheap, financially accessible to almost anyone. What took months or years and millions of dollars can now be done in hours or days, with a few thousand dollars. The accessibility of the components of a cyber enterprise, from the equipment to the APIs,[154] means that global participants in cyberspace literally can come from any of the nearly 200 countries around the world.

The ubiquity of the cyber-realm means that almost everyone is a stakeholder; and stakeholder protection in virtually all regulation means reduced efficacy, value, and efficiency in the delivery of goods and services—without disputes over the net value of fully justified regulation. Regulations may protect certain stakeholders, which may be necessary and worthwhile, but severely disfavor others. To illustrate with the illogical extreme, protecting pedestrians by limiting cars to a driving speed of five miles per hour, or making all scissors kindergarten-safe, reduces risks; but it also results in a much less useful product for a broad range of society.

Thus, the cyber-realm is massively different from even its most similar historical innovation forebears. There is no doubt that many of its challenges to regulators will be unique and will require new thinking. But realistically, exploiting any opportunities to use existing regulatory rules and tools will make the task easier. Writing new, untested legal language is always risky. And totally new institutions always have a lot to learn, and experience can be a hard teacher.

We reflect now on some of the boxes that successful cyber-realm regulation will need to check, and what will be entailed in doing so.

GUIDELINES FOR REGULATING INNOVATION: CYBERSPACE AS A CASE IN POINT

From our two proxy activities, maritime and space, flows an elegant framework for emergent technologies and their best-practice "regulatory

---

154 An application programming interface (API) is a documented set or library of "packaged" programs for building computer software programs. APIs help with communication between various system components. A programmer uses various APIs as his building blocks to create computer programs.

rules of the road." Some of these items reflect the unique facets of the cyber-realm phenomenon. Others follow longer-term regulatory practice, but still show, to a lesser or greater degree, the uniqueness for cyberspace. All taken together, we believe, constitute an accurate and useful roadmap to successful cyber-realm regulation—understanding that even this now seemingly familiar territory has not yet been fully explored.

1. *Who should be the Regulator?*

   On the basis of the experience of maritime law and outer space, the United States should establish a single national-level cyber regulator.

   Some might argue that there should be a shared regulatory responsibility with separate regulators for each of the multiple cyberspace platforms. We believe that the potential benefits of specialization would be limited, because the various platforms are much more alike than different. A single regulator would be preferable because the more consistent the rule making, the better—which generally means having fewer rule makers and therefore less fragmentation.

   That regulator should be located at the national level because, given the unique challenges around cyber retribution, the regulator will need to be particularly well equipped to handle not only private-sector participants, civil offenders, and criminals, but also nation-state and other public actors.[155] In many countries, it is virtually impossible to distinguish cyber activity undertaken by the private sector from that undertaken by the public sector. For that reason, cyber regulation needs to be a matter of nation-state policy, rather than a commercial or social activity. Across national borders, cooperation is critical; and relevant laws and the regulations must align with this reality. And if cyber regulation is to pass a cost-benefit test—to do more material good than harm and to provide value for the stakeholders—there must be consistency across national boundaries, and the ability to enforce the guidelines.

   Furthermore, the regulator must have the skills and resources to enforce the regulations. From a practical perspective, laws and regulations that are consistent and enforceable must be made at

155 Recent US security agency findings that foreign powers have used cyberspace to attempt to discredit our system of government are pointed examples. Office of the Director of National Intelligence, *Assessing Russian Activities and Intentions in Recent US Elections*, January 6, 2017 (https://www.dni.gov/files/documents/ICA_2017_01.pdf).

the national level. Cyberspace is virtually limitless, and inconsistency and fragmentation from a multiplicity of conflicting regulations and overseers in all the subnational jurisdictions will create uncertainty and inefficiency, and be difficult to enforce. The United States would be best served by only one national policy administered by only one specific arm of government, not by local or state laws. Fragmentation of oversight and accountability will weaken effectiveness.

In response to the vacuum of leadership on the federal level, individual states have begun to develop their own approaches. These include incubators and sandboxes (not unique ideas; in Switzerland in 2017, the Canton of Zug independently set a cantonal priority to encourage commercial cyber development with "safe harbor" provisions). Some may find it admirable that states, such as Arizona in 2018, have stepped up to take responsibility and have tried to innovate. But this does not change our conviction that the best results would come with a single federal regulator.

Given the border-eradicating effect of the cyber-realm, some might think that a national regulator would not go far enough, and that international agreements and treaties would be the ideal. The precedents of maritime and outer-space regulation would seem to endorse that view. Maritime and space regulation have some protocols that have been followed (like the role of the CMI), but several major initiatives have failed to achieve international agreement (as discussed above). Expectations for the effectiveness of an international regime therefore should be tempered. Furthermore, cyberspace entails massive challenges of enforcement, exceeding maritime and space rules, and effective enforcement is an absolute prerequisite for regulatory success. Some nation-state actors might well conspicuously pursue their own interests over the collective interests of all stakeholders, flouting global rules. International regulation might be hoped or planned for, but it cannot be relied on in the foreseeable future.

However, we still can learn some lessons from current institutions. As one example, as with maritime law, cyber actors will follow the law of the country where they are domiciled. Thus, American actors, regardless of where they are or whom they touch, would be expected to use an American court, and not the courts of other jurisdictions in which they operate.

2. *Screens: What cyber activities should be regulated? What should be the depth and scope of regulation?*

   Historically, the catalyst for creating rules of the road has been material activity that draws public attention—usually local rather than global. The initial framework for regulation was based on customary behavior that could be identified and communicated. The process began spontaneously but then was codified.

   As we suggested above, there could be regulatory failings in cyberspace whose consequence would be no worse than inconvenience. Such instances would not surpass a reasonable materiality threshold in terms of the seriousness, nature, size, scale, or scope of the impact. Government should hold back from regulation where there is no strong argument for it, because regulation tends to affect economic growth. Rather, formal regulatory activity normally would require some degree of impact on public activity or safety, or some invasion of personal data or identity damage.

   As a first step in the process of regulation, one way to set a standard would be to restrict regulation to situations where a public authority already requires some form of license. If you need a license, then you need to meet minimum cyber standards. This approach is not perfect, because it probably misses some activity that should be captured, and may include activity to which cyber risk is irrelevant. Over time, it may become possible to address both of these issues, but the licensing standard might be a reasonable starting point.

3. *Responsibilities or regulations*?

   Can we live with voluntary market practice, or must regulatory standards be mandatory?

   Good cyber hygiene is the number one protection against cyber risks. Cyber hygiene involves such basics as limiting and sunsetting access; proper disposal of nonpublic information on a timely basis; vigorous vetting and auditing of third-party providers of services and equipment; and draconian limitation on the use of externally sourced equipment such as "thumb drives" and personal smart devices. However, it is not clear that all (or any) of these "best practices" should be mandated by regulation.

   More generally, for market actors to choose to adhere to voluntary standards, the informal practice or "rule of the road" must be mutually beneficial and provide real value, and the various parties must be able to enforce customary practice. A strong market actor might maintain certain rules in its favor, but only so long as it could enforce them through fiscal or physical means. If standards are needed for societal reasons but do not reach that level of self-interest, then formal regulation will be necessary.

4. *What are the core cyber rules?*

Cyberspace's power and reach require regulations to go beyond the obvious "thou shalt not steal or damage." Because of the challenges of attribution, mitigation, and retribution, the laws and regulations must focus on the key areas of vulnerability; there is too much more ground to cover every issue. Protecting public safety, privacy, and digital information should be at the top of the list. These would be followed by risks of manipulation and violation of others' rights.

Rules of the road would need to address cyber specifics such as storage of Internet service provider (ISP) addresses; tracking and targeting; data-scrapping rules; and data storage. Basically, any actor who obtains data in any form becomes fully accountable for its safe, respectful handling.

None of this is easy. For example, full transparency disclosure must occur up front, when content is "sponsored" or usage is being tracked for data mining. Standards must include obtaining and retaining data, and agreeing on what level of consent (active vs. passive) is required to scrape and save data. In general, is it acceptable to assume that if one clicks on or uses a site, such information can be used—either in a generic fashion to evaluate trends, or in a specific manner to push activity deemed relevant back to the user or the IP address? What permission is sufficient to go forward? Is silence permission? Or must there be an explicit approval? Regulations are likely to require periodic secure disposal of any nonpublic information that is no longer necessary for legitimate business operations.

A critically significant cyber risk comes from the increasing use of third-party vendors. While both the public and private sectors struggle to control and oversee their own cyber activity, they introduce new cyber risk through their increasing reliance on third-party suppliers and vendors. These third-party players may themselves rely on multiple levels of providers of parts or services, almost a proverbial "Russian nesting doll" of cyber risk. As difficult as it is to manage cyber risk fully contained within an organization, the complexity and challenge is far greater with multiple third-party suppliers.

Regulations may need to prohibit or limit the use of third-party suppliers and vendors for certain goods and services. Is this practical and enforceable? How do you stop thumb drives? To save cost, many firms mandate that their staff use their own electronic devices ("use your own cell phones") to conduct company business. If a market participant is significant in size or potentially critical to security, should the regulators require that everything from services to equipment either be in-house or sourced only from approved vendors?

Already, managements and boards are liable for key regulated activity. Cyber-focused regulations likely will extend these areas of accountability to cyber risks that range from poor internal cyber hygiene to imprudent vendor practices; or buying equipment or services from a contractor that introduces cyber malware into the environment. Materiality will be an important screen in this regard. For example, if a restaurant closes, the impact is dramatically different than if a dam collapses; if a hospital fails due to its records being stolen, its equipment rendered useless, and patients' medical records made public; or if an airplane falls from the sky. New York State has gone so far as to list its views of what a cyber framework should include on the basis of a risk assessment.[156]

---

156 Following is New York State's proposed checklist of necessary topics to be covered by any organization's cyber framework, based on a risk assessment:

a) information security;
b) data governance and classification;
c) asset inventory and device management;
d) access controls and identity management;
e) business continuity and disaster recovery planning and resources;
f) systems operations and availability concerns;
g) systems and network security;
h) systems and network monitoring;
i) systems and application development and quality assurance;
j) physical security and environmental controls;
k) customer data privacy;
l) vendor and third-party service provider management;
m) risk assessment; and
n) incident response.

New York State also specifies data retention (and disposal).

The less mature an activity, the greater the likelihood that a principles-based approach will be preferable to a more rigidly defined rules-based approach. The speed of change in the cyber-realm calls for principles-based regulation. Detailed rules-based regulation would be too rigid to accommodate the rapid pace of change. Rules would be literally outdated and outmoded before they were published, or they would have to be so rushed and vague as to provide minimal direction to regulators.

As discussed in the context of maritime and space activity, this cyber regulator will need to create a balance of principles and rules based on a combination of US and international laws, flowing from customary practice. A dedicated cyber court might or might not be set up to handle the complexities of cyber activity.

Cyber-realm regulation will need to promote immediate escalation and sharing of troublesome issues to both government authorities and peers. Timely response will be critical. Cyber rules need to make shared communications across industry participants mandatory. Sharing insights and intelligence—cooperation as a default behavior—will be a bulwark against intruders and attackers.

5. *Mitigation regulation requirements*:

   As discussed above in the section on "responsible" behavior, it is good cyber practice to have at a minimum in documented form: a cybersecurity plan; cyber contingency steps; and cyber reporting protocols, to include mandated cyber "event" escalation to management, the board, public authorities, and perhaps peer organizations.

   These recommendations present an opportunity to leverage customary practices. Cyber insurance exists, providing a template for expected cyber oversight. Regulations could use cyber insurance as a guideline. Historical examples of this approach abound. Possible models include the insurance industry's campaign for mandating automatic safety restraint systems (seatbelts).[157]

   How will the enterprise protect itself, through a contingency plan, to remain viable either in terms of ongoing operations or financial solvency? (Possible methods include insurance or reserves, but other tools are possible.) To increase the likelihood of business continuity,

157 *Motor Vehicle Manufacturers Association of the United States, Inc. v. State Farm Mutual Automobile Insurance Company*.

relevant stress tests, back-up plans, and perhaps even living wills could be required (hopefully avoiding the mistake that banking regulators made in ranking volume over quality; less is more).

6. *Require that all stakeholders have a voice, and include subject-matter experts in the regulatory conversation.*

   Creating something simple and understandable in an environment in which the topic is growing, and where the number of subject matter experts may be limited, will be difficult. As we discussed in Chapter 5, cyberspace itself should facilitate the longstanding requirement for public comment in the development of regulations; but this potential has not been exploited. In the cyber-realm, as much as or more than in any other field, regulators will desperately need the input of stakeholders and subject-matter experts. It behooves cyber regulators to recognize both that need and the potential of the people they are regulating to fulfill it.

7. *Keep rules and regulations to a minimum.*

   In regulation, as in many other human endeavors, there is an unfortunate tendency to measure output by the pound. We have in financial regulation a costly manifestation of that tendency. It should not be repeated in cyberspace. Cyber regulators must make their work comprehensible if compliance is to be possible, and communicate clearly what the regulations are. And to be comprehensible, those regulations must be within the grasp of one cyber actor, or at most a very small team of them. Brevity is valuable; length and volume are an evil and will make the regulations at best ineffective and at worst destructive. Market actors will need forward guidance from regulators, likely in the forms of frequently asked questions (FAQs), templates, and the like.

   As part of the creation of laws and regulations, there should be a specific targeted search for existing laws or regulations that may cover some or all of the cyber issues being addressed, given that cyber activity may often touch on other commerce. The existing law or regulation should be used to the extent possible; as seldom as possible should a new law or regulation be created. The reason is simply that legal language that has not yet been tested in court always carries the risk of some unwelcome surprise should it be challenged. In the event of overlap (or even worse, inconsistency and conflict) between the regulations, the existing regulation should simply be referenced and used for cyber oversight.

Clearly, the use of existing regulations for cyberspace, on the one hand, and clarity and brevity, on the other, might well be in conflict. Considerable effort will be necessary to get cyber regulation right; and the reach and impact of the cyber-realm make that effort a high priority.

8. *Provide sufficient funding and other resources for execution and enforcement of the regulations.*

   Given the easy access to and the rewards of cyber technology today, cyber commerce is a nation-state priority for several countries, on the scale of their national defense and infrastructure. This is far beyond the priority assigned in the United States, despite the importance of cyber communications to legions of US businesses.

   Instead, the US approach to the cyber-realm has in the view of many lagged behind that of other countries. The United States has fallen behind or been seriously challenged not only by the obvious large countries such as China[158] and Russia[159], but also even smaller countries such as North Korea[160] and Israel.[161] Even small Estonia has a national policy based on leveraged cyber activity to drive its economy.[162] While the United States has claimed to focus on cyberspace, some have likened the difference between our nation's efforts and others' to that between a college athletic program and a professional sports team. (Less charitable comparisons liken the difference in resources to that between a high school football program and an NFL football team.)

   Presidents Bush and Obama both tried to move legislation. When the US Senate failed to pass the Cybersecurity Act of 2012 that

158 Zi Yang, "China Is Massively Expanding Its Cyber Capabilities," *Asia Times*, October 2, 2017.

159 David Bond, "More Countries Are Learning from Russia's Cyber Tactics," *Financial Times*, March 15, 2018.

160 Emma Chanlett-Avery, Liana W. Rosen, John W. Rollins, and Catherine A. Theohary, "North Korean Cyber Capabilities: In Brief," Congressional Research Service, August 3, 2017 https://fas.org/sgp/crs/row/R44912.pdf.

161 Christopher P. Skroupa, "Cyber Warfare—Reasons Why Israel Leads the Charge," *Forbes*, September 7, 2017.

162 Damien McGuinness, "How a Cyber Attack Transformed Estonia," BBC, April 7, 2017.

> August, Presidential Policy Directive 20 was signed in secret. Directive 20 supported government-driven cyber activity of both a defensive and an offensive nature.[163] The Snowden disclosures,[164] which shook the national security world, and inaction by Congress, drove the Obama Administration to publish a brief set of cyber principles.[165]

Cybersecurity and regulation efforts will not pay for themselves. It will be necessary to reconcile cyber needs with overall fiscal responsibility. When our nation's elected policymakers sit down to create a comprehensive budget reform plan—which they should, and soon—cyber funding should be a part of the mix. When weighed against other priorities, even in our current dire fiscal situation, we believe, cybersecurity as an issue will stand up well.

---

163 The Administration released the following "FACT SHEET ON PRESIDENTIAL POLICY DIRECTIVE 20":

- The President recently signed a classified Presidential directive relating to cyber operations.
- Because the policy is classified, we cannot discuss all of the elements contained in it.
- This policy is part of the Administration's focus on cybersecurity as a top priority.
- The policy takes into account the evolution of the threat and our growing experience.
- The policy establishes principles and processes for the use of cyber operations so that cyber tools are integrated with the full array of national security tools we have at our disposal.
- The policy provides a whole-of-government approach consistent with the values that we promote domestically and internationally as we have previously articulated in the International Strategy for Cyberspace.
- The goal of these principles and processes is to enable more effective planning, development, and use of our capabilities.
- The policy enables us to be flexible, while also exercising restraint in dealing with the threats we face.
- It is our policy that we shall undertake the least action necessary to mitigate threats and that we will prioritize network defense and law enforcement as preferred courses of action.
- All processes outlined in this policy will be conducted in a manner consistent with the US Constitution and other applicable law and policies.

164 Lawfare Institute, "Snowden Revelations," Lawfareblog.com.

165 Commission on Enhancing National Cybersecurity, *Report on Securing and Growing the Digital Economy*, December 1, 2016, https://fas.org/irp/offdocs/ppd/ppd-20.pdf.

9. *Require both up-front impact analysis and formal periodic impact review to ensure that the regulations deliver what is expected.*

   The scale, scope, and effectiveness of the regulations must be reviewed on a frequent basis (at least every 12 months). There should be a formal discussion among all relevant actors in that process as to whether cyber-realm activities should be dropped from regulation or added.

   In addition to new laws and regulations to address cyber activity, the nation needs a dispassionate review of several existing laws that may now be anachronisms, such as the Computer Fraud and Abuse Act. The Department of Commerce has tried to establish minimum workable standards for customary behavior and guidelines, if not more formal regulations. But the department has experienced limited success.

   Some would argue for a "sunset" date with automatic expiry, therefore requiring a proactive event to renew a cyber regulation. We are sympathetic with the ultimate goal. But we believe that sound periodic review would trump automatic sunsets. Given necessary process for either regulations or underlying legislation, the busywork required to continue sound practice could entail a significant cost and harmful delay. Even worse, in the realm of legislation, "must-pass" bills to avoid automatic sunsets, even if the underlying law is supported by consensus, can create the occasion for unrelated demands or "riders," causing enormous mischief. However, failing necessary affirmative review, a sunset requirement would be necessary.

10. *Ensure a practical, affordable and pragmatic means of overseeing and enforcing the regulations.*

    As we have noted repeatedly, effective oversight is the *sine qua non* of successful regulation. At the same time, successful regulation will balance oversight with economic advancement and growth—not stifling growth and development, but not allowing the unfettered unleashing of a toxic Pandora's box. Sound regulation will not stop every unfortunate development, but it will do more good than harm.

SUMMARY AND CONCLUSIONS

History teaches us that new technologies can build to the level of public interest and impact such that compliance with evolving behavioral standards—customary "rules of the road"—becomes important. However, conflicts among the interests of different market actors might inhibit compliance. Recent developments indicate that cyberspace has clearly reached the inflection point where standards are essential, and also that some private entities and even nation-states will not follow voluntary standards. Some measure of regulation is needed, but challenges of attaining accurate attribution and appropriate retribution will be extreme and even unique.

The experience of the development of maritime and outer-space commerce, as well as of regulatory first principles, provides guidelines to produce an initial set of cyber regulations. The content of these recommendations suggests that the first regulations start with those activities that already require licensing by a public body. The items regulated must be conspicuously material. Some practices might be strongly recommended, but not necessarily a proper subject of regulation. The terms of cyber insurance, where available, might be important indicators of best practices for regulation. It is clear that significant additional investment in cybersecurity by both public offices and private concerns is needed. We believe that the need will justify that greater investment, even in the context of today's federal budgetary stringency.

APPENDIX: INCUBATORS—ACCELERATORS—SANDBOXES . . . *OH MY*!

New financial-technology (FinTech) enterprises provoke frequent debate over cyber regulation. Various entities, public and private, have created devices to develop new FinTechs[166] and bring them to market. Because similar pre-cyber financial service providers are commonly regulated, because they entail considerable financial risk, regulation of these FinTechs seems appropriate to many. However, the FinTechs

166 For purposes of this section, the single term **FinTechs** will encompass both the financial technology companies that provide revenue-generating products and operational support/services for financial institutions (**FinTechs**) and financial technology companies that provide tools to manage/support the audit/compliance/regulatory activities (**RegTechs**).

are different from conventional service providers, and because of the concern that conventional regulation might stifle new and potentially beneficial technologies, both regulators and market actors have sought alternative low-risk environments in which the FinTechs can be tested and grow. These same devices might apply to other cyber innovations as well. Three approaches to this objective are mentioned frequently:

- Incubators
- Accelerators
- Sandboxes

These terms have made their way into the tech vernacular and are used fairly casually and often without great discipline or definition. This short section is meant to provide high-level, generic descriptions of these three common terms.

As a brief preliminary taxonomy, incubators are used for FinTechs at the earliest stage of development. Accelerators are used for somewhat more mature entities, and sandboxes are used for FinTechs almost ready to enter full operation. We will discuss these three types of business-development devices in that order.

Incubators

Incubators support startups that are still in formation, may not necessarily require investment capital, and tend to be part of the local startup community already. They are startups that need basic initial help to convert a concept or idea into a workable business model (and thus are very much focused on commercialization, rather than basic R&D). That assistance may include identifying and building the necessary infrastructure, conducting market research, and providing other components required to get the firm or concept to market. Their timeline to commercialization may be long, or they are so early that some of the basics have not yet been addressed.

In their simplest form, incubators are funding vehicles that work with a startup that has just an innovative idea. However, some incubators may stay involved with the firm all the way to formal funding and product launch. Incubators can be either private- or public-sector activities.

Private-sector-driven incubators often prioritize investor financial returns, as venture capitalists would do.

Public-sector incubators can vary widely. They may be:

- economic development agencies;
- governmental or political entities, such as a country, state, province, or canton (real-world examples include Singapore and UK governmental entities; the state of Arizona in the United States; the province of Ottawa in Canada; and the canton of Zug in Switzerland);
- medical groups;
- governmental regulators; or
- universities, public or private (or they may take other forms).

Note that when governmental entities become involved in business nurturing under the guise of supporting public purposes, there is an immediate escalation of political concerns and challenges. Purposes of a public-domain incubator can vary from trying to create jobs for the local economy to building a trove of patents and other sustaining revenue flows for the community. Legacy private institutions or firms may fear (or at least claim) that the publicly supported incubator is taking sides among business entities to the disadvantage of the incumbents by financing the development of their competition with public taxpayer funds. Other critics might see this as the state deciding which technologies are nurtured with taxpayer dollars from effectively bottomless pockets, and which other enterprises are disadvantaged due to lack of funding.

Incubators operate on an open-ended timeline. They focus less on a startup's growth rate, and more on helping it become self-sufficient and sustainable. It is not uncommon for incubators to mentor startups for one to two years, sometimes even longer. This much longer, patient view of incubator candidates is an important distinction, because accelerators rarely will consider prospects that have years of development and investment ahead of them before they might become self-sustaining.

Incubator incumbents often arrive via referrals. Participants in an incubator usually will co-locate to the incubator's location. The founder(s) frequently will rent space at the incubator on a significantly subsidized basis. The shared location means that founder(s) often find themselves aligned for professional purposes with other startups in the incubator. Few if any of them will have similar initiatives underway. The co-location benefit of being with other startups is the shared learning experience of what it takes to move from the embryonic stage of just an idea to the birth of an operating company.

The focus of the incubator will be to move from an initial idea to a working business plan. This requires practical technical support from reliable market and legal information to creating the operational and management teams necessary to execute the business plan.

Startups going into an incubator have often not had their first formal funding round. Some have suggested that an incubator's goal can be summarized as getting a startup ready for its first investment stage, or to move on to an accelerator.

Accelerators

The techniques of accelerators and incubators in helping startups to grow their businesses are significantly similar. The lines between these two are not distinct.[167] Both programs provide guidance and counseling (including legal) to startups, and back-office support, and also will advance their business models and strategies. The main goal is to groom the startup to become valuable in the eyes of investors. Both accelerators and incubators help startups attain success by providing certain financial assistance and access to resources—some basic such as space and access to industry-subject-matter experts. Both can provide environments in which regulators might forbear enforcement, in the interests of giving the new business a chance to succeed. Still, for entrepreneurs, there are some very important differences.

Accelerators focus on scaling a business that is usually at least at the prototype stage, while incubators accept entrepreneurs still at the idea stage. Business founders apply to participate in accelerators. The better-known accelerators have an acceptance rate below that of Stanford or the Ivy League undergraduate schools. Being seen as an investible candidate is a critical acceptance criterion. Applicants also must be willing to relocate or co-locate proximate to the accelerator for the length of the commitment. Once acceptance is granted, there may be a modest investment from the accelerator (sometimes the first outside money for the startup), but the main value comes from the coaching that the mentors provide. An accelerator's advisers may take a small portion of equity (5 to 10 percent), but often the driver for the mentors is the "giving back."

---

167 With some apologies, we need to point out that there are other vehicles as well, such as so-called innovation labs. Innovation labs tend to be corporate and frequently internally focusing. Therefore, for our purposes here, we focus on accelerators and incubators as the dominant forms of help for startups.

Accelerators match up subject-matter experts with startups and provide them a discrete time to leverage these competencies (the timing is often in days, weeks, and sometimes months, but almost never years—much less than the gestation periods with incubators). Startups entering accelerators have often already achieved their first funding, and when exiting an accelerator are often poised to obtain their second round of funding.

Accelerators advance a startup's pace and build on the foundation it has already created. The main goal and contribution of an accelerator is to increase the pace of "proof of concept," helping a startup to cut the time to become sustainable from years down to months, by leveraging the lessons that small and medium-sized enterprises (SMEs) have already learned. Most startups could benefit from being in an incubator, because its benefits are basic. Fewer startups are sufficiently advanced for an accelerator.

Accelerators often align with industry/corporate partners; thus the entrepreneurs/startups that are selected usually will have an affinity with the partners and their objectives. Accelerators will often also provide a pitch platform for the startups as they are ready to leave. A good accelerator provides startups with the tools to attract investment capital.

Sandboxes

What is a **FinTech** Regulatory **Sandbox**? It is some grant of regulatory latitude that facilitates the development and testing of innovative financial technology ideas, processes, and products under the watchful eye of a regulator.

"Sandbox" is the generic term or concept for testing how a new idea, process, or product may work. A sandbox defines the testing environment and agreement among all parties. Sandboxes can range from the highly academic and theoretical, where no real-world exposure is allowed (we can think of this type of sandbox as being *a clean room laboratory sandbox*), all the way to what might be termed "safe harbor" sandboxes, where products and processes can be offered to the public under agreed-upon terms. The agreement with the FinTech describes specifically what is permissible in terms of many factors that might include number of clients; type of clients; duration of the test period; specific quantity or dollar-amount ceilings; and the like. In this type of regulatory sandbox, real clients and customers are exposed to the products and processes. The commitment from the regulators is a "safe harbor" promise that as long as the FinTech adheres to the agreed-upon parameters and criteria it will not be subjected to regulatory rebuke or charges.

There are many variations and permutations of sandboxes between these two extremes of purely academic versus real-world with a regulatory "safe harbor."

As always, there are trade-offs for all parties in terms of the amount of practical learning that comes from a particular sandbox arrangement versus the degrees of risk that the individual parties must accept and to which they will be exposed. The theoretical ("laboratory") sandbox, where a concept is tested in an enclosed environment without real-world participants, provides limited information and limited learning, but does not create a significant level of risk for the regulators (or the public). The safe-harbor sandbox obvious entails more risk.[168]

How much regulatory latitude companies are given in using the sandbox will depend on the risk appetite of the regulators, and the public-policy priorities that either support or restrict the regulators. The operative distinction here between a "beta" product testing and a sandbox is that the latter operates under regulatory scrutiny and within specific permissions and parameters.

Regulators who are encouraged to support innovation may therefore use a sandbox approach to facilitate the development of beneficial new products and processes. The sandbox helps startups to achieve their goal in a prudential manner with more benefits than harm. Besides providing a window of opportunity for these new products or processes to be tested, the regulatory sandbox approach often waives or lessens the licensing and other regulatory requirements that could both delay significantly new product launches and add massive upfront costs.

There are skeptics to the sandbox approach. These are often legacy institutions, who argue that in the spirit of level playing fields these startups even in the sandbox stage should have to shoulder the full regulatory burden that they carried when they themselves were founded.

The regulatory sandbox concept is a global phenomenon, with countries from Australia to Switzerland actively promoting sandboxes. The first sandbox attribution is often given to the UK for their 2015

---

168 Note that the term *sandbox* is sometimes applied to industry initiatives, but given that these are commercial and might be analogous to the proverbial industrial "skunk works," these industry sandboxes are not addressed here and have limited regulatory impact.

efforts. However, as noted, each regulatory sandbox operates under different strictures depending on local issues and interests.

Given the complexity and challenges of new technology, there has been an understandable reluctance to swiftly introduce sandboxes, with their consequent reduction of certain regulatory requirements. The result not just in the United States but around the world has been the risk of a fragmentation of policy (and of controls, and even the creation of regulatory arbitrage opportunities). In the United States, an example would be that certain states such as Arizona and Illinois in 2018 began promoting their own sandboxes. Even a comparatively compact country like Switzerland has experienced this issue: the Swiss Central Bank moves cautiously on FinTechs, but the Canton of Zug recognizes them as an opportunity and supports them as a cantonal priority.

We believe strongly that one national policy on sandboxes is in the nation's clear interest, and that fragmentation creates inefficiencies and inherently expands the potential for risk. Individual state initiatives pose considerable interstate and federal issues (particularly in a borderless cyberworld) in terms of whether approvals granted by a state will be recognized by other states or at the federal level. Thus, we again strongly recommend federal action and initiative to reduce unnecessary and inefficient issues and risks, as in the UK (the Financial Conduct Authority) and Singapore (the Monetary Authority of Singapore).

However, as a topical example, Arizona's sandbox contains many of the key attributes that most generic sandboxes have. We list those items below. (It is interesting that Arizona's attorney general has taken the leadership role in approving or granting applications.)
The key provisions of Arizona's FinTech sandbox include:

- *acceptance of applications from late July 2018 until July 2028.*
- *administration by the state attorney general's office.*
- *acceptance of companies with products that would normally require licensing from Arizona's Department of Financial Institutions, such as money transmitters, consumer lenders, debt management companies, mortgage brokers, and deferred presentment companies.*
- *plans from applicants to monitor and test their products, as well as to protect consumers. The test period is two years with a possible one-year extension.*

- *information from applicants on the benefits and risks to consumers of using their products, and on ways in which the innovation is different from other products or services available in the state.*
- *legal limits on the number of users of a product or service to 10,000 Arizona residents unless the company can show it has the capitalization and risk management capacity to handle up to 17,500 users.*
- *limits on consumer loan transactions to a maximum value of $15,000 for individual loans and a total of $50,000 in aggregate loans per consumer.*
- *limits on money transmission products or services to a maximum value of $2,500 per transaction and no more than $25,000 in aggregate transactions per consumer. These amounts can be increased to $15,000 per transaction and up to $50,000 in total if the company demonstrates adequate capitalization and risk management.*
- *compliance with all other Arizona laws, including those on consumer fraud and any other state laws applicable to financial products or services as determined by the attorney general.*
- *specific disclosures to consumers before providing the product.*
- *no exemption of the participant from compliance with federal consumer financial services laws, but it must be "deemed to possess an appropriate license under the laws of this state for purposes of any provision of federal law requiring state licensure or authorization." In other words, the provisions of 18 U.S.C. § 1960 making it a federal crime to operate without a required state money transmitter license are deemed satisfied, at least according to the terms of the Arizona law.*
- *the attorney general may enter into agreements with state, federal, or foreign regulators to allow entities authorized to operate in sandboxes in other jurisdictions to be recognized as sandbox participants in Arizona.*

Arizona's legislation includes a "passporting" provision, something currently available under European Union law between member states, which would allow a participant in Arizona's sandbox to operate in other jurisdictions with similar programs and vice-versa.

As always, some practical matters must be addressed in terms of new regulatory initiatives. Regulatory sandboxes are new and therefore constitute an additive "burden." Regulators will need funding and training so that they are fully skilled and can provide attention to these sandboxes. Regulators cannot possibly support sandboxes in their spare time and from their current resources.

A supportive sandbox structure that facilitates the testing of new ideas under the supervision of regulatory oversight has many benefits. Two of the most important are that it keeps useful and beneficial products and processes in the nation's markets; and it avoids driving new technology either into the shadows and outside of control and oversight, or into foreign markets. A sandbox that encourages FinTechs by lowering the various regulatory barriers and costs in a prudent manner increases economic well-being and also reduces risks.

8

REGULATING HEALTH CARE

Health care is among the most heavily regulated industries in the United States. Some would allege that regulation is the reason why health care costs are rising more rapidly than virtually any other prices in the economy, while others believe that still greater regulation would solve many of our nation's problems with access to, and cost and quality of, health care. We believe that with respect to the need for and efficacy of regulation, health care bears some textbook characteristics, but is in other respects unique. And as in most other regulated industries, regulation can be done poorly, or it can be done well.

We also believe, however, that the fundamental source of the current unsustainable cost growth is the way in which the health care sector is organized. The sector's misaligned incentives create an irresistible bias toward excessive cost and but a second-class level of quality. Absent structural reform, the best efforts toward regulating the system as it is organized today will fail.

WHY REGULATE HEALTH CARE?

Those who doubt the need for regulating the health care industry (at least to the degree practiced today), and who indeed believe that a more free-market orientation would solve many of its problems, might come close to agreeing that the major health care market imperfection is third-party payment. From this perspective, all of the individual regulatory challenges, from licensing to prescription drugs and more, originate in this market deficiency.

The contention is that in the United States, by and large, people consume health care but insurers pay for it. (This system includes not only private insurance, which was motivated in substantial part by a federal tax subsidy for employer financing of coverage, but also direct government provision of insurance—of which Medicare and Medicaid, enacted in 1965, are the major part.) Therefore, according to the perspective faulting the third-party-payment system, people have the incentive to consume more health care than they would choose if they were paying the bill themselves. Some might add that this incentive would lead to overtreatment, which can be harmful, as well as merely encouraging very low-value but harmless treatments, which just waste money.

If you accept this diagnosis, then the remedy would include less regulation. In particular, the nation should free people to accept more personal financial responsibility for their health care. Requirements for people to buy relatively comprehensive coverage would be deemed counterproductive, as would be standards for minimum levels of coverage (like the "essential health benefits" [or EHBs] required under the Affordable Care Act [also known as the ACA, or "Obamacare"]). Instead, people should be allowed to save their own money in "health savings accounts" (HSAs) and to save money by choosing their own health care treatments and providers. Because those funds will be available without tax or penalty for any purpose in retirement, people will not spend the money frivolously. For protection beyond their HSAs, people should have access to high-deductible "consumer-directed health plans" (CDHPs). The first dollars' worth of care can come out of the HSA, and therefore out of the consumer's (pre-tax) pocket, so people will be motivated to economize on everyday care. But if serious illnesses arise and costs exceed the deductible amount, insurance will pay dollar-for-dollar, so people will not have to pay for truly catastrophic and essential care.

We agree, with reservations.

There is no doubt that health care's third-party payment is unusual, if not unique. And there is no doubt that its incentives can be perverse. Consumers who had third-party payment for automobiles, for example, would rationally acquire new cars every week.

But cars are not health care. Our society takes no offense that a given individual cannot afford a Cadillac. We are, however, offended when an individual suffers and dies because of inability to afford care.

Our physicians take an oath to provide care, and provider institutions are required by law to deliver at least some level of care regardless of ability to pay. Medicaid provides care to the indigent at public expense.

More technically, the biggest part of health costs is treatment of serious chronic conditions, like heart disease, Alzheimer's disease, or cancer. People are unlikely to respond to the third-party-payment incentive by lining up for repeat transplant surgeries. Where people allegedly claim benefits too often is for everyday ailments, like the common cold, rather than by staying home and trying chicken soup, bed rest, and over-the-counter remedies. Many comprehensive health insurance plans address that problem not with very high deductibles, but rather by requiring modest co-pays. (The co-pays can be waived to encourage enrollees to seek preventive care.) And the evidence shows that our nation does not face a health care cost crunch because of office visits for the sniffles.

Where CDHP and HSA advocates might argue that their approach would be more effective is in the choice among high-cost treatments for serious illnesses. With CDHPs and HSAs, it is argued, people will choose less-expensive treatments, to save money for themselves. But this argument stands on one weak leg as well, because treatments for serious illnesses typically far exceed the deductible out-of-pocket ceilings of any CDHP. Therefore, people won't save any cash by economizing on truly expensive catastrophic care. Furthermore, when beset by serious illnesses, people tend to focus much more on survival than on shopping for lower prices, for either themselves or their loved ones. People choose more-intensive, more-expensive care to save their lives, not cheaper care to save money. And when serious illnesses require timely care, people rarely take the time to shop for a 10 percent savings on a major surgery. When people do forgo care under high-deductible plans, it tends to be preventive care that could prevent higher costs in the long run.[169] This is not terribly surprising. One argument for the CDHP is that it discourages "routine" care; the distinction between "routine" care and "preventive" care is less than obvious.

We do accept that third-party-payment incentives matter, and that market-oriented systems would help to control health costs. However, we believe that shrinking insurance coverage and direct consumer responsibility for doctor and hospital bills is not the best answer, for

169 RAND Corporation, *High-Deductible Health Plans Cut Spending but Also Reduce Preventive Care*, Research Brief RB-9588.

all of the reasons cited above. We favor instead responsible choices among health *insurance plans*. That would require a fundamentally restructured market. We believe that this form of competition would inspire innovation and motivate all plans to deliver greater quality, to both attract customers and succeed in the marketplace. The different regulation of that market for health care would be accomplished by restructuring the market rather than by addressing any pre-existing need for revision of regulation. (One evergreen issue in regulation, likely applicable where reforms of the present system are in place, is risk adjustment. Plans that accept unhealthy people should receive appropriate compensation. However, such plans should not for that reason attempt to characterize the people they cover as less healthy than they are. Government and regulators need to identify the ailments of insured individuals accurately to prevent overpayment of plans and providers. We anticipate that this would be less of an issue, but an issue nonetheless, in a competitive system with potentially larger regional enrollments that will therefore be more-typical risk pools. Another continuing need would be to loosen restraints that prevent successful health plans from expanding across state lines. Today, a plan that delivers high-value, quality care in one state faces barriers to moving their successful model to other states, which would drive competition and improvement in those new venues.) That discussion has been addressed elsewhere.[170] CED's recommendations for health care restructuring are included in the box that immediately follows.

170 CED, *Adjusting the Prescription*. Substantively, if every family could acquire a low-priced, high-quality (and comprehensive) health insurance plan of its choice at no out-of-pocket cost, and were responsible for the incremental cost if it chose a more-expensive plan, then every plan would need to attract cost-conscious family consumers to survive. And every provider would need to offer high-quality, low-cost services to attract insurance plans to affiliate with them. Providers of plans that could not attract cost-conscious consumers would not succeed. The pressure of competition in health care would have the same salutary effect that it does in every other market —raising quality and reducing price.

CED Policy Recommendations

CED has developed recommendations that harness market forces under both the Affordable Care Act and Medicare.

Affordable Care Act:

- Replace the ACA's complex subsidy mechanism, which imposes a heavy compliance burden on and may mislead families with modest incomes and has proved difficult to administer accurately.
- Restructure the ACA exchange system to align more closely with cohesive geographic health care market areas.
- Broaden the exchange populations to increase the numbers of enrollees and also the risk diversity, especially in small geographic areas.
- Expand the ACA's increase in consumer choice of insurance plans—which is the key to competition and innovation.
- Remove the ACA's unpopular mandates—and their complex exemptions—to compel the purchase of insurance.
- Replace the ACA's income-conditioned premium subsidies with a "fixed-dollar" refundable tax credit, usable only to purchase insurance.
- Eliminate the unnecessary individual and employer mandates.
- Reform the tort system, using new data and analysis to formulate rebuttable standards of sound practice. Create specialized expert courts to facilitate more timely and less costly decisions.

Medicare:

- Eliminate the Medicare Advantage price benchmark based on traditional Medicare's fee-for-service cost, and provide enrollees with a premium subsidy.
- Increase the income-conditioning of Part B and Part D premiums, including a temporary Part B premium reduction for lower-middle-income seniors.
- Risk-adjust premium revenue for plans.
- In rural areas, allow Medicare beneficiaries to enroll in traditional Medicare at no additional out-of-pocket cost, until Medicare Advantage plans meet a minimum threshold of availability.

As real as third-party-payment incentives are, we believe that regulation of some aspects of today's health care system, and of any feasible future alternative, is in fact more justified for two other reasons than the third-party-payment system. These logically lead to a different approach to regulation than does the third-party-payment system.

The first reason why health care delivery must be regulated is that health care is a true "merit good"—that is, society has a clear interest in citizens' using it. Our society values life. Our health care providers take oaths to protect life, and we have laws requiring that some level of care be given regardless of ability to pay, and we have a program (Medicaid) explicitly created to pay for care for those with low incomes. Some forms of preventive care can ward off serious conditions that would be costly to society if individuals could not pay. A market in which individuals will be served regardless of ability to pay requires regulation to maintain order and fairness.

Another reason for regulation is that health care is complex beyond the training of the typical layperson. Typical citizens contact doctors because they need service from professional health care providers. Moreover, insurance is as legally complex as health care. Other forms of insurance, such as life insurance and property and casualty insurance, also are regulated, for the very same reason.

These arguments in favor of regulation do not prioritize individuals' financial responsibility for their own individual medical services, as did the rationale for third-party payment. (In fact, the complex legalities involved in health care would provide an argument against individual choice among health care treatments and providers motivated by financial limitations.) But these justifications for regulation require consideration of further important issues. We highlight two, both relevant to forms of market power.

Market Concentration

To paraphrase the old political saying, all health care is local.[171] This is a slight distortion, because technology, particularly Internet technology and the near-instantaneous transmission of digital information, is making possible remote delivery of medical care. But the vast majority of care today requires physical proximity between the patient and the provider.

171 "All politics is local," typically attributed to the late former House Speaker Thomas P. "Tip" O'Neill of Massachusetts. Tip O'Neill and Gary Hymel, *All Politics Is Local: And Other Rules of the Game* (Holbrook, MA: Adams Media Corporation, 1995).

This constraint limits the ability of individuals to shop for health care outside of a particular geographic area.[172] Compounding the physical constraint is state regulation of health insurance. Different options for coverage, and therefore possibly for care, may be allowed or denied to people in different states.

Thus concentration of ownership of facilities for the delivery of health care can allow some plans and providers to charge higher prices. As one example, there have been allegations of a monopoly of hospital beds in an area of California.[173] A similar dispute has arisen in Massachusetts.[174] Such allegations imply that monopoly constitutes a barrier to entry into that health care market, allowing the monopoly to charge higher prices. But this potential damage is compounded because the monopoly can afford to be lax in providing potentially efficiency-improving innovation, given that market-disrupting competitors cannot gain a foothold in that regional market. Constructing new hospitals to enter the market may not be a viable option if that new hospital-bed capacity would largely exceed the need in that region. Therefore, the public suffers from both higher prices for a given technological level of care, and less technological and organizational development than it might enjoy otherwise.

As in every potential instance of an abuse of market power, finding remedies can be difficult. There is good reason why challenges to mergers that may yield market power are more common than are actions against existing market arrangements. Remedies to existing market power of firms are always the subject of intense adjudication; the disruptions to accessibility of a vital service such as medical care may impose greater costs than any foreseeable long-term benefits (appropriately discounted). A further complication is that there is no single pressure point to engage a remedy to market power—precisely because "all health care is local," and all insurance regulation is (by state), as well. Divestitures of hospitals by a large chain, or requirements that a hospital allocate beds and admitting privileges to a competing health care plan,

---

172 Limits, but certainly does not eliminate.

173 "The California Attorney General and Sutter Health Face Off in an Antitrust Lawsuit"; Chad Terhune, "California Sues Giant Sutter Health, Where Study Found Prices 25% Higher," *Kaiser Health News.*

174 Avik Roy, "Hospital Monopolies: The Biggest Driver of Health Costs That Nobody Talks About," *Forbes,* August 22, 2011; Scott Allen and Marcella Bombardieri, "A Handshake That Made Healthcare History," *Boston Globe*, December 28, 2008.

might be indicated; but the terms would have to be finely crafted to yield true and effective competition.

Another example of market power arises under Medicare and Medicaid, where providers often are reimbursed according to the service provided. Medical professionals thus can earn more by providing more services, which they sometimes accomplish in part by purchasing other service providers (like a physician purchasing a magnetic imaging provider, or perhaps just a machine). Such professionals might sometimes manipulate diagnoses to justify additional scans, provide the service, and then bill Medicare. There are regulations against such self-dealing (including the "Stark Law"), but enforcing such regulation can result in hand-to-hand combat between the providers and the administrators, who must comb through complex detail to determine whether services are justified, and whether the choice of provider is cost effective. We believe that a structural remedy such as CED's proposal might provide the best way to avoid these problems. If a plan's providers perform excess services in costly venues, then the plan will not be cost competitive. It will be in the plan's interest to use its expertise to ensure that services are accurately chosen and are delivered in the most cost-efficient way.

Pharmaceuticals

A related instance of market power exists in the field of pharmaceuticals. Prescription drugs are a comparatively small (9.8 percent in 2016) share of total US health expenditures, and drug costs have not grown that quickly (they were also 9.8 percent of total health expenditures in 1960, though they were as low as 4.7 percent in 1980, and as high as 10.4 percent in 2006[175]).

Prescription drug costs have been a source of public angst, however, for other reasons. Many of a typical person's health care costs are bundled into an insurance premium, itself divided between the employer and the employee, with even the employee's share ignored in the deductions section of the payroll stub (often electronic). Furthermore, the amounts of those payroll deductions usually remain stable and predictable over a calendar year. Co-pays for physician encounters usually are nominal as well as known ahead of time. In contrast, prescription drugs are necessary when an illness strikes at short notice, at prices that are not known beforehand, which must be paid in cash out of the patient's bank

175 Centers for Medicare and Medicaid Services National Health Expenditures Data.

balance instantly. And even for continuous-maintenance prescriptions, prices can change in unpredictable ways. The cost of a new prescription may be surprisingly high, given the trend toward more-personalized biologic pharmaceuticals. Sometimes these drugs approach life-or-death necessities, in which case a high price tag can be enormously worrisome.

And finally, there are bad actors who have purchased existing low-production-cost drugs accessible from only one pharmaceutical company, and then exploited that monopoly position to charge prohibitive prices.[176] This echoes age-old allegations of predatory pricing in their end-game stages, when a seller exploits an ill-earned monopoly position to charge outlandish prices and earn spectacular profits. Although such malefactors in some instances had no real prior connection to the pharmaceutical industry, that entire industry was tarnished by their behavior.

The economics of the pharmaceutical industry is laced with uncertainty. Researchers and companies have little idea what the development of the next drug will cost. And up to the last minute, utter failure remains possible. In this sense, the pursuit of a new pharmaceutical might resemble the exploration for and drilling of an oil well. The key difference is the potential life-or-death value of the pharmaceutical. For all these reasons, no reserve of money would be seen as enough for a pharmaceutical company for the development of tomorrow's drug, and in pursuit of that potentially life-saving innovation, no price would be seen as too much for today's drug. But today's drug can save lives, thus posing an irresolvable conflict in pricing.

Research indicates that pharmaceutical innovation is tied to drug company profits; drug research is cost-constrained.[177] Some react by advocating that pharmaceutical research be nationalized in the federal government's health-research institutions.[178] This would in effect socialize all of the research risk, so that the pharmaceutical industry would operate solely as a manufacturing and distributing business. But such a move would entail enormous risk. Private research has kept the United States in the lead in pharmaceutical innovation. (There has been some closure in innovation among nations over time, but that is to be expected—just like convergence in overall economic performance.) Concentrating much

176 Luke Timmerman, "A Timeline of the Turing Pharma Controversy," *Forbes*, September 23, 2015.

177 Dana P. Goldman et al., *Regulating Drug Prices: US Policy Alternatives in a Global Context*, RAND, 2008.

178 Dean Baker, "End Patent Monopolies on Drugs," *New York Times*, January 10, 2016.

of the function of drug development in the federal government could sacrifice the momentum of the progress of all recent decades, and the benefits of private competition—including not only the profit incentive, but also the diversity of approaches to problems that might lead to better solutions by the winners. A single entity, especially a government, could be more regimented, and research "by the book" might miss productive alternative approaches to particular problems. That is why our system always has relied on the private sector for product development (as opposed to basic research) whenever possible, and there is no clear reason why drug research should be a total exception.

There is another potential path to greater public benefit through improvement of the patent system. But this entails an eternal, structural tradeoff between the incentive to the innovator, through longer patent protection, and the benefit to society through more rapid diffusion of the innovation into other producers' products, through shorter patent lives. Some have argued that protection for pharmaceuticals under patent law extends for too long a time, and that if patents expired sooner, more prescription drugs would go off-patent and become available as cheaper generics. Though this is precisely why patents are not made eternal, it ignores the demonstrated relationship by which the incentives of a period of profit under patent encourages the search for new drugs. The benefits of both this incentive for research and the possibility of earlier distribution after patent expiration are real, and the tradeoff between the two is unavoidable. There is no simple answer for the best duration of a patent.

There is an arguable case that patent law has been manipulated in pharmaceuticals. Some claim that small and nonsubstantive modifications of drugs have been used as a pretext for the extension of patents. Similar allegations have been raised with respect to combinations of two drugs, each of which is about to go off-patent. There have been attempts in effect to sell patents to native American tribes, and then claim the tribes' sovereign status as perpetual protection for the monopoly rights. "Trolls" have attempted to claim patents merely by filing for small variations on existing patents, without doing any substantive research themselves. Clearly, sound patent-law enforcement and regulation are necessary.

Another alternative could be some form of government risk-sharing for drug development. Because finance is a demonstrated constraint on pharmaceutical development, government conceivably could share in the financing of research and development of prescription drugs, in exchange for a share of the profits on the eventual sales. Profits could be recycled into the program. In other private industries, such government involvement would be inappropriate. Some might argue that the justifiably positive aspect of pharmaceuticals, the life-or-death and preventive benefits of healing, could justify such a course.

This idea has some appeal, but also substantial risk. Pharmaceutical companies would have an understandable incentive to choose tactically among their research portfolios as to which drugs they would put forward for government risk-sharing. After some exploration of the relative prospects, private firms might reserve their most promising drug ideas for themselves alone; government might be left with the riskiest and least-promising projects. The government portfolio would not represent the entire industry and likely would be much riskier. And government would be left with politically contentious and perilous decisions as to which project to finance, and how to price any resulting pharmaceuticals. Various interests would try to influence government decisions about where to allocate taxpayer money; crony capitalism could enjoy a field day. To recoup its investment, government would have to impose higher prices; if it did, government would be open to political criticism that it did not reduce prices as expected. The public might not accept a government's argument that if it did not charge high prices, such prescription drugs would not be developed at all; after all, the public has not accepted that argument from private pharmaceutical firms. Claims of political motivations could be expected regarding which disease groups and which private firms would be supported with public funds.

The current Administration has issued its own package of pharmaceutical-policy proposals, which is billed as providing price relief to the consumer.[179] Some of the components of the plan are still ideas rather than specific proposals.[180] The strongest parts would seem to be those that emphasize greater competition, such as by preventing patent abuse or increasing bargaining at the stages of marketing and distribution. There is greater uncertainty about provisions that would encourage pharmaceutical companies to raise prices overseas, which would require international agreements, often with foreign governments.

---

179 "President Donald J. Trump's Blueprint To Lower Drug Prices"; Alex M. Azar II, Scott Gottlieb, and Seema Verma, "Help Is on the Way for Americans Facing High Drug Prices."

180 Emma Court, "Your Guide to the Trump Drug Price Plan: Who It Affects and How," *MarketWatch*, May 14, 2018.

More bargaining between Medicare and Medicaid and pharmaceutical companies would also become necessary, which may be problematic if there is such need for a patent-protected drug that the federal government would be unable to walk away from the bargaining table and therefore would have little leverage.

Again, there is reason to believe that a fully restructured and reformed health insurance market, along the lines of CED's proposal, might be the most positive possible step. Health insurance plans would have every incentive to use their knowledge base and purchasing power to choose the most cost-effective existing prescription drugs, and to encourage the development of new pharmaceuticals that will reduce the cost of solving health problems.[181] And if bad actors try to exploit a monopoly position on a simple drug, the prospect of large plans shifting all of their demand to an alternative producer might force a moderation of prices to a level closer to production cost. However, this example makes clear why some degree of standardization of coverages across competing plans would be necessary. Plans could be tempted to provide less generous coverage of some or all pharmaceuticals, and thereby to offer (and advertise) lower premiums. Enrollees might learn about the higher out-of-pocket costs of pharmaceuticals only after they already were committed to the plan.

In sum, there are important, controversial regulatory issues in health care. Improvements are surely possible. However, in our opinion, it would be a serious mistake to believe that all of the nation's health care problems, including the growing cost of care, could be solved through changes in regulation. Our problems are more fundamental and more structural. But even after those flaws are addressed, important new issues of regulation will inevitably appear.

181 Anna Wilde Mathews, "Detective Work: Reading Fine Print, Insurers Question Studies of Drugs," *Wall Street Journal*, August 24, 2005, p. 1.

9

"SOCIAL" REGULATION

Traditional economic regulation—including antitrust enforcement and guidelines for profits and prices in public utilities and other regulated industries (often "natural monopolies")—dates back to the nineteenth century. But what is called "social" regulation has progressed from its creation to perhaps the major place in the US regulatory framework in little more than 40 years.

"Social" regulation is difficult to define. It is not clearly distinguishable from "economic" regulation, is not purely non-economic, and is not totally devoid of dollars in either its costs or its benefits. It is often labeled "health, safety and environmental" regulation. We might restrict that term to "health and safety" regulation, because the environmental component generally has as its objective people's health and safety.

And beginning from that perspective, perhaps the clearest (though not totally clear) distinction of social regulation is that its benefits are not measured directly in dollars. Economic regulation of, say, electric power generation is imposed to reduce the influence of a natural monopoly, and thereby to increase the production of electric power and to lower its price. Because electric power is bought and sold in a free marketplace, we can relatively easily assign a value to that additional power production, and we can measure the savings of existing consumers. Thus, the benefit of that economic regulation can be measured and stated in a straightforward way, in dollars.

Not so with safety regulation, say, that is intended to reduce pollution from electric power generation (more on that below). Another social regulation requires the installation and use of seatbelts in automobiles. The cost of the seatbelts is straightforwardly monetary. (The cost of requiring and enforcing the use of seatbelts is admittedly somewhat less so.)

However, the benefits of seatbelt regulations are far more obscure. Some lives are saved. How much are those lives worth, in dollars? (More on that in a moment.) Some injuries may be avoided; the severity of other injuries may be lessened. What is that worth? Presumably some medical costs are avoided, and those can be estimated straightforwardly. But what about the avoided pain and suffering? Those surely have some value. How is it possible to measure that value? In court, it is typically assumed to be some multiple of medical costs; but that is clearly arbitrary. Then we proceed to the truly complex or speculative: What about injuries that might be worsened by seatbelts? Are any accidents caused by restraint on drivers' movements, or by a sense of invulnerability because drivers are wearing seatbelts?[182] Complete data gathering and careful analysis are essential, both of which cost money.

But perhaps the knottiest issue in every analysis of every branch of social regulation is valuing a human life. Installing seat belts, or making workplace tools safer, saves human lives but costs money. Are these expenditures worthwhile?

Some individuals will respond reflexively that the value of life is infinite, that human life is priceless. But they don't truly believe that. How do we know? Because anyone who truly believes that the value of life is infinite will devote every dollar of income (and perhaps every available borrowed dollar) beyond the maintenance of life to protect and preserve life—his or her own, and every fellow citizen's. Few people have been observed to forgo all recreational or otherwise frivolous expenditures and instead to direct all of their discretionary income to the minimization of risk to themselves and others. Thus, no one truly believes, or acts logically upon the belief, that the value of life is infinite.

Many questions arise. Should different lives be valued differently—for example, the young versus the old? One possible approach is to estimate future earnings and use that number as a guidepost. But does that mean that the lives of the retired are worthless? Most (probably all) Americans would reject that. One controversial approach to the young would be to estimate future earnings, but also to deduct estimated expenses of child rearing (such as education). The ironic result is that

182 Sam Peltzman wrote a controversial paper in 1975, arguing that drivers became more aggressive because of the apparent safety in wearing seatbelts, and so had more accidents (resulting in fewer fatalities because of the protection afforded by the seatbelts). He comments on his finding in "Sam Peltzman Thinks You Should Belt Up," *Chicago Booth* Review, November 27, 2016, http://review.chicagobooth.edu/economics/2016/article/sam-peltzman-thinks-you-should-belt.

with reasonable discounting for the time value of money, the expected net value of earnings compared with the expenses of rearing today's young children could well be negative. (Parents and grandparents will not be persuaded.) Most analysts would recommend that alternative life values and alternative discount rates be used to produce a range of estimated cost-benefit ratios. That might avoid reliance on a single absurd estimate—but it also fails to produce the single definitive estimate that most policymakers instinctively want.

So careful analysis of the lifesaving effects of social regulations is essential. More obviously, such analysis is necessary to determine where an extra dollar of regulatory cost will be most productive in saving lives. One potential initiative—seatbelts, versus safer workplace ladders, versus some other requirement—might prove most productive. Or none of them might be justified. Such calculations must be extended to regulation that reduces injuries and illnesses (like occupational safety and health), or noise pollution, or other social "bads."

These judgments are made through cost-benefit analysis, which abounds within the field of social regulation. They are the subject of intense dispute.

However, rapidly advancing technology may shift the ground rules for some of the hitherto most controversial fields of environmental regulation. These changes may well substantially improve consumer welfare, but they also raise bedeviling issues in regulatory policy.

In this chapter, we will discuss some of the accomplishments of social regulation. But we will also present two examples of difficulty experienced in implementing social regulation. We will then point out two related areas where technological change could greatly simplify what are now troublesome issues in social regulation.

As we discussed in our survey of the history of regulation, free-market competition is the best "regulation," and technological change can sometimes create competition where once there was none. Markets that are imperfect can hold opportunity and can attract innovators and entrepreneurs who perceive it. Such is the prospect in the examples we cite below. The economy may not always be so fortunate, and technology may not always coincide with knotty regulatory problems; but we should look for such opportunities and grasp them when they appear.

ACCOMPLISHMENTS OF SOCIAL REGULATION

Health, safety, and environmental regulation has been, and likely will remain, highly controversial. Complaints about intrusive workplace inspections, and costly nuisance requirements on product designs, are legion.

The elimination of risk in life is, of course, impossible. All modes of transportation entail risk. Common foods and beverages can cause all manner of disease; and disease is in the daily environments of all Americans. Regulation can only try to reduce those risks, not to end them.

Regulation entails costs. Safer workplace tools and safer consumer products cost money. Sound regulatory policy will weigh those costs against the benefits of reduced injury and illness. Such comparisons require the kinds of difficult analyses that estimate lives saved, and injuries and diseases avoided, and value those uncertain benefits over sometimes-long periods of time in the future. The estimation of costs is generally simpler, dealing with dollars spent in the here and now.

Official estimates of benefit-cost analyses tend to indicate positive results (greater benefits than costs).[183] This is not surprising, in that those analyses are used to determine which regulations will be issued. It is also less than fully reassuring, because (as we noted above) one area where the federal government has fallen behind the state of the art is in collecting data and evaluating the success of regulations after they are put in place. It is possible that ex-post review, as opposed to the official accumulation of original estimates, would show less-satisfactory results. Furthermore, methods and practices differ significantly across agencies, making conclusions tenuous.

Another perspective—more superficial, but perhaps more consistent with popular perception—would come from data on the achievement of some of the headline objectives of social regulation. It can be difficult or impossible to determine whether progress in any of these areas is the result of regulation itself or, rather, to totally extraneous developments, including conscientious behavior on the part of private entities that would have been undertaken even without regulation. Thus, these developments must be taken as indicative, rather than dispositive.

---

183 The most recent annual report was Office of Information and Regulatory Affairs, Office of Management and Budget, *2017 Draft Report to Congress on the Benefits and Costs of Federal Regulations and Agency Compliance with the Unfunded Mandates Reform Act*.

But to provide some sense of the degree of progress, we might start with workplace accidents. The Occupational Safety and Health Administration of the Department of Labor is mentioned with some frequency as intrusive and disruptive of business. However, the record for nonfatal workplace injuries is arguably encouraging (see figure 9.1).

The rate of incidence of injuries on the job is on a steady downtrend. The picture for fatal injuries is not so clearly favorable, however, as shown in figure 9.2.

FIGURE 9.1 **Nonfatal occupational injury and illness incidence rates by case type, private industry, 2003-17**

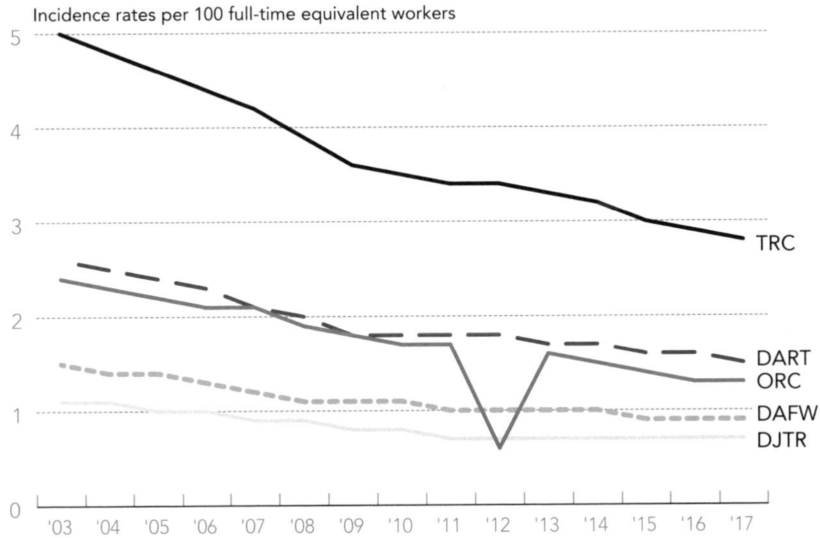

TRC (Total recordable cases)
DART (Cases with days away from work, job transfer, or restriction)
ORC (Other recordable cases)
DAFW (Cases with days away from work)
DJTR (Cases with days of job transfer or restriction only)

Source: U.S. Bureau of Labor Statistics, 2018.

FIGURE 9.2 **Number of fatal work injuries by employee status (2003-2017)**

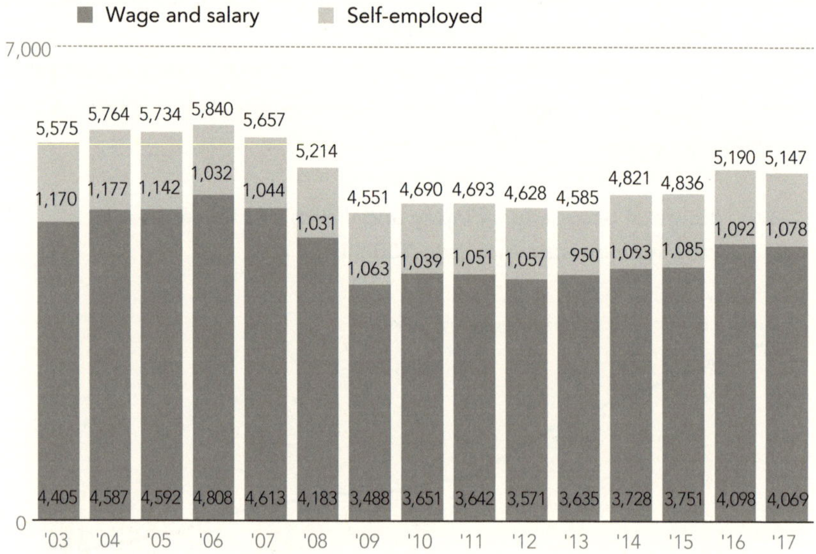

Source: U.S. Bureau of Labor Statistics, 2017.

Note, however, that these figures are presented in absolute numbers, not in incidence rates per 100 full-time workers, as are the figures for nonfatal injuries. (This is reflected in the steep drop in injuries over 2007-2009, as the financial crisis cut down on employment and work.) The number of payroll jobs in the economy rose by about 12 percent over 2003-2017, whereas the number of fatal accidents dropped by about 8 percent. Thus, the improvement of workplace safety over the long haul remains impressive. (Again, however, it is speculative to assign this improvement to workplace safety rules, when many other factors—such as changes in the nature of work, or efforts by employers—might contribute.) Still, the increases in fatalities over 2013-2017 exceed the growth of the workforce and so might be a source of concern.

Another issue area where some arguable success has been achieved is roadway fatalities. Here the reasonable denominator of the statistic is the number of deaths per vehicle mile traveled, to take into account the degree of risk undertaken on the highways. And here again, as evident in figure 9.3, the results are favorable.

FIGURE 9.3 **Fatalities and fatality rate per 100 million VMT, by year, 1975-2016**

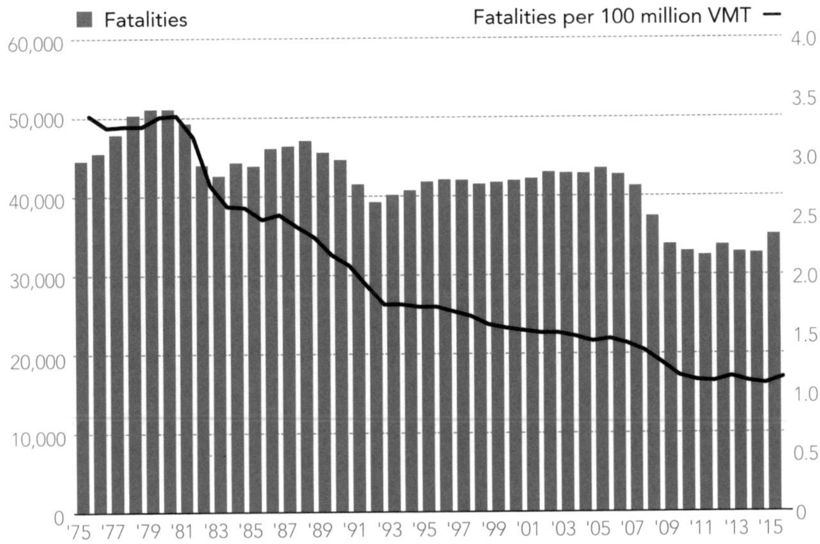

Sources: Fatality Analysis Reporting System (FARS) 1975-2015 Final File, 2016 ARF; Vehicle Miles Traveled (VMT): Federal Highway Administration (FHWA).

The number of highway fatalities increased over 2014-16, perhaps worryingly so. But the change in the fatality rate per mile traveled was small, as the strong economy resulted in more highway traffic. Again, there is no real way to assign this improvement to regulation, as opposed to improvements in, say, vehicle design that manufacturers would have undertaken anyway. On the other hand, perhaps the focus of regulators on crash-test results and ratings in their communications with the public have encouraged manufacturers to put more effort into safety.

Yet another possible indicator of the success of safety regulation arises in air travel safety. Crashes have become sufficiently rare that they appear as blips in the data. In fact, over the latest seven years of US data, there have been no fatalities at all (see Table 1).

TABLE 1 **Passenger Injuries and Injury Rates, 1998 through 2017, for US Air Carriers Operating Under 14 CFR 121**[a]

Year	Passenger Injuries[b]		Passenger Enplanements (millions)	Million Passenger Enplanements per Passenger Fatality
	Fatalities	Serious Injuries		
1998	0	12	650	No Fatalities
1999	10	46	676	67.6
2000	83	13	701	8.4
2001[c]	483	7	629	2.5
2002	0	11	619	No Fatalities
2003	19	10	654	34.4
2004	11	3	711	64.6
2005	18	2	743	41.3
2006	47	4	747	15.9
2007	0	3	770	No Fatalities
2008	0	6	745	No Fatalities
2009	45	14	706	15.7
2010	0	5	723	No Fatalities
2011	0	4	734	No Fatalities
2012	0	3	740	No Fatalities
2013	0	1	746	No Fatalities
2014	0	0	766	No Fatalities
2015	0	8	801	No Fatalities
2016	0	4	826	No Fatalities
2017[d]	0	1	851	No Fatalities

Source: National Transportation Safety Board, http://www.ntsb.gov/investigations/data/documents/aviationaccidentstatistics_1998-2017_20181019.xlsx

Notes:

a Since March 20, 1997, aircraft with 10 or more seats used in scheduled passenger service have been operated under 14 CFR 121.

b Injuries exclude flight crew and cabin crew.

c An illegal act was responsible for an occurrence in this category during this year. These acts, such as suicide, sabotage, and terrorism are included in the totals for fatalities but are excluded for the purpose of fatality rate computation. Only the number of people that died on board each airplane used during the September 11, 2001, terrorist acts is provided in this table; the resulting ground fatalities are not reflected.

d 2017 data are preliminary.

One area in which apparent results have been less encouraging is instances of foodborne disease. The Centers for Disease Control suggest no real improvement in the incidence of illness caused by food.[184] Clearly, the task of inspecting a growing food supply, in which flows across borders are increasing, is daunting. Recent reports of the identification of problems in the food supply before illnesses resulted are promising.

Again, it is hard to draw conclusions on the complex question of causality. For example, it is impossible to know how much the efforts of growers and producers would have contributed to the safety of the US food supply without federal safety inspections and regulation. It is equally impossible to know whether foodborne illness would have been significantly more prevalent were it not for federal inspections. It is clear, however, as OMB concluded in its annual cost-benefit report, that there were at least indicators of success in areas where regulation addresses risks to life. These indications provide at least some encouragement about the effectiveness of social regulation.

On the other hand, there are some areas where social regulation achieves arguably less success.

Aircraft Noise Reduction

A past effort to improve society's well-being through reduction of airplane noise has become a case study in the difficulty of the design of successful social regulation.[185] This difficulty rests upon multiple aspects of the design task. Policymakers and regulators must identify all of the costs, and all of the benefits, of a proposed regulation. And beyond that, they must consider all of the options available to address the underlying problem. There may be several alternatives that achieve a positive balance of benefits and costs, but only one that achieves the best balance. And that alternative may or may not be politically acceptable because of attributes of its design. Economists might formulate an "optimal" construct that voters as a group would not understand or accept.

Steven Morrison, Tara Watson, and Clifford Winston analyzed the effects of a rule that required aircraft purchased before a certain date, subject to one set of noise abatement rules, to be either scrapped or upgraded to a later and more-stringent set of noise reduction rules by

184 CDC, *Estimates of Foodborne Illness in the United States*.

185 Steven A. Morrison, Tara Watson, and Clifford Winston, *Fundamental Flaws of Social Regulation: The Case Study of Airplane Noise*, AEI-Brookings Joint Center for Regulatory Studies Working Paper 98-2, September 1998.

a later date. The authors performed a cost-benefit analysis (which had not been done prior to the release of the rule) and also critiqued the design of the rule relative to potential alternatives.

The issuance of a rule to reduce aircraft noise raises all of the difficulties of regulatory policymaking. Benefits of values like noise reduction are largely diffuse and indistinct. Noise itself is difficult to measure (being subject to a relative scale, rather than absolute values). Noise reduction yields likely improvements in health, for example, but those are difficult to identify and assess. Approximating such benefits requires heroic assumptions. One way chosen by researchers into this issue has been to assume that all benefits are capitalized into home values. Even that simplified monetization requires very rough estimation of changes in values of the relatively small number of affected homes, which are not necessarily subject to resale, relative to the values of unaffected homes in a changing and uncertain real estate market. And of course, some homes near airports are affected more than others by noise patterns, and the vast majority were purchased before the rule change in question would come into effect, in a free market and in full cognizance of the prior noise levels.

Reasonable analysis of a social regulation requires consideration of the costs of a rule. The primary cost of the airplane noise rule was the reduction of value of all of the aircraft covered by the rule—most of which, incidentally, had been purchased by the airlines before the rule was announced. Because all of those aircraft would become unusable without a retrofit of equipment to reduce noise, the airlines that owned those aircraft would incur a cost of either replacement or repair, and therefore a loss of the value of those aircraft if the airlines chose to sell them in the interim. The authors found that the estimated reduction in aircraft value summed up to be twice as large as the estimated increase in the values of the affected homes. The conclusion was that the rule was not economically justified; it imposed a greater cost (to one party, the airlines) than it provided a benefit (to a second party, the affected homeowners).

So Morrison, Watson, and Winston considered what economists would call an "optimal" regulation, one that would match the benefits precisely to the costs. What they suggest is a tax on the use of the older-generation, noisier planes to equal the social cost of the noise from each specific flight, to be transferred dollar-for-dollar to the precise homeowners who are adversely affected by that flight. Such a tax-and-transfer rule would by its definition have costs equal to benefits. But the benefits (and the costs) would be much smaller; the benefits would be about 4 percent as large as those of the actual rule. The airlines would have a choice: They could retire the noisy plane (or retrofit it with noise-reducing hardware) and pay no tax; or they could pay the tax. Given that the tax likely would be only about 2 percent the size of the decline in aircraft value from the actual rule, it would be most likely that the airlines would keep the noisy planes in the air and pay the tax.

This "optimal solution" is much more a thought exercise than an actual proposal; it would be virtually impossible to identify the actual parties damaged by the incremental noise from each flight, and to calculate their precise loss. But this exercise delivers a lesson: Social regulation is very difficult to accomplish properly. The authors observe that in many real-world episodes, the benefits for any individual household can be very small.

This exercise, which is still read in classroom considerations of social regulation, did have an impact. If you think about it, the analysis is the kind of "ex-post review" that experts ask for. In part because of this lesson, full cost-benefit analysis is now more common than it was in the time of this actual airplane noise rule. And policymakers now, at least if they follow their checklists imposed in presidential executive orders, do consider both alternative forms of regulation, and alternatives to regulation (including not regulating at all), before they impose rules on the public.[186]

INFRASTRUCTURE APPROVALS

The private sector uses public infrastructure—roadways, air traffic facilities, water and sewer capacity, and other investment—to do business and create jobs. This highlights the cooperative nature of the public and private sectors. The private sector generates income, growth,

186 Interestingly, Congress recently passed legislation to allow previously prohibited supersonic flight over the United States. Such flights were not allowed because of the "sonic boom" that is created when an aircraft exceeds the speed of sound. The legislation reflects not only a reduced concern about such noise, but also some technological progress in designing "low-boom" supersonic aircraft, which are claimed to be quieter. This development might be a credit to the effect of regulation in incentivizing innovation, or alternatively might be characterized as the end of a period of regulation stifling legitimate business activity. David Reid, "Lawmakers Pave the Way for the Return of Supersonic Flight," CNBC, September 24, 2018.

and employment, but cannot succeed without the groundwork built by the public sector, notably including sound regulation. The public sector facilitates growth, but cannot achieve this on its own; the private sector must step up in the environment that the public sector facilitates.

One area where this cooperation too often breaks down is in approvals for infrastructure projects. There have been numerous instances of delay in taking projects from design to implementation.[187] In at least one notorious example, a major roadway tunneling project was delayed so long that it was ultimately cancelled.[188]

The problems of clearance delay are not necessarily caused by one faulty regulation. Central to the issue is the National Environmental Policy Act (NEPA), which was created and implemented in company with the White House Council on Environmental Quality (CEQ), with a clear intention of facilitating comparatively brief and speedy review. CEQ regulations assume book-length review documents. Instead, over time, reviews of contemplated projects have come to fill or even overflow a bookshelf.

Rather than stemming from one regulation, delays have resulted from the accretion of multiple levels of clearance, in terms of both subject areas of review and levels of government. Some projects surely raise issues that cut across multiple disciplines, such as water quality, land wildlife habitat, and air quality. And different jurisdictions may be affected by a single project. However, the requirement for multiple review and clearance can unwittingly create multiple choke points and veto authorities. If multiple reviews and approvals are needed, then the pace of the project clearance becomes the pace of the slowest reviewing entity; and the fate of the project is determined by the reviewer that is most easily moved to reject the project—however material (or not) that entity's concern might be. Even worse, conflicting requirements from different agencies can trap potential projects in unresolvable conflict.

The same conceptual problem arises when multiple levels of government, including multiple states or multiple local jurisdictions, or several of both, become involved. Again, a single project can well affect several political jurisdictions, but none is well served if all are constrained by the slowest actor and the highest hurdle.

---

187 Philip K. Howard, "Two Years Not Ten Years: Redesigning Infrastructure Approvals," *Common Good*, September 2015.

188 Howard, "Two Years Not Ten Years: Redesigning Infrastructure Approvals," p. 6.

Delay is costly, across multiple dimensions. A highway project might improve the flow of traffic and reduce air pollution, but pollution mounts while the project sits on the drawing board. And with delay, costs mount. General price inflation is important, but so is the cost that contractors and suppliers must add as they sit idle after they had anticipated the start of work. If they must break off to do other business so that they can survive, that can cascade into further delay when approval is finally granted—or perhaps increase cost still more if the project authority must replace a no-longer-available low bidder with a more costly supplier.

And any instance of delay can be worsened if a project winds up in court. Across multiple political jurisdictions and multiple subject issues, the legal process can add orders of magnitude to the project time. A frequent line of argument in legal challenge is that the project review did not give full hearing to one particular complaint. Forestalling such arguments can require substantive review documents to become longer and longer, taking more and more time.

If somehow time could be stopped, such a process of review could in some respects be justifiable. Somewhere in the labyrinth of complex reality might be a point of concern that could affect a project decision. But while the approval process parses the complexities, society loses the value that the project can provide. Furthermore, in this imperfect world, every decision entails advantages and disadvantages. The current system of multiple vetoes allows a project to be stopped, or at least delayed, for the smallest of disadvantages, regardless of the net advantage that the project could deliver.

There are multiple required remedies for this multi-faceted problem. In place of a process with numerous substantive decision points, there needs to be a decision locus, which collects multiple reviews produced on a deadline and with volume constraints, and weighs those reviews to reach a conclusion. Interstate projects should be adjudicated in this same fashion at the federal level—hearing and appropriately weighing state and local reviews in a timely manner and produced to an appropriate depth of detail. And resorting to the judicial process should not be allowed for mere difference of opinion with the clearance decision; it should instead be restricted to true malfeasance in the process.

Electric Power Generation

From the early days of electric power generation, the most cost-effective method has been centralized generation of power with a grid to distribute that power to all households and businesses within a technologically efficient reach.[189] Both the power-generation facility and the grid were so costly that it would be economically inefficient, if not infeasible, to have multiple producers and distributors competing against one another to ensure a competitive market and therefore fair prices and ample production. Thus, there was a natural and unavoidable monopoly for power providers, and therefore regulation was needed to ensure that a single producer earned a fair return from its investment and incentives to pursue technological improvements, and for consumers to get a fair price for the amount of power they want.

Pollution—in terms of sulphur dioxide, nitrogen, particulates, and other contaminants that caused "smog" and health problems—became an issue of increasing seriousness in the 1950s and 1960s.[190] At that point, the economic regulation of electric power generation of the earlier days became overshadowed by environmental ("social") regulation, prominently with the creation of the Environmental Protection Agency under President Richard M. Nixon in 1970.[191]

Major innovations in regulation yielded positive results—especially through a cap-and-trade restraint on sulphur dioxide, plus technological innovations motivated in part by regulatory requirements that in turn motivated cleaner power generation. (A push toward greater fuel conservation because of the international oil crisis of the early 1970s helped as well.) The nation made significant progress against smog (though challenges remained),[192] particulate pollution was also greatly reduced (including by new regulation in the 1990s),[193] and although environmental regulation remained controversial, it was, on its own terms, highly successful in reducing "air pollution" as it was then understood.

---

189 Based on resistance in those wires, economies of scale of the generating facility, and other factors.

190 Especially in California. See Daniel Nussbaum, "Bad Air Days," *Los Angeles Times*, July 19, 1998; and "Smog Alert," *Los Angeles Times*, June 26, 2007.

191 But because smog was a localized phenomenon, state and even local governments became involved as well.

192 EPA, 1990 Clean Air Act Amendment Summary: Title I.

193 EPA, Summary of Executive Order 13045.

However, a new alleged threat from power generation, carbon dioxide, rose to prominence in the 1990s, and "global warming" or "climate change" became the new most prominent environmental issue. Because carbon emissions have truly global effects, federal government regulation (including international negotiations) was the locus of much of the effort, although California has continued its efforts as an environmental leader, and other states and localities have taken action as well.[194]

Thus, continuing the trend from the 1950s through the 1990s and to this day, and although economic regulation of electric power generation (especially rate setting) has sometimes been a public issue, "electricity regulation" has most prominently meant reducing pollution—be it smog or carbon emissions—through environmental or social regulation.

Climate change has remained a controversial issue. It is probably fair to say that the consensus of scientific experts has been that the Earth's environment is warming on average, and that an important cause has been the cumulative volume of carbon emissions in the atmosphere.[195] That said, some scientists disagree, and some opinion leaders maintain that the notion of human-induced climate change is an economically destructive myth.[196] As a result, the environmental regulation of carbon emissions through electric power generation has become a bitterly disputed public issue. Policy initiatives have included direct and indirect regulation of or restrictions on coal-fired power plants (the previous Presidential administration's "Clean Power Plan"),[197] subsidies for basic research and technology development,[198] and deployment of both

194 See EPA, *History of Reducing Air Pollution from Transportation in the United States* and "Why California Gets to Write Its Own Auto Emissions Standards: 5 Questions Answered," *The Conversation*, April 6, 2018.

195 NASA, "Scientific Consensus: Earth's Climate Is Warming," last updated November 15, 2018.

196 Katie Tubb, "5 Facts the Left Isn't Trumpeting About Paris and Climate Change," Heritage Foundation, December 4, 2015; "Global Warming Petition Project"; Open Source Systems, Science, Solutions, "31,000 Scientists Say 'No Convincing Evidence.'"

197 Union of Concerned Scientists, "The Clean Power Act," last updated November 1, 2018; "President Trump's Energy Independence Policy," March 28, 2017.

198 Department of Energy, "Successes of the Recovery Act," January 2012.

distributed and centralized solar power generation.[199] Several of these initiatives have been rejected over recent years.[200]

Furthermore, as China has gained considerable market share through allegedly illegally subsidized exports of renewable electric power generation equipment, countervailing duties have been imposed, raising the price of non-carbon-emitting electric power generation equipment.[201] Those subsidies allegedly put US producers at an insurmountable competitive disadvantage, given that the "deep pockets" of a firm supported by a government (with enormous ability to borrow) would allow "predatory pricing" that would force US firms to run unsustainable losses to try to remain price competitive, and eventually to go out of business.

However, despite these adverse developments, the rapid pace of technological improvement in the utility- and household-scale generation of electric power from solar and wind energy has caused the cost of renewable power to fall relative to fossil-fuel centralized generation.[202] Lazard, the financial advisory and asset management firm, has estimated the unsubsidized cost of power generation from various sources over time and has found a downward trend in generation from wind and from commercial- and industrial-scale solar energy.[203]

199 William Pentland, "Federal Subsidies for Solar and Wind Fell Sharply in Recent Years, Says New Report," *Forbes*, April 29, 2018.

200 "President Trump's Energy Independency Policy," March 28, 2017.

201 Doug Palmer, "US Sets Steep Final Duties on Chinese Solar Panels," Reuters, October 10, 2012.

202 See David Feldman, Jack Hoskins, and Robert Margolis, *Solar Industry Update*, National Renewable Energy Laboratory, May 2018, p. 46, for data from 2014 to 2017; and Geoffrey Carr, "Sunny Uplands," *The Economist*, November 21, 2012 for the longer-term trend graph.

203 "Lazard's Levelized Cost of Energy Analysis – Version 11.0," © November 2017.

FIGURE 9.4 **Unsubsidized levelized cost of energy—wind & solar photovoltaic (PV) (historical)**

Over the last eight years, wind and solar PV have become increasingly cost-competitive with conventional generation technologies, on an unsubsidized basis, in light of material declines in the pricing of system components (e.g., panels, inverters, racking, turbines, etc.), and dramatic improvements in efficiency, among other factors.

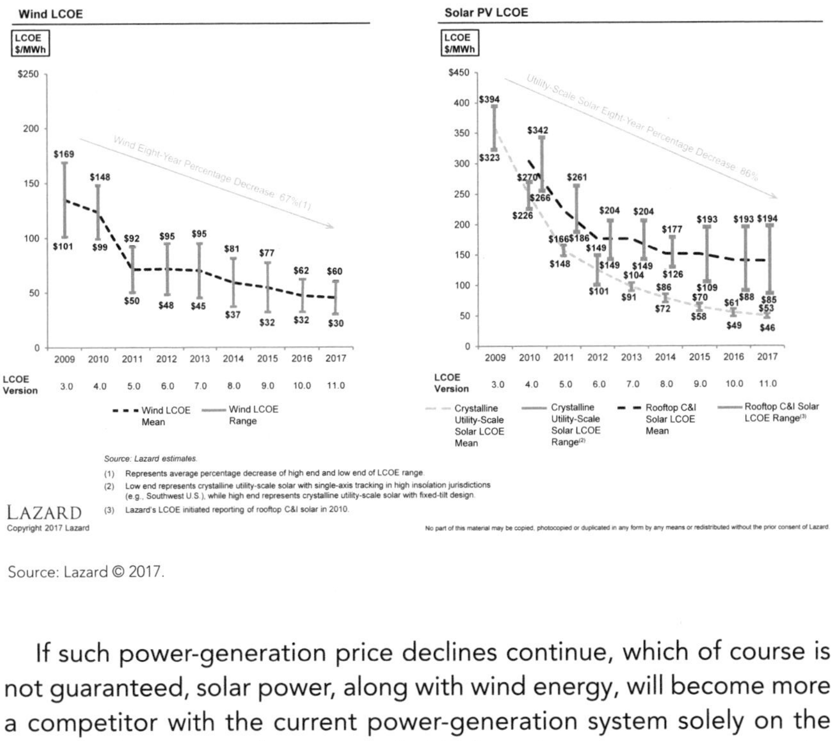

Source: Lazard © 2017.

If such power-generation price declines continue, which of course is not guaranteed, solar power, along with wind energy, will become more a competitor with the current power-generation system solely on the ground of price— without any subsidy for solar power, or any penalty for "the social price of carbon"[204] imposed upon centralized fossil-fuel electric power generation. The Edison Electric Institute, the association that represents US investor-owned electric companies, published a paper in 2013 that recognized that this trend has implications for the organization—and we would argue for the regulation, or reduction thereof—of the electric power industry:

204 "The social cost of carbon is an estimate of the monetized damages caused by a one-ton increase in greenhouse gas emissions in a given year." Ted Gayer, "The Social Costs of Carbon," testimony, Brookings Institution, February 28, 2017.

> Recent technological and economic changes are expected to challenge and transform the electric utility industry. These changes (or "disruptive challenges") arise due to a convergence of factors, including: falling costs of distributed generation and other distributed energy resources (DER); an enhanced focus on development of new DER technologies; increasing customer, regulatory, and political interest in demand-side management technologies (DSM); government programs to incentivize selected technologies; the declining price of natural gas; slowing economic growth trends; and rising electricity prices in certain areas of the country. Taken together, these factors are potential "game changers" to the US electric utility industry, and are likely to dramatically impact customers, employees, investors, and the availability of capital to fund future investment. The timing of such transformative changes is unclear, but with the potential for technological innovation (e.g., solar photo-voltaic or PV) becoming economically viable due to this confluence of forces, the industry and its stakeholders must proactively assess the impacts and alternatives available to address disruptive challenges in a timely manner.[205]

The accounting and consulting firm Ernest & Young Global Limited (EY) estimates that the decline in the cost of off-grid energy will proceed beyond cost and performance parity with grid-delivered energy and will reach the point where the cost of transporting electricity exceeds the cost of generating and storing it locally by 2039 in the northeast United States.[206] This time frame is a veritable heartbeat given the long lifetimes of electric utility facilities, and of the grid itself.

These prospects are subject to enormous uncertainty. Past declines in prices of renewable energy need not continue; some have drawn an analogy between the pace of price decline of photovoltaic power cells and that of semiconductors, but the technologies of the two are not

---

205 Peter Kind, "Disruptive Challenges: Financial Implications and Strategic Responses to a Changing Retail Electricity Business," prepared for Edison Electric Institute, January 2013.

206 Benoit Laclau, "When Energy Customers Go Off-Grid, Will Utilities Be Left in the Dark?" EY, June 7, 2018.

identical.[207] Meanwhile, conventional power generation is not standing still, but increasing its productivity. However, as an immature industry, renewable energy likely has more technological headroom than the well-tilled fields of conventional energy generation and transmission. New materials have been invented to allow wind turbines to stand in salt-ocean waters for decades; new materials also are likely to be developed to facilitate other forms of renewable power generation and storage. (However, people may be reluctant to buy into any such rapidly changing technology for fear that they will have invested in soon-obsolete hardware that falls behind a declining cost curve.)

Clearly such developments would mark a sea change in both the perception and the substance of energy regulation. The change of perception would be stark. Instead of a politically contentious imposition of pain in the form of higher electric power prices over a controversial scientific theory, electric power regulation would become again a simple issue of economic regulation—and that regulation would be markedly narrower in scope than it is today. However, the nature of that regulation would need to change equally markedly to achieve the most efficient economic outcome both over the long term and, perhaps even more notably, in a transition period between two different power-generation regimes.

This prospect raises a whole family of issues. Among the greatest complexities and challenges are the roles of the power grid and existing public utilities. Reliability will be important to all stakeholders, especially vital infrastructure (such as hospitals, police, and firefighting), and experts will debate the merits of alternative energy sources and approaches to ensure resilience. Peak time-of-day and weather-condition availabilities of renewable energy and demand for energy do not necessarily coincide, meaning that the development of storage technology will be important; and technological progress on storage and on renewable-generation technology also need not coincide. Simultaneous financing of the unamortized costs of the existing infrastructure and of new technologies will be a puzzle.

Are there good answers? How can our regulatory system guide us toward the lowest-cost, most economically efficient future of electric power?

---

207 Michael Kanellos, "Why Solar Is, and Isn't, Like the Chip Industry," Greentech Media, August 17, 2010. For that matter, the improvements in the speed of computer processors have hit natural limits, and the same could happen in photovoltaics.

The enormous technological uncertainty militates against any complete and certain answer. However, there are some "no regrets" options. To the degree possible, utilities should encourage conservation rather than adding greater centralized generating capacity, because that capacity may prove to be redundant in the not-too-distant future. Part of that effort should be using time-of-day and other techniques to minimize the peak load. Furthermore, we need research into "mini-grids" and small-scale local generating capacity that could provide resilient backup power in the event of interruptions of distributed generation because of weather events or other contingencies. We need careful thought about alternatives for the configuration and organization of a distributed power regime: Should people be free to own their own equipment on their side of the electricity meter? Or should utilities lease equipment to homeowners—again, on the homeowner's side of the meter? How can the power industry handle geographically diverse capacities of renewable energy, and of demand for power? Could there be fair and economically efficient terms for households generating their own excess power to sell it to the grid?

The extraordinarily long-lived capital in the existing power industry makes these decisions important. Regulatory policy should facilitate such "no regrets" policies: avoiding the purchase of assets that society soon may not need; aiding policies that reduce peak loads, and thus the need for additional capacity; engaging stakeholders in debate about fair treatment of sales of distributed energy to the grid; and the like.

Notably, however, the nation is apparently making a transition from a time when rising prices and environmental problems confronted us with alternative bad regulatory choices, to a time when advances in technology provide our regulatory system with alternative good ones. If technology allows, renewable power might not only reduce the conflict over environmental regulation of electric power, but might also ease issues in traditional rate-of-return regulation, because competition among alternative providers of distributed energy and centrally generated power could move the entire market closer to textbook-perfect competition. Thus, as in the case of the early railroads, technology might again solve hitherto vexing and persistent regulatory problems.

Associated advances in automobile technology may push that fortunate trend even further.

AUTO EMISSIONS REGULATION

The status of environmental regulation of automobiles is similar in some respects to that of electricity generation. And for our current purposes, technological change holds the same prospect of making what is now an often-contentious issue of "social" regulation into a much more tractable economic question—with the prospect of some knotty issues of transition beforehand.

Auto emissions regulation began with emphasis on clean air, particulates, and smog and achieved meaningful success on those fronts. Additional concern centered on petroleum consumption, because of price and reliance on potentially hostile foreign sources of the resource. There was some sense of success on that front as well, but a roller-coaster ride of sentiment ensued. Price declines in the late 1980s were good news; conflict in Iraq and Kuwait in the early 1990s, and again in Iraq in the early 2000s, was bad news, as was the sharp run-up of prices coinciding with the outbreak of the financial crisis in the late 2000s. The substantial increase in US potential and actual production through horizontal drilling and hydraulic fracturing ("fracking") greatly reduced concerns about prices, supply, and the political reliability of its sources. However, lurking in the background has been the newest environmental concern of global climate change, allegedly caused by carbon emissions. In the post-horizontal drilling environment of comparative security with respect to petroleum quantity and price, the notion that Americans would need to economize on oil consumption because of controversial environmental concerns grated on some. Prominently, the current administration's rollbacks of the just previously accepted fuel-efficiency agreement highlighted this tension.

On the other side, there are some forces behind gasoline efficiency. The pressures for fuel efficiency, including through the corporate average fuel economy (CAFE) regulations, arguably motivated some of the undeniable technological progress in that direction. Such progress continues. To some degree, progress is shared between electric power generation and zero-emission (at the stage of operation, not necessarily in the generation of the electric power, at least at this time) vehicles; and as a result, electric cars have come closer to satisfying consumer demands.

There are notable differences of opinion about the prospects for renewable-powered vehicles. Some are skeptical, based especially on the current state of what appears still to be an immature technology.[208] Others are more sanguine, noting that the immaturity of the technology leaves headroom for improvement. They cite opportunities including synergies between the development of residential and vehicle electric power, and between electric power and vehicle autonomy, which offer higher levels of consumer satisfaction—including improved mobility for older persons, reduced fatigue on long trips, quicker taxi availability, and better parcel delivery.

No one knows how these competing technological forces will resolve themselves. There is no doubt that progress in improving conventionally powered vehicles will continue. But EY projects, on the optimistic side, that in 2025 electric vehicles will achieve price and performance parity with internal-combustion-engine cars worldwide.[209] Their interpretation rests on steady progress rather than assumed breakthroughs.

A major difference between electric-power generation and electric vehicles is that electricity is a totally homogeneous product (or service), whereas electric (for that matter, all) vehicles are differentiated products that must satisfy multiple dimensions of consumer taste. Technological progress in electricity generation has reduced price (and improved reliability), and if price can fall below the level of centralized fossil-fuel-generated electric power, and reliability of service can be assured, one would expect that consumers in that particular market area would be willing to move to generation with renewables. In contrast, even though some index of attributes might suggest market domination for electric vehicles, some consumers with different patterns of taste and different performance priorities might not be satisfied.

One key attribute of electric vehicles is driving range. The vast majority of automobile miles are driven within a small number of miles of the owner's home. Still, many consumers feel concern about running out of power while away from home, or what is known as "range anxiety." Technology is directed to allaying that fear. Fast-charge batteries, interchangeable batteries (such that a driver could pull up to a "fueling" station and exchange his battery for an identical freshly charged battery for just a charging fee), and greater battery capacities are all possible. Today's hybrid cars, with gasoline engines that can both recharge

208 Simon Alvarez, "BMW Exec Expresses Reservations on Electric Car Battery Costs: 'It's a Nightmare,'" Teslarati, October 8, 2018.

209 Benoit Leclau, "The Countdown Is On to When the Utilities Sector Reaches Three Tipping Points on a Journey to a New Energy Ecosystem," EY, June 7, 2018.

batteries and power the vehicle, are one answer; but ideally consumers would not need to pay for and carry along the internal combustion engine and its gasoline (both of which also displace potential passenger room and cargo capacity while weighing on the vehicle's performance and economy).

Unlike centrally generated electric power in today's world, the prices and characteristics of automobiles are not regulated (beyond safety-related matters). Thus, one might argue that regulators can just sit back and allow the market to evolve, and not worry about regulatory policy. To a considerable degree, that is true. The exceptional conditions are that there are synergies between distributed home electric power generation and electric automobiles, and potential barriers to entry for new automobile technologies. Added to those, perhaps, is the environmental issue of climate change.

There are potential synergies between electric vehicles and the growing use of renewable (and especially distributed) home electric power. Once distributed electric power is available, a consumer's electric vehicle can be charged at zero marginal resource cost, and with zero greenhouse gas emissions. (Today, ostensibly clean electric vehicles might be powered, ultimately, by coal-generated electricity.) The further synergy is that vehicle batteries can be used for home energy storage for night hours and times of overcast weather, thereby making distributed home electric power generation more reliable.[210] This would make renewable distributed home power generation more attractive and would facilitate the conversion from centralized fossil-fuel generation. Apart from the climate change amelioration (for those who share that concern), it would also save consumers money. So if society were to decide that home-generated electric power should be encouraged for environmental reasons, facilitating a changeover to electric vehicles would advance that purpose.

All of this has implications for regulation. The nation now regulates vehicles—in "social" or environmental regulation—for emissions, and so one might argue that existing regulation is a stake in the ground for

210 Because home electricity storage is less load-critical than is powering an electric vehicle, there is also potential (already being realized in some instances) for used vehicle batteries, which might otherwise need to be discarded and might contain hazardous materials, to be simply repurposed for home storage. See David Stringer and Jie Ma, "Where Three Million Electric Vehicle Batteries Will Go When They Retire," *Bloomberg Businessweek*, June 27, 2018 and, indirectly, Katie Fehrenbacher, "The Big Potential of Used Electric Car Batteries," *Fortune*, August 25, 2016.

potential intervention to facilitate, or at least not impede, a changeover to electric vehicles. Such a changeover obviously would simplify existing environmental regulation of automobiles enormously; many current standards would simply fall away. (This would be true only to the extent that the electric power that charges automobiles is renewable.) A danger would be that government intervention would step in too soon, enshrining an immature technology that could be improved. That outcome should be avoided at all costs. Enormous amounts of business and household investment could be wasted and environmental benefit could be lost.

One way to make the market work—at least from the perspective of those who believe that human-induced climate change is real, and a real threat—would be to both reduce and simplify current regulation by replacing CAFE standards with higher taxation of gasoline. The CAFE standards, coupled with cheap gasoline (at least by global standards), create the perverse incentives of encouraging (at least relatively) the purchase of a bigger, heavier, lower-fuel efficiency vehicle, and then driving it on frequent occasions. After all, if gasoline is cheap, there is little penalty for buying a comfortable car and then using it even for very short trips. If instead gasoline were costlier (including to the extent necessary to provide full financing for maintenance of existing roadways and the construction of new ones, which the current level of gasoline taxation demonstrably does not achieve), consumers would have more incentive to buy fuel-efficient cars, and then to consider public transportation or even walking for shorter trips. Economists would endorse that strategy on the basis of both budget-revenue sufficiency and environmental responsibility.

Environmental regulation of the automobile is highly controversial. Beyond wanting cheap automobiles and cheap fuel (as well as cheap everything else, of course), many Americans would be concerned about raising the cost of commuting to downtown jobs for low-wage workers who are forced into remote suburbs by the cost of housing. There would also be concern about raising the cost of driving for rural Americans who live in remote locations. And then consider our environmental worries as well. But as technological progress reduces the cost of distributed generation of renewable electricity and makes electric vehicles more cost-competitive with internal-combustion power, at least some of the challenges of social regulation will be eased.

We noted earlier that the best regulation is market-based competition, and that technology sometimes advances it. If entrepreneurs and innovators see investment returns that can be exploited and bid down, they will do so. In this process, they can solve some of the knottiest problems in the economy. It happened in the deregulation of transportation and energy in the 1970s and 1980s, and it can happen again in the environmental regulation of this decade. Necessity is the mother of invention, and nowhere is this clearer than in the energy innovation of this day.

There have been important accomplishments in product and workplace safety, as well as the environment. But apart from those developments, given the difficulty of valuing a human life, assessing the risks of accident or disease, and weighing the nuisance costs of noise and other by-products of modern life, social regulation will remain a source of controversy.

10

ANTITRUST

Antitrust enforcement has been an important part of US regulatory policy since the nineteenth century, and this is likely to continue. There are conditions under which antitrust is an essential element in overall economic policy. However, antitrust can be a blunt instrument, and it can be difficult to use effectively in today's rapidly changing competitive environment. Forward in time, antitrust authority must be exercised with care to maximize US prosperity.

THEORETICAL UNDERPINNINGS

Antitrust policy has firm and clear roots in economic theory. The ideal and most straightforward textbook image of a product or service market is composed of many buyers and many sellers—so many that no one buyer or seller is large enough to control the market, and collaboration among them to control the market is impossible. No buyer or seller possesses any more knowledge of the product or the market than any other. The goods or services are relatively uniform and are sold through a simple bidding process. This competition drives prices down to the marginal cost of production, the lowest feasible level, and maximizes output. With the highest possible output and the lowest possible price, society's well-being is maximized. Such "perfect competition" is the best of all possible worlds, and any government or other civil authority would be well advised to leave the workings of such a market alone.

Market Imperfections and Abuse of Market Power

However, the assumptions of perfect competition are sometimes (perhaps often) violated, at least to some degree. Among the earliest recognized flaws in markets was the concentration of ownership of production capacity; either one seller ("monopoly") or only a few sellers ("oligopoly") controlled a market. Typically, under those conditions, the sellers could raise prices—even at the cost of reducing sales, though by a lower percentage—and thereby increase profits at the expense of consumers.[211, 212]

Such behavior was troubling in the short run, but even more problematic in the long run. Sellers with "deep pockets" from past profits could use that wealth to monopolize scarce resources and thereby cut off opportunities for other firms to enter the market and reduce prices to the benefit of consumers. One technique for preventing competition was for large firms to temporarily reduce local market prices even below cost, to bleed dry any new, small potential competitors, running them out of business—a practice called "predatory pricing." Any such exploitation of "barriers to entry" for new competitors can be doubly destructive if the prospective competitors seek to bring new and superior technology to the marketplace. In those instances, society can be deprived of innovation, technological improvement, and productivity growth merely because of incumbent interests' "deep pockets," themselves filled with profits from monopolies or oligopolies. Superior new technologies that could have succeeded in the marketplace are never given a fair chance. In general, monopolists or oligopolists could skew markets to their personal or corporate benefit.

Beyond predatory pricing, another potential abuse is "crony capitalism."[213] Monopolists or oligopolists might use their deep pockets to influence the political process and fend off competition. One such device has been to influence regulation; for example, to cut off the

---

211 Collusion by multiple firms toward this end is called "price fixing."

212 One or a few buyers also sometimes could exercise enough power in a market to be able to hold prices down. Market domination by buyers, rather than sellers, such as in the case of large employers' holding wages down in local markets, is known in the textbooks as "monopsony" or "oligopsony."

213 CED, *Crony Capitalism: Unhealthy Relations between Business and Government* (Washington, DC: October 14, 2015); and Steve Odland and Joseph J. Minarik, *Sustaining Capitalism: Bipartisan Solutions to Restore Trust & Prosperity*, The Conference Board, 2017, chapter 2.

access of prospective competitors to market. They might allege that new technologies are unsafe or otherwise disadvantageous to consumers. Thus, consumer protection can become an argument for preventing consumers from enjoying the benefits of competition—and one more argument for vigilance in our political system to prevent crony capitalism.

In the broader picture, monopoly or oligopoly power can be highly damaging. Market power can be a money machine, and that money can buy anything, including political power. Through crony capitalism, monopoly can perpetuate itself, reducing the prosperity of consumers and workers today, and reducing the innovation and economic growth that determine living standards tomorrow. And all the while, manipulation of our political life can demoralize and degrade our democracy.

Imposition by monopoly or oligopoly of significant burdens on consumers stimulated enactment of the earliest pieces of antitrust legislation in American history. The railroads and oil in the nineteenth century and "big steel" in the twentieth century inspired classics of the "muckraking" literature, which led to breakthrough legislation such as the Interstate Commerce Act of 1887, the Sherman Antitrust Act of 1890, the Clayton Antitrust Act of 1914, the Federal Trade Commission Act of 1914, the Robinson-Patman Act of 1936, and the Celler-Kefauver Act of 1950. Oversight of issues related to antitrust has been exercised not only by the broad scope of the Federal Trade Commission and the Antitrust Division of the Department of Justice, but also in focused industry segments of the Federal Communications Commission and by the Securities and Exchange Commission. In recent years, many would say that those laws of decades ago are the totality of the nation's antitrust policy, and that our policy is not implemented through the courts or newer legislation.

There are other, more subtle ways in which firms can exercise their market power to the disadvantage of consumers. They have attempted mergers to monopolize markets, but mergers are subject to antitrust review and have on some occasions been prohibited.[214] Firms have sometimes attempted to keep market segments separate and to "price discriminate," that is, to sell at different prices to different consumers, taking advantage (some would say) of those willing and able to pay. Firms have been prohibited from requiring prospective purchasers who

214 For just one example, see Michael J. de la Merced and Rachel Abrams, "Office Depot and Staples Call Off Merger after Judge Blocks It," *New York Times*, May 10, 2016.

wish to buy a product over which the seller has a monopoly to buy other products from the same seller when the purchaser might prefer to buy elsewhere (a practice called "block booking").

Courts have attempted to remedy such abuse of consumers in various ways. Some years ago, large firms that were judged to constitute monopolies and to engage in anti-competitive behavior were broken up by court decisions. Standard Oil was one example. The same kind of divestiture was required of AT&T in its adjudged monopoly of telephone communications in a court case that was filed in 1974 and settled by a consent decree in 1982. In other instances, governmental authorities have identified specific behaviors (like block booking) as unequivocal monopolistic abuses and have prohibited them outright, without structural remedies.

But courts rarely impose the most aggressive structural remedies (like breaking up Standard Oil and AT&T), surely at least in part because they disrupt the functioning of the economy. The basis of the Standard Oil decision was a perceived extreme imbalance that could be corrected only with such a radical mid-stream transformation. The AT&T divestiture was considered in the same light, with rapid technological change arguably requiring a quantum intervention to keep the industry in step with the times (including innovations overseas). At one point in the 1990s, the courts considered breaking up Microsoft because of the far-reaching power of its control over computer operating systems. But the courts backed away and instead required access to source code so that other vendors could write effective utility programs that could work with Windows. Several court actions have since then revisited that decision to ascertain continued compliance.

Current antitrust enforcement has been less of an intervention into the status quo, and more of a review of proposed mergers before they occur. The prevailing mindset in the courts apparently has been that firms might acceptably earn market share in day-to-day competition, benefiting consumers as they gain that ground by offering the best value. However, buying market share by consolidating existing firms should not be allowed and can be prevented by denying approval of mergers.[215] Recent examples include the proposed mergers of Time Warner and Comcast, and of Office Depot and Staples.

In addition, however, this new attitude surely rests on enormous recent technological and economic change in many industries. Technological change is breaking down many barriers between markets, intensifying competition, and reducing the power of any individual firm to monopolize a market, as traditionally understood, in a wide range of business categories.

One clear example is the growing prevalence of online sales, in retailing and in wholesale trade. It is easier for buyers to compare prices, which is forcing firms to be competitive, and is driving margins down. There might be valid concern about a firm achieving significant prevalence, even domination, over bricks-and-mortar retailing in a particular product line in a particular geographic area. However, all of that firm's customers likely have at least one alternative online vendor as a source. And even further, with that (or those) online vendor(s) forced to reveal all prices in the course of doing business, the customer can easily find the best price. Therefore, even an apparently dominant bricks-and-mortar vendor might be fighting for survival against Internet-based competitors.

There has been similar intensification of competition in other markets. The growth of international trade is an example. Half a century ago, the US automobile industry was seen by many as an oligopoly (benevolent or not) dominated by three large firms. Auto design was seen as largely static, employment terms were set by an industrywide contract with organized labor, and price competition was believed to be somewhere between polite and nil. Today, in stark contrast—and although the number of US producers has hardly changed—multiple US and foreign producers battle for market share with a plethora of designs. Sellers, except for niche submarkets, are perceived to have minimal pricing power. Allegations of antitrust offense are highly unlikely, even though arguably US production is no less concentrated today than it was in the 1960s. The recent rise of potential additional suppliers of autonomous

215 One example of the refinement of the mindset about market power is a permissiveness about so-called vertical mergers, under which, say, a production firm would merge with a sales firm that sold its products. Understanding that the consumer has only so much demand for the product, antitrust authorities have come to see that mergers along the production chain do not increase market power over the consumer; they can only, perhaps, increase the efficiencies of the production and marketing of the product, to the potential benefit of everyone.

vehicles, and the struggles of traditional automakers to positional themselves to compete in this changing marketplace, only amplifies this conclusion.

In the case of auto production, the notion of an absence of monopoly power is hardly controversial. However, in the example of bricks-and-mortar versus online retailing, controversy is far more likely. Recent merger applications have been rejected on the ground that they would lead to monopolization, while the applicants have argued that they needed greater size to survive the online marketing proliferation.

The key concept in these issues is the "relevant market." A firm that dominates a particular market can extract extra profits from the consumers who are reliant on the good or service sold in that market. However, if these consumers have good alternatives, even though the alternatives might not be identical, sellers in that market will not be able to exploit those consumers. A simplistic example: If one seller monopolizes the market for peaches, but consumers who see high-and-rising prices for peaches would be more than willing to step across the store aisle and buy pears, oranges, grapes, or bananas instead, then a monopoly over peach production may be totally benign.

In short, if a good or service has many substitutes, then its relevant market includes those substitutes. Market power in just one part of a relevant market may not be market power at all.

The relevant market has a geographic dimension as well. Monopoly over a local market area for, say, perishable food could be a real issue. But in today's technological environment, a bricks-and-mortar store for nonperishable products has competition from a host of online sellers.

There are reasons to believe that "trusts"—the market power once exercised by "the oil trust," "the railroad trust," "the meat-packing trust"—are a decreasing issue in today's economy. For one thing, trusts raised prices. In the economy of the last three decades, inflation has been an ebbing problem. In fact, the concern of the last decade was, if anything, not too much inflation but too little.[216] Economists with historical perspective will say that even the largest firms have less "market power," or in different words "pricing power," than in years gone by.

Part of the reason is globalization. Years ago, US producers dominated US markets, with no challenge in sight. Under those circumstances,

216 Inflation will rise again; but when it does, it will likely be more attributable to government's macroeconomic—or even trade—policy mistakes than to powerful firms flexing their muscles at the expense of their customers.

prices were limited as much by a risk of customer (that is, voter) anger leading to antitrust action as they were by competition. In today's economy, a broad range of industrial sectors—even some services, as well as goods—are at competitive risk. Firms must compete to protect market share today and to ward off new competitors tomorrow. And that competitive pressure will not ease in the foreseeable future. Just about any glimmer of market power in the United States today would elicit foreign competitors tomorrow.

Part of that pressure comes, directly or indirectly, from technology. New product and service ideas, from home and abroad, challenge existing ones. Technologies are exploited and copied at a dizzying pace. The consumer's discretionary dollar is enticed by an enormous range of new choices, and the prices of necessities are stabilized by ever-more-efficient production.

The intensity of competition and technological pressure has pushed economic change to an unprecedented and still-accelerating pace. As just one indication of this near-turmoil, of the "Fortune 500" firms of 1955, only 60 remained on that list as of 2017.[217] Some firms that would have been thought by many to be monopolistic or oligopolistic abusers of market power were rather, in the fullness of time, proven to be vulnerable to competition through globalization, technological advancement, changing consumer needs or tastes, or to many other factors.[218] Thus, a snapshot of the business world at any given moment might show an apparently stable industrial titan that is on the brink of, or even enduring competitive assault and decline. Reacting to such a snapshot to impose structural antitrust remedies for that perceived market power might result in costly economic disruption that serves no ultimately useful purpose. The best enforcement of truly effective and neutral antitrust in today's economy may well be the force of technological progress and falling barriers to trade and competition, rather than government intervention into rapidly advancing markets.

There are dissenting voices.[219] A more concerned view is that large Internet enterprises (epitomized by Amazon) hold enormous potential

217 Mark J. Perry, "Only 53 US Companies Have Been on the Fortune 500 since 1955, Thanks to the Creative Destruction That Fuels Economic Prosperity," *Ideas*, American Enterprise Institute, May 23, 2018.

218 Recent examples might include General Electric and Kodak.

219 Lina M. Khan, "Amazon's Antitrust Paradox," *Yale Law Journal*, vol. 126, no. 3, January 2017, pp. 710-805.

market power. If smaller producers and sellers must market through a single Internet platform, this argument goes, then that platform holds enormous power over them. The platform could cut off their lifeline and take over their place in the market, using its enormous financial resources to replicate such businesses. The platform could then raise prices and exploit consumers.

This argument could go back and forth for some time. One side might begin by saying that such Internet vendors sell at razor-thin margins, benefiting consumers. If an Internet vendor began to sell at exploitative prices, given the instantaneous availability of information, its brand would be damaged immediately, and other sellers would enter the market and take its market share. And in any event, this argument would go, it would be highly questionable to seek a disruptive remedy against an enterprise on the ground of possible abuse of market power that has not yet occurred. The counterargument would be that a business such as Amazon could accumulate enough wealth and a strong enough place in the market that once it began to abuse the consumer, no competitor could possibly gain a foothold. Those concerned about the size of such a firm would fear that it could raise prices just to the level that would keep competitors out of the market, which they would contend would be above a truly competitive level.

Some might add that some Internet firms are large enough and powerful enough that they have the ability to hire labor at very low wages, strengthening the trend toward economic inequality. Others might counter that such a firm selling at very thin margins would by definition need to raise prices to finance higher wages, and that those higher prices imposed on consumers would go to workers who by definition have already willingly accepted their jobs at lower wages. These defenders of existing large Internet firms would further argue that any such large firm should be judged on the basis of its actual behavior in the labor market, not according to what it might do in the future.

This debate very much reflects the spirit of these times, which are dominated by strongly held positions that are at least tinged with ideology. Perhaps the most fraught decision on the table is whether strong firms should be judged according to what they might do, rather than what they actually have done.

CONCLUSION

US economic and political history is marked by examples of firms using market power to profit and even to govern by proxy at the expense of the public good. That sadly earned experience has taught us the need for vigilance against the exercise of monopoly and oligopoly power, in the political arena as well as the marketplace.

But at the same time, more-recent economic history is replete with examples of growing technology and a shrinking world bringing down the mighty—and then doing it again. We see pressure on producers and sellers to keep pace with their competition, and a steady or even declining price of a rising standard of living. Our economy has problems, to be sure. Many Americans have not kept up with the demands on workers imposed by galloping technology, and wage growth has been disappointing—very much in the wake of, but even before, the financial crisis. But unlike in the past, those problems have not been caused by individual, identifiable, all-powerful firms. The motive force has not been market power, but rather a powerful market demand for skills.

We believe that antitrust belongs in the economic policy quiver, accessible when it is needed. But it should stay there until that time.

CONCLUSION

We believe that our nation can improve its collective well-being by improving regulation—not necessarily with more regulation or less regulation, but certainly with *smart* regulation.

The bad news is that regulatory policy has been deficient for many years. To some extent, the culprit has been either inattention or questionable direction from the policymaking level. To perhaps an even greater extent, poor outcomes have resulted from inadequate resources and an unwillingness to see regulation as an ongoing process that must be studied, managed, and updated over time. It has been easy to "set it and forget it," and to assume that regulations once made will be perfect and will remain so over time—however much the surrounding world, and its technology, might change. And technology is changing, thereby rendering some regulations outdated and impeding our nation's economic development.

The good news, however, is that these shortcomings leave enormous room for improvement. Though the United States was once considered the gold standard of regulatory practice, it has been falling behind the state of the art. We could do much better in some important respects by motivating ourselves to recapture the lead.

There is much at stake. For the prosperity of our nation and its people, and for our nation's position of leadership in the world, regulation must allow our economy to stay on the cutting edge of global competition. This is not a stationary target; the world is changing constantly in many dimensions, technology and demographics among them. As technology advances, and the rest of the world advances, US regulation must remain in step.

How could we accomplish that? This survey of regulatory history and practice provides some answers. Below we will emphasize, in list format, broad, general lessons, but will also refer to some specific regulatory issue areas that we discussed above.

1. *At the basic level and above all, markets work.* Market-driven competition works. Regulation should intervene only when markets fail (or ideally before they do). And sometimes markets do fail—but market failure should be a firm test, honored diligently. Its categories encompass: true monopoly; depletion of common resources (like fish populations) or proliferation of public "bads" (like pollution); and threats to public safety by a race to the bottom on product quality, or a lack of consumer information. All of these should require regulation. But if an industry is generating jobs and incomes without causing such problems, then regulation is not necessary. It should neither protect nor penalize success.

   And the basics are especially important in the regulation of financial services, a sector of the economy much on people's minds today. We firmly believe that the financial crisis arose from elementary mistakes, with some financial players and regulators forgetting or ignoring some of the most important principles of financial behavior. Bank boards and managers and regulators need to learn from that history, and to make that learning a part of their institutional playbooks going forward, for good.

2. *Free-market competition can be the best regulation.* Competition cannot solve every problem; it will not replenish an overfished waterway, for example. But there is no better remedy for abuse of market power than an entrepreneur with a new competing technology. The growth of truck and air transport ended what was once a choking railroad monopoly. The same can be true of natural monopolies. Regulators should see if the development of renewable energy, especially if it can be distributed rather than centralized, can solve both the enduring environmental concerns of pollution and the headaches of public-utility rate setting.

   And regulators should take seriously the option of not regulating. That can mean deciding that there is no good regulatory option. But not regulating does not necessarily mean not acting. In some instances, the best response to a market failure might be another tool. For one example, our society has determined that smoking is a public health hazard. We could respond collectively by pure regulation. But the policymaking process has determined that an important part (though not all) of our policy response should be a substantial tax on purchases of tobacco products. Yes, our body politic tends to recoil collectively at any suggestion of imposing or raising taxes. And yes, common sense regulation (like restrictions on smoking in public places) continues. But the tobacco tax has been a rousing success at discouraging smoking, especially among the younger population that is more sensitive to price. There are other instances where tax policy can be an important contributor to public policy, with less of an administrative or compliance burden, and less distortion of economic behavior, than regulations would cause.

3. *Regulation should, wherever possible, be based on defined objectives and be tied to outcomes and performance. And properly implemented, broad principles are better than narrow rules.* Regulatory goals are best if they are defined in terms of quantitative targets (which is not always possible). What matters is results: substance, not form. But micromanaging rules will encourage form rather than substance; that is, getting the box checked without the effort and expense of ensuring that performance hits the target. And when one market player finds the loophole in the detailed rules, others will be driven through it in a race to the bottom, because those who exploit the loopholes will succeed, but in the wrong game.

   Principles can be exploited as well. Perhaps the greatest concern is that regulators will overstep their bounds by seeing any action as in violation of poorly interpreted principles. Regulators may even be rewarded for playing "gotcha." That is why quantitative targets, when they can be formulated in clear and objective terms, are best; meeting the well-defined objectives can be a safe harbor, not subject to misinterpretation, or to process requirements that preclude efficiency and innovation.

4. *The regulatory burden is greater than the sum of its parts.* When regulations are piled upon one another, it can be hard for market stakeholders to get to the bottom of things. This becomes all the more problematic when federal regulations pile on state regulations, and the regulations of our global trading partners. Some regulatory agencies (OSHA, for one) have attempted to communicate to particular regulated entities what their responsibilities are, to save them from sifting through the entire Federal Register all by themselves. But the mass of regulations can easily be intimidating, depending on the situation of a particular business, for example. Policymakers should be conscious of this problem.

The regulatory process provides special treatment to "significant" regulations—generally those that entail at least $100 million in costs. But costs well below $100 million can sink a lot of small businesses, and even some comparatively large ones. Regulators need to decide whether the problems they seek to solve are truly material. Not regulating should always be an option, and the impact of one more regulation on the total mass of regulations needs to be considered as a cost in benefit-cost analysis. And regulators and lawmakers should be conscious that even in a regulation where the benefits exceed the costs, the benefits may not go to those who bear the costs, and therefore may not help those who bear the costs to pay them.

This point is especially important in social regulation. When the regulatory process pursues small benefits that are hard to measure in monetary terms, regulators should take great care. This is not to say that social regulations are not justified, only that we must be sure that they are truly material.

5. *Do not try to regulate on the cheap.* Good regulation costs (some) money, but it can save much more than it costs. Regulating agencies need good personnel, with strong leadership and training, so that they can learn from the past even without having lived it. Regulatory agencies need to be sure that individual regulators are rewarded for sound decisions, not for issuing citations or imposing fines through overly narrow interpretations of the rules. Regulators with the sound judgment to use (and not abuse) regulatory principles, and who seek to make their regulatees and the markets in which they operate stronger and better, will get the best results.

   In some specialized fields (such as finance), the "penny-wise-and-pound-foolish" approach can be particularly destructive. Skill-short public regulators will not be able to keep up with better-trained and more-experienced private-sector managers. Regulatory agencies in other countries are empowered to pay market rates to hire talent. The United States does so to a limited extent; more such flexibility is needed.

6. *Draw on the experience of public stakeholders.* Public comment on proposed rules is a part of the regulatory process. But there is evidence that regulators do not fully capitalize on this resource. Internet technology does allow a flood of superficial comment and complaint, but it also allows the identification of genuine experience

and insight in the comment process. Regulated entities know what makes compliance easy or hard. Truly using such public input can yield better results.

7. *Review and revise continuously*. Because of constant changes in technology, regulations—those based on rules, but even those based on principles—require constant review. And public policy can always be improved, as new ideas open new doors and new possibilities. We believe that the regulatory process should include a process of continuous review and revision. This is not a one-time task, and it should not be assigned to a part-time commission. It is a serious obligation that will continue forever.

   We believe that an informed process of review is best. If politics cannot provide that systematic process, then we would reluctantly acknowledge that a requirement for automatic sunsets of regulations would be necessary. Any sunset process would need to avoid wasted time on opportunistic "hostage-taking" over the renewal process for sound and uncontroversial regulations.

8. *Beware of pride of authorship*. Two heads are better than one. It can be fruitless to ask the authors of regulations what they think about their own regulations, even after enough time for the facts and circumstances to change. Fresh eyes and open minds are needed. We suggest that OIRA be expanded to undertake regulatory review independently, rather than counting on the agencies that created the regulations to grade their own homework.

9. *Bad regulation entails multiple costs*. Bad regulations result in winners as well as losers. Those in a position to take advantage of bad regulations will become vested interests in them. As a prominent example, some stakeholders resisted the ultimately successful deregulation of transportation and telecommunications of the 1970s and early 1980s, because even though it benefited most people in society, it disadvantaged these others. It is preferable to review existing regulations regularly, before they begin to detract from economic efficiency.

   In addition, bad regulation can divert the regulatory system's attention from real and dangerous problems. As an example, financial regulation during the building of the financial crisis should have focused on the liquidity of the critical institutions: Could they raise the cash they needed to maintain safety and soundness in a fast-building crisis? Instead, regulation focused on other indicators until it was too late.

10. *Sound regulation can be bipartisan.* Improving regulation will not be easy. It will require a united effort in Washington. But that is one of the most hopeful notes in this story. Regulatory reform once was a bipartisan cause, and the results from the early 1970s through the early 1980s were overwhelmingly positive. Most Americans today—with absolutely no distinction between Republicans and Democrats— would unite in opposition if the federal government set high minimum prices for airline tickets, or required that trucks and freight trains cross the country empty, or prohibited consumers from choosing their own telephone equipment. And yet for years, such was the (regulatory) law of the land.

    That law was changed when Republicans and Democrats realized that the nation could do better, and that both could benefit from that better America. We believe that our elected policymakers of both parties could find such opportunities again—and perhaps could build upon that success to work together on other problems that our nation faces today.

    We are not politically naïve. We recognize that for all of the political tensions that we (and everyone else) perceived in Washington four decades ago, hostilities today are far, far worse. We understand that all of the smart money is on infighting and gridlock. If forced to bet, we would put our money there too.

    But we remain hopeful and committed to creating "a more perfect union." In years past, when Americans faced adversity, they took a collective deep breath, set aside partisanship, and found ways to work together in their common interest—and in the interest of their children and grandchildren, and of American generations to come. We believe that Americans can do so again.

    The stakes four decades ago were high. But now, in many ways, they are even higher. Today, our nation's leadership is challenged around the world. We cannot lose this leadership—especially in prosperity and commerce—lest we lose our lead in statecraft as well. We need better regulatory policy to maintain our global advantage. We call on our policymakers to meet this imperative.

DETAILED CED POLICY STATEMENTS

1. The Structural Threats to Capitalism—And the Structure of a Solution

Odland, Steve, and Joseph J. Minarik. *Sustaining Capitalism: Bipartisan Solutions to Restore Trust and Prosperity*. Committee for Economic Development, 2017.

Tackling Economic Inequality, Boosting Opportunity: A Blueprint for Business (Arlington, VA: Committee for Economic Development, April 6, 2016), www.ced.org/pdf/CED-Inequality-Report.pdf.

Leadership and Shared Purpose for America's Future (Washington, DC: Committee for Economic Development, October 22, 2008), www.ced.org/reports/single/leadership-and-shared-purpose-for-americas-future.

2. Crony Capitalism

The Landscape of Campaign Contributions: Campaign Finance After Citizens United (Arlington, VA: Committee for Economic Development, July 10, 2017), https://www.ced.org/reports/the-landscape-of-campaign-contributions1.

New Mexico Business Leaders Survey (Arlington, VA: Committee for Economic Development, February 8, 2017), www.ced.org/reports/new-mexico-business-leaders-survey.

Crony Capitalism: Unhealthy Relations Between Business and Government (Arlington, VA: Committee for Economic Development, October 14, 2015), www.ced.org/pdf/CED_-_Crony_Capitalism_-_Report.pdf.

Ben W. Heineman Jr., *Restoring Trust in Corporate Governance: The Six Essential Tasks of Boards of Directors and Business Leaders* (Washington, DC: Committee for Economic Development, January 25, 2010), www.ced.org/reports/single/restoring-trust-in-corporate-governance.

Private Enterprise, Public Trust: The State of Corporate America After Sarbanes-Oxley (Washington, DC: Committee for Economic Development, March 21, 2006), www.ced.org/reports/single/private-enterprise-public-trust-the-state-of-corporate-america-after-s.

3. Focusing on Long-Term Value: Reversing Business Short-Termism

Helping Skilled Workers Return to Work Following a Career Break: Tapping Under-Utilized Talent to Grow the Economy (Arlington, VA: Committee for Economic Development, April 11, 2018), https://www.ced.org/reports/helping-skilled-workers-return-to-work-following-a-career-break.

Fixing America's Roads & Bridges (Arlington, VA: Committee for Economic Development, March 29, 2017), https://www.ced.org/reports/fixing-americas-roads-bridges.

The Economic Impact of the Food and Beverage Industry (Arlington, VA: Committee for Economic Development, March 20, 2017), https://www.ced.org/foodandbev.

Every Other One: More Women on Corporate Boards (Washington, DC: Committee for Economic Development, November 13, 2014), www.ced.org/reports/single/every-other-one-more-women-on-corporate-boards.

Business Statesmanship and Sustainable Capitalism: Can Corporate Leaders Help Put America and American Business Back on Track? (Washington, DC: Committee for Economic Development, May 28, 2013), www.ced.org/pdf/Business_Statesman_Working_Paper_Final.pdf.

Fulfilling the Promise: How More Women on Corporate Boards Would Make America and American Companies More Competitive (Washington, DC: Committee for Economic Development, June 26, 2012), www.ced.org/reports/single/fulfilling-the-promise.

Ben W. Heineman, Jr. and Stephen Davis, *Are Institutional Investors Part of the Problem or Part of the Solution?* (Washington, DC: Committee for Economic Development, October 3, 2011), www.ced.org/reports/single/are-institutional-investors-part-of-the-problem-or-part-of-the-solution.

Rebuilding Corporate Leadership: How Directors Can Link Long-Term Performance with Public Goals (Washington, DC: Committee for Economic Development, February 18, 2009), www.ced.org/reports/single/rebuilding-corporate-leadership-how-directors-can-link-long-term-perfo.

Built to Last: Focusing Corporations on Long-Term Performance (Washington, DC: Committee for Economic Development, June 27, 2007), www.ced.org/reports/single/built-to-last-focusing-corporations-on-long-term-performance.

4. Reform Education

Building Supports for Successful Transitions into the Workforce: Community Conversations with Business Leaders and Parents (Arlington, VA: Committee for Economic Development, March 26, 2018), https://www.ced.org/reports/building-supports-for-workforce-transitions.

Charting a Path Forward for Charter Schools (Arlington, VA: Committee for Economic Development, February 13, 2018), https://www.ced.org/reports/a-path-forward-for-charter-schools.

Apprenticeship in Brief (Arlington, VA: Committee for Economic Development, December 6, 2017), https://www.ced.org/reports/apprenticeship-in-brief.

How to Reinvigorate Higher Education for the 21st Century (Arlington, VA: Committee for Economic Development, November 15, 2017), https://www.ced.org/reports/hea-reauthorization.

Pathways to High-Quality Child Care: The Workforce Investment Credit (Arlington, VA: Committee for Economic Development, August 31, 2017), https://www.ced.org/reports/early-learning/pathways-to-high-quality-child-care.

Child Care in State Economies (Arlington, VA: Committee for Economic Development, August 1, 2015), www.ced.org/childcareimpact.

The Role of Business in Promoting Education Attainment: A National Imperative (Arlington, VA: Committee for Economic Development, April 22, 2015), www.ced.org/pdf/20150714_Lumina.pdf.

How Business Leaders Can Support College- and Career-Readiness: Staying the Course on Common Core (Washington, DC: Committee for Economic Development, November 12, 2014), www.ced.org/pdf/White_Paper.pdf.

William R. Doyle, *A New Partnership: Reshaping the Federal and State Commitment to Need-Based Aid* (Washington, DC: Committee for Economic Development, January 24, 2013), www.ced.org/reports/single/a-new-partnership-the-road-to-reshaping-federal-state-financial-aid.

Unfinished Business: Continued Investment in Child Care and Early Education Is Critical to Business and America's Future (Washington, DC: Committee for Economic Development, June 26, 2012), www.ced.org/pdf/Unfinished-Business.pdf.

Boosting Postsecondary Education Performance (Washington, DC: Committee for Economic Development, April 30, 2012), www.ced.org/reports/single/boosting-postsecondary-education-performance.

Harnessing Openness to Improve Research, Teaching and Learning in Higher Education (Washington, DC: Committee for Economic Development, November 5, 2009), www.ced.org/reports/single/harnessing-openness-to-improve-research-teaching-and-learning-in-higher-edu.

Teacher Compensation and Teacher Quality (Washington, DC: Committee for Economic Development, October 1, 2009), www.ced.org/reports/single/teacher-compensation-and-teacher-quality.

The Economic Promise of Investing in High-Quality Preschool: Using Early Education to Improve Economic Growth and the Fiscal Sustainability of States and the Nation

(Washington, DC: Committee for Economic Development, June 26, 2006), www.ced.org/reports/single/the-economic-promise-of-investing-in-high-quality-preschool.

Education for Global Leadership: The Importance of International Studies and Foreign Language Education for U.S. Economic and National Security (Washington, DC: Committee for Economic Development, May 17, 2006), www.ced.org/reports/single/education-for-global-leadership.

Ellen Galinsky, *The Economic Benefits of High-Quality Early Childhood Programs: What Makes the Difference?* (Washington, DC: Committee for Economic Development, February 15, 2006), www.ced.org/reports/single/the-economic-benefits-of-high-quality-early-childhood-programs-what-makes-t.

Cracks in the Education Pipeline: A Business Leader's Guide to Higher Education Reform (Washington, DC: Committee for Economic Development, June 14, 2005), www.ced.org/reports/single/cracks-in-the-education-pipeline-a-business-leaders-guide-to-higher-educati.

5. Making Washington Work

Let the Voters Choose: Solving the Problem of Partisan Gerrymandering (Arlington, VA: Committee for Economic Development, March 13, 2018), https://www.ced.org/reports/solving-the-problem-of-partisan-gerrymandering.

Choosing Justice? The Need for Judicial Selection Reform (Arlington, VA: Committee for Economic Development, November 18, 2015), www.ced.org/reports/single/choosing-justice-the-need-for-judicial-selection-reform.

Anthony Corrado, *Hiding in Plain Sight: The Problem of Transparency in Political Finance* (Washington, DC: Committee for Economic Development, July 24, 2013), www.ced.org/reports/single/hiding-in-plain-sight-the-problem-of-transparency-in-political-finance.

After Citizens United: Improving Accountability in Political Finance (Washington, DC: Committee for Economic Development, September 26, 2011), www.ced.org/pdf/After-Citizens-United.pdf.

Hidden Money: The Need for Transparency in Political Finance (Washington, DC: Committee for Economic Development, September 26, 2011), www.ced.org/reports/single/hidden-money-the-need-for-transparency-in-political-finance.

Partial Justice: The Peril of Judicial Elections (Washington, DC: Committee for Economic Development, September 26, 2011), www.ced.org/reports/single/partial-justice-hidden-money-and-after-citizens-united.

Building on Reform: A Business Proposal to Strengthen Election Finance (Washington, DC: Committee for Economic Development, April 5, 2005), www.ced.org/reports/single/building-on-reform-a-business-proposal-to-strengthen-campaign-finance.

6. A Prescription for Fiscal Health

Debt 101: A CED Introductory Series (Arlington, VA: Committee for Economic Development, 2018), https://www.ced.org/reports#debt-101-series.

Time to Face Up: The Growing Urgency for Tackling Our Nation's Debt (Arlington, VA: Committee for Economic Development, April 26, 2018), https://www.ced.org/reports/time-to-face-up.

Corporate Income Tax Reform in 2017? (Arlington, VA: Committee for Economic Development, March 9, 2017), https://www.ced.org/reports/corporate-income-tax-reform-in-2017.

Adjusting the Prescription: Improving the ACA Medicare (Arlington, VA: Committee for Economic Development, March 9, 2017), https://www.ced.org/reports/improving-the-affordable-care-act.

Modernizing Medicare (Arlington, VA: Committee for Economic Development, October 19, 2016), www.ced.org/reports/single/modernizing-medicare.

Adjusting the Prescription: CED Recommendations for Health Care Reform (Arlington, VA: Committee for Economic Development, April 23, 2015), www.ced.org/reports/single/adjusting-the-prescription-ced-recommendations-for-health-care-reform.

Alain C. Enthoven, *To Reform Medicare, Reform Incentives and Organization* (Washington, DC: Committee for Economic Development, November 4, 2011), www.ced.org/reports/single/to-reform-medicare-reform-incentives-and-organization.

This Way Down—To a Debt Crisis (Washington, DC: Committee for Economic Development, January 25, 2011), www.ced.org/reports/single/this-way-down-to-a-debt-crisis.

Harnessing Openness to Transform America's Health Care (Washington, DC: Committee for Economic Development, December 19, 2008), www.ced.org/reports/single/harnessing-openness-to-transform-american-health-care.

Quality, Affordable Health Care for All: Moving Beyond the Employer-Based Health-Insurance System (Washington, DC: Committee for Economic Development, November 14, 2007), www.ced.org/reports/single/quality-affordable-health-care-for-all-moving-beyond-the-employer-base.

The Employer-based Health-Insurance System (EBI) Is At Risk: What We Must Do About It (Washington, DC: Committee for Economic Development, July 17, 2007), www.ced.org/reports/single/the-employer-based-health-insurance-system-ebi-is-at-risk-what-we-must-do-a.

A New Tax Framework: A Blueprint for Averting a Fiscal Crisis (Washington, DC: Committee for Economic Development, September 23, 2005), www.ced.org/reports/single/a-new-tax-framework-a-blueprint-for-averting-a-fiscal-crisis.

Fixing Social Security: A CED Policy Update (Washington, DC: Committee for Economic Development, May 18, 2005), www.ced.org/reports/single/fixing-social-security-a-ced-policy-update.

The Emerging Budget Crisis: Urgent Fiscal Choices (Washington, DC: Committee for Economic Development, May 13, 2005), www.ced.org/reports/single/the-emerging-budget-crisis-urgent-fiscal-choices.

7. Regulation to Build Trust in Capitalism

Regulation & The Economy: The Relationship and How to Improve It (Arlington, VA: Committee for Economic Development, September 27, 2017), https://www.ced.org/reports/regulation-and-the-economy.

8. Sustainable Capitalism and the Global Economy

The Power of More Foreign-Born Workers: How Raising Immigration Levels Can Boost US Economic Growth (Arlington, VA: Committee for Economic Development, January 17, 2018), https://www.ced.org/reports/power-of-more-immigration.

Trade under Attack (Arlington, VA: Committee for Economic Development, August 31, 2017), https://www.ced.org/reports/trade-under-attack.

Immigration Policy That Works (Arlington, VA: Committee for Economic Development, June 14, 2017), https://www.ced.org/reports/immigration-policy-that-works.

In Support of International Trade: Business Leaders Speak Out (Washington, DC: Committee for Economic Development, October 7, 2009), www.ced.org/reports/single/in-support-of-international-trade-business-leaders-speak-out.

Reducing Risks from Global Imbalances (Washington, DC: Committee for Economic Development, September 7, 2007), www.ced.org/reports/single/reducing-risks-from-global-imbalances.

Public-Private Partnerships for Development: A Handbook for Business (Washington, DC: Committee for Economic Development, July 19, 2006), www.ced.org/reports/single/public-private-partnerships-for-development-a-handbook-for-business.

Reducing Global Poverty: Encouraging Private Investment in Infrastructure (Washington, DC: Committee for Economic Development, July 19, 2006), www.ced.org/reports/single/reducing-global-poverty-encouraging-private-investment-in-infrastructure.

Making Trade Work: Straight Talk on Jobs, Trade, and Adjustments (Washington, DC: Committee for Economic Development, June 1, 2005), www.ced.org/reports/single/making-trade-work-straight-talk-on-jobs-trade-and-adjustment.

INDEX

M

N

Q

R

W

Y